TALES FROM THE COURTROOM

Other books by Brian Harris include:

The Literature of the Law, Blackstone Press, (now Oxford University Press), 1998

Injustice, Sutton Publishing, (now The History Press), 2006

Intolerance, Wildy, Simmonds and Hill, 2008

Passion, Poison and Power, Wildy, Simmonds and Hill, 2010

Reviews

The Literature of the Law

'a splendid anthology ... packed with good things' Robert Bruce. THE TIMES
'... an admirable book, every layman should read it' NEW LAW JOURNAL

Injustice

'... an excellent and ... unique book'
Adrian Turner. JUSTICE OF THE PEACE REVIEW
'... plainly the result of real scholarship .... I strongly recommend it' Nigel Pascoe QC. COUNSEL magazine.

Intolerance

'should inspire any number of debates, arguments and disputes, not just among the legal fraternity, but among a much wider readership ...'

Phillip Taylor MBE and Elizabeth Taylor of Richmond Green Chambers

Passion, Poison and Power

'... Harris's assessment of the evidence leads him to intriguing and convincing hypotheses about who was actually responsible for Overbury's murder.'

Elisabeth Stevenson. LAW GAZETTE.

Brian Harris OBE QC

Tales from the Courtroom

Tales from the Courtroom

Copyright © 2013 Brian Harris

The right of Brian Harris to be identified as the Author of this Work has been asserted by him in accordance with the Copyright, Designs and Patents Act 1988.

All rights reserved. No part of this book may be reproduced, stored in a retrieval system, or transmitted, in any form or by any means, electronic, mechanical, photocopying, recording or otherwise, without the consent of the copyright owner. Such a written permission must also be obtained before any part of this publication is stored in a retrieval system of any nature.

ISBN-13: 978-1480111721
ISBN-10: 1480111724

Typeset with LaTeX using the memoir class and custom Python scripts

For my son Neil

Contents

Contents vii

Introduction ix

Acknowledgements xiii

1 **CRIME AND PUNISHMENT** 1
   1.1 PRIMITIVE LAW 1
   1.2 THE SENTENCE OF THE COURT 15
   1.3 THE LONG ARM OF THE LAW 31

2 **THE ACCUSED** 41
   2.1 A GALLERY OF ROGUES (NOT ALL OF THEM LOVEABLE) 41
   2.2 GUILTY BUT INNOCENT (OR THE WRONGLY CONVICTED) 59
   2.3 THOSE WHO GOT AWAY (OR THE WRONGLY ACQUITTED) 85
   2.4 UNSOLVED MYSTERIES 98

3 **GOING TO LAW** 113
   3.1 'PUBLISH AND BE DAMNED' 113
   3.2 MARTIANS IN COURT 128
   3.3 WEIRD WILLS 130
   3.4 SCANDAL! 132
   3.5 GOD'S AWKWARD SQUAD 156

4 **DISCONTENT** 165
   4.1 'UNEASY LIES THE HEAD' 165

	4.2	WAR'S ALARMS	179
	4.3	THE VOICE OF PROTEST	196

5 LIBERTY   235
     5.1   FREEBORN ENGLISHMEN 236
     5.2   SLAVERY 244

6 THE LAWYERS   251
     6.1   THE BENCH 251
     6.2   CONTEMPT OF COURT 262
     6.3   HOMER NODDING 266
     6.4   THE PRACTITIONERS 293

7 'THE DUSTY PURLIEUS OF THE LAW'   313
     7.1   THE COURTS 313
     7.2   THE INNS OF COURT 317

8 LAWS AND LAW MAKING   325

9 LAW AND THE SUPERNATURAL or, Who can resist a ghost story?   341

10 LAUGHTER IN COURT   349

11 VALEDICTORY   357

Index   361

Introduction

The English have always had a love/hate relationship with the law, viewing it both as an object of fascination and frustration. The man in the street goes to it for his personal and business affairs, but is put off by its complexity, its arcane customs and, above all, its cost. But none of these has stopped him from turning to the courts for protection against powerful individuals, corporations, even ministers of the Crown (who don't like it one bit). Robert Bolt put the point plainly in his play, *A Man for All Seasons*. After Sir Thomas More's future son-in-law urged him to sweep aside the law rather than give the Devil his due he angrily snapped back, 'This country's planted thick with laws and if you cut them down ... do you really think you could stand upright in the winds that would blow then?'

The people best qualified to judge the merits of a legal system are, not the lawyers, but those who go to it for justice and those who find themselves caught up in it against their will. What follows, therefore is an attempt to explain the origins, practices, achievements and problems of the law through a patchwork of individual 'tales' of people whose lives have been touched by the courts - mostly British courts, but with a pinch of alien cases thrown in for good measure - together with some notes on the courts themselves and the other institutions in which the lawyers ply their trade.

The tales have been selected for their intrinsic interest, but also for the lessons which can be drawn from them, whether concerning the diversity – sometimes the unknowability - of human conduct, the nature of justice and how the law has been used by brave men and women to make life better for us all. But how should the stories be arranged? Lord Justice Scrutton once admonished counsel: 'We are having some difficulty in following your submissions and wonder whether you might like to put them in some sort of order. Logical order would obviously be best, but this is clearly not to be hoped for. Alternatively you might consider a chronological presentation. But if this is also too much to ask, at least try alphabetical.'[1]

Taking this advice to heart, I begin with a brief discussion of some of the more interesting (read 'gruesome') laws of days gone by, before turning to the always fascinating subject of crime. The cases in this section are designed to illustrate Mr Justice Megarry's remark that 'the path of the law is strewn with examples of open and shut cases which, somehow, were not; of unanswerable charges which, in the event, were completely answered; of inexplicable conduct which was fully explained; of fixed and unalterable determinations that, by discussion, suffered a change.'[2] They include a collection of rogues who paid the penalty for their misdeeds, of unfortunates who were wrongly convicted, even a few who were lucky enough to have been wrongly acquitted.

Contrary to the picture so often painted in fiction, not all crimes are cleared up satisfactorily, a sad fact that I seek to demonstrate by a number of 'unsolved mysteries', like the murder of a magistrate which nearly ended the career, even the life, of Samuel Pepys, and the puzzle of whether a famous French revolutionary was the same man who was convicted of theft from an English museum.

The criminal courts are usually seen as the high drama of the law, but civil proceedings can be every bit as emotionally charged. Take for example the historian whose extreme right wing views were laid bare in a libel action, or the clash between religion and science which took place on a courtroom lawn. I was tickled by the story of the man who sought

---

[1] Quoted by Sir Michael Kerr in 'As Far as I Remember'. Hart Publishing, 2002.
[2] *John v Rees*, 1969.

to sue the Devil, and the 'Martian' who tried to sue almost everyone else. And I was particularly heartened by the way in which the modern law of cremation was brought about by the exertions of an eccentric Welsh doctor and a Hindu ex-soldier.

Scandalous conduct, though not a crime, features all too often in the court lists and is, of course, well represented here. Among such cases are the 'delicate investigation' of a queen of England, and the affair of 'the poet, the prig and the prime minister'. This chapter is rounded of with a selection of the endlessly entertaining peccadilloes of the clergy.

England has had more than its fair share of tumult and disorder, from the Peasants' revolt of the fourteenth century to the Newport uprising of the nineteenth, from Peterloo to the Pop Gun conspiracy – all of which ended up in the courts, and now find their place in this book. But if the law has been used as an instrument of oppression it can also be a powerful agent for reform. Indeed, the fight for liberty (nowadays rebranded as human rights) could fairly be said to have been an invention of the common law. The right to a fair trial, for example, was achieved by ordinary people like the two Quakers who bravely stood up to a bullying judge, and innovative advocates like William Garrow of 'Garrow's Law' fame. And, of course, it was the law, specifically English law, that helped rid the world of its most cruel institution.

Inescapably, it is the lawyer, on and off the Bench, who is at the heart of this book. Judges of days gone by have dispensed their own forms of justice eccentrically, even brutally, though closer examination reveals that not all of them were as wicked as they are sometimes depicted. A few members of the judiciary - often the brightest – have found the task uncongenial and walked away to do other things. As for the advocates, the blowsy rhetoric of the Victorian barrister has given way to today's understated style of presentation. Which does not mean that present-day lawyers lack wit. Consider, for example, the courtroom triumphs of 'Gorgeous George', or the longest speech in forensic history, which began with probably the best opening line. Ever.

More than most, the law is a profession which has taken its character from the buildings from which it sprang, as I have tried to show by pen portraits of some of the more interesting. The book ends with an attempt to explain why the law remains so devilishly complex, followed by a brief diversion into the supernatural and a few examples of that two edged sword, legal humour.

Many stories in this collection came fresh to me, like that of the sinister Air Loom gang, the German lawyers who maintained a proper concern for human rights throughout two World Wars, and our own Parliament's peculiar concern for the rights of outlaws – which continues to this day. I hope that the reader will be as fascinated as I was by the strange laws which governed pirates, and by England's only licensed torture chamber.

Despite all my efforts to impose order on a disorderly subject some readers may prefer to dip into the book serendipitously, moving smoothly from tragedy to farce, from the almost unbelievable story of the Whit Monday murders to the *Da Vinci Code's* day in court, from the longest trial in history to the shortest judgment, from the Queen's corset to the King's feast; 'until they think warm days will never cease'.

Tennyson wrote of the lawyers who were 'fresh from brawling courts/And dusty purlieus of the law.' The law has many dusty purlieus, but I am determined that the following pages shall not be among them.

B.H.

1 February 2013

Acknowledgements

This book has benefitted greatly from the wise comments and emendations of Andrew Carnes, John Crowle, and John Spencer. The remaining errors and infelicities I claim for myself.

It has been designed and prepared for press by my son, Neil. The cover illustration of the Temple Church was drawn by the late John Walkerdine.

I hope that my wife, Jan will forgive me for the lonely hours she has suffered while I have enjoyed myself writing.

Chapter 1

CRIME AND PUNISHMENT

1.1 PRIMITIVE LAW

Primitive law was, well, primitive.

> *It is nearly a millennium since England was last invaded and it is easy to forget that conquerors may have cause to fear the people they have just conquered.*

Englishry

In the Summer of 1944 the Second SS Panzer Division ('Das Reich') were engaged in an epic march from the Mediterranean to Normandy in a desperate attempt to stem the Allied invasion. After crippling attacks from the Maquis the frustrated Germans announced that for every one of their soldiers killed ten Frenchmen would be hanged and their bodies thrown in the river. This draconian order did not stop the attacks and in reprisal the SS destroyed the town of Oradour sur Glane and massacred its 642 inhabitants.

As it was in occupied France, so it was in eleventh century England. After the Norman conquest the victors found themselves looking over their shoulders for vengeful Anglo-Saxons. Fortunately, their retaliation took a milder form than that of the Nazis.

In order to discourage the natives from murdering their newly acquired overlords Duke William ordered that whenever a murdered body turned up the hundred (or township) in which it was found should pay a heavy fine, known as 'murdrum', unless the killer was produced for justice or the deceased could be shown to have been of English birth. The process of proving that the dead man was not Norman was known as the presentment of Englishry, and usually took the form of the cadaver being identified by two of his relatives. In Wales and Ireland the process was known respectively as 'Presentment of Welshry' and 'Irishry'.

In fact, William was merely continuing an earlier practice, known as frankpledge, which King Canute had set up in order to protect what was left of his army after he had sent the bulk of it home to Denmark.

Englishry fell into disuse in the time of Richard I but lingered on until 1341 as a source of royal revenue.

Right up until the eighteenth century animals, as well as humans, could find themselves in the dock accused of crime.

Pigs in the dock

Between 1120 and 1741 there were ninety-two prosecutions of animals in France. It was no laughing matter; in 1457, for example, a sow and her six young pigs were tried at Lavegny on the charge of having killed and partially eaten a child. The sow was convicted and condemned to death, but the little ones were acquitted on the grounds of their tender age, the bad example of their mother, and the absence of any direct evidence that they had taken part in the unnatural feast.

Other animals, even insects, found themselves in similar plight throughout western Europe during the Middle Ages.

The practice of putting animals on trial died out in the eighteenth century, but it enjoyed one last bizarre flourish - in Hartlepool of all places. When a French ship was wrecked offshore during the Napoleonic wars the only survivor was a monkey dressed - for reasons we can only speculate on - in a French uniform. Following a summary trial on the beach the poor creature was convicted of being a spy, sentenced to death and hanged from the mast of a fishing boat on the Headland. To this day the local Rugby Union team are known as the Monkeyhangers and Hartlepool United F.C.'s mascot is a monkey called H'Angus the Monkey.

Before the Vikings brought trial by jury to these shores people resorted to magic to determine guilt or innocence. Water and fire figured prominently among the instruments used.

Buoyant Witches and Hot Ploughshares

The ordeal (or judgement) by water was brought to England by the Anglo Saxons half way through the first century AD.[1] It consisted of throwing the accused, bound, into a pool or river. Anyone who floated was deemed guilty, taken out and hanged. If he sank he was declared innocent and pulled out of the water. Just to be sure, he was also banished from the kingdom. There is little agreement about the theory behind this nonsense. Some argued that witches floated because they had renounced baptism; others that they were supernaturally light. James VI of Scotland claimed in his book, *Daemonologie* that water was so pure an element that it repelled the guilty.

Hardly more attractive than the ordeal by water was the ordeal by fire, a practice which can be traced as far back as the Bible. This involved the accused walking barefoot and

---

[1] The practice was codified in 1166 by the Assize of Clarendon, a sitting of the royal council.

blindfold over red hot ploughshares. To survive uninjured was regarded as God's witness to his innocence. The most famous example of this, though by far the least representative, was the case of Emma of Normandy, mother of Edward the Confessor, who was accused of having had an affair with Alwyne, Bishop of Winchester, her near relation. To test her innocence King Ethelred condemned her to the ordeal by fire. After walking with bandaged eyes over nine red hot ploughshares she is said to have asked when the ordeal was going to begin.

Ploughshares seem to have been reserved for the upper classes; the rest had to make do with putting their hand into a vessel filled with scalding water and picking out a stone 'which was hung into it by a string by a hand's breadth'. A bandage was applied to the scalded arm and removed after three days. If the skin was undamaged the accused was considered to be innocent.

Many of these practices came to an end in 1215 when an Edict of the Lateran Council stopped priests from taking part in them, but the practice of ducking witches continued well into the seventeenth century.

But they have continued in other parts of the world. In 2006, for example, in the Indian state of Rajasthan it was reported that one hundred and fifty men were ordered by their village elders to dip their hands into boiling oil to prove their innocence after rice and wheat had been stolen from a local school. Fifty who refused to do so were held responsible for the crimes. What happened to them is not recorded.[2]

---

[2] *Dublin Independent*, 19 September 2006.

> One of the most feared orders of mediaeval times was a declaration of outlawry. Few outside Westminster are aware that legislation concerning this ancient practice still appears on the Order Papers of Parliament on a regular basis.

The wolves' heads

In Anglo Saxon times anyone who failed to turn up at court or was otherwise in contempt of court could be declared an outlaw, which meant that he would be denied the protection of the law. It was a crime to give an outlaw food or shelter, and to kill him was no murder. The writ of outlawry contained the feared words, *'caput gerat lupinum'*: 'treat his as a wolf's head', and people were paid five shillings for every outlaw's head they produced, or well over £3,000 in today's money.

The practice of outlawry gradually died out as it became more difficult to evade justice. Nevertheless, to this day the business of each Session of the UK Parliament still begins with a reading in the House of Commons of the Outlawries Bill. The Bill's stated purpose is 'for the more effectual preventing clandestine Outlawries'.[3] The Bill is read before every Queen's speech, but is not printed and never gets to be debated. The sole purpose of this arcane procedure seems to be to put the monarch in her place by asserting the right of the Commons to debate a subject of its own choosing before getting down to more serious business.

The Outlawries Bill has actually served a real purpose on a few occasions. In 1763, for example, John Wilkes MP used it to complain of his imprisonment, and in 1794 the playwright, Richard Brinsley Sheridan MP used it to protest against the continued suspension of Habeas Corpus.[4]

---

[3] A 'clandestine outlawry' was a judgment of outlawry made without due process of law.

[4] The equivalent to the Outlawries Bill in the House of Lords is the Select Vestries Bill. A select vestry is the parish committee held in the vestry or priest's robing room.

Despite widespread use of the word, 'outlaw' in the American West the legal concept of outlawry never existed in the New World, except for the crime of treason, for which it was preserved by an Act of 1777.

> *The right of a criminal to claim sanctuary from the church has been known since Biblical times. It has been offered in England since at least 600 AD, both by the church and the king.*

Sanctuary

There were two forms of sanctuary. General sanctuary, which was available only in churches and monasteries, offered refuge to those accused of any felony punishable by death except sacrilege and treason. Peculiar sanctuary on the other hand, which was granted by the king, protected even those guilty of treason.

To claim general sanctuary it was necessary to go through some ritual, such as sitting on a stone called a frith seat, or touching a knocker on the church door. (There is a fine example of this at Durham cathedral which takes the form of a ring held between the teeth of a monstrous head.) Once the fugitive left sanctuary he could not go back.

After 40 days someone in general sanctuary had the option of standing trial for his offence or surrendering unarmed to the Coroner and agreeing to, 'abjure the realm', that is, to leave England. If he chose to go he would be instructed to '... cast off your own clothing, which will be confiscated and sold. You will wear only an ungirdled garment of crude sackcloth and you will walk bareheaded, carrying a wooden cross before you, made with your own hands from wood in the churchyard. You will tell passers-by what you are and you must take care not to stray from the highway nor stay in one place more than one night. If you fail, people are justly entitled to treat you as the wolf and behead you. And if you ever set foot in England again, you will be outlaw and your head forfeit to any man who can lift a sword'.

The most famous sanctuary of all was only re-discovered in modern times.

The mighty tower

When the Middlesex Guildhall was being built in 1913 the contractors hit a problem. Just below the surface they came across the foundations of what was once the sanctuary tower and belfry of Westminster Abbey. The mighty tower had been 290 feet square with walls 25 feet thick, built on oak piles driven deep into the sand of what was then Thorney Island. In Norman times the building had been a sanctuary, along with the churchyard and adjoining close, including the aptly named Thieving Lane, now part of Prince's Street.[5]

In its time the tower had protected many notable people, among them Elizabeth Woodville, the Queen of Edward IV who in the year 1471, escaped from the Tower, and registered herself and her companions there as Sanctuary women. It was here 'in great penury, and forsaken of all her friends,' she gave birth to a son, Edward, who was 'born in sorrow and baptised like a poor man's child.'[6] The poet, John Skelton, tutor and, supposedly, poet Laureate to Henry VIII, is said to have 'fled thither to escape the vengeance of Cardinal Wolsey, whom he had lampooned in verses which show more dulness (sic) than malice.' Another who sought sanctuary at Westminster was the corrupt chief justice Tresilian, whose sorry end is described below.

---

[5] *'Westminster Abbey: The sanctuary and almonry', Old and New London:* Volume 3 (1878).

[6] It did not do him much good. Though he became king at the age of thirteen his reign lasted only a matter of weeks before he died, seemingly murdered, as one of the Princes in the Tower.

Judicial corruption was a commonplace in mediaeval times, but it did not always go unpunished.

The corrupt chief justice

When the Chief Justice of the King's Bench was murdered during the Peasant's Revolt King Richard II appointed a Cornish lawyer by the name of Robert Tresilian in his stead. Tresilian repaid the favour by hanging over 500 of the captured rebels in what came to be called the Bloody Assize.

Tresilian used his office of chief justice to feather his own nest by selling justice to the highest bidder. But it all came to an end when, in a dispute between the king and his nobles Tresilian unwisely sided with the king. After Richard was defeated at the battle of Radcot Bridge the nobles took control of the 'Merciless Parliament' which duly summoned a number of the king's supporters to appear before them. One of them was Tresilian who was accused both of treason and of corruption. The chief justice fled London for Bristol, only to return later in secret.

Unable to find him, the nobles put Tresilian on trial in his absence, convicted him and sentenced him to death. Shortly afterwards he was spotted on the roof of a house opposite Westminster Tower watching the comings and goings of Parliament. A search of the building found him, disguised with a false beard and hiding under a table. He was dragged out by the mob to shouts of 'We have him'. He tried to claim sanctuary, but his pleas were ignored and he was taken on a hurdle to Tyburn where he had to be 'goaded [onto the gallows] by sticks and whips'.

Even at the last minute the old peculator had one trick up his sleeve. He told his captors, 'While I carry a certain something around me, I am not able to die.' His clothes were swiftly stripped off him, revealing 'particular instructions with particular signs depicted in them, in the manner of astronomical characters; and one depicted a demon's head, many others were inscribed with demons' names'. The tawdry charms were removed and he was hanged naked. Just to be sure, they cut his throat.

The right of sanctuary gradually fell into disrepute and was finally done away with by king James I.

> As well as the official sanctuaries there have also been a few places in which criminals were able to ply their trade without fear of the law. Lord Justice Sedley alluded to the most famous of them recently when he criticized the Act of Parliament which created the Serious Organized Crime Agency. By this Act, he said, the state had set out to create an Alsatia, 'a region of executive action free of judicial oversight.'[7] The comment evoked a curious feature of London's past.

Alsatia

During the seventeenth century the term, 'Alsatia'[8] referred to certain discrete areas of London where thieves and debtors lived largely free from arrest. The most famous of them was the liberty (or district) of Whitefriars, which stretched from Fleet Street to the banks of the Thames, between the Temple and St Bride's church. When Henry VIII suppressed the Carmelite Order ownership of this area became unclear. A charter of 1608 acknowledged a measure of self-government, but otherwise it seemed to be under no one's control and soon became inhabited by absconding debtors and other ne'er-do-wells. (The eponymous hero of Sir Walter Scott's novel, *The Fortunes of Nigel* was said to have sought sanctuary there.)

Alsatia was not the only such area, but it was the most notorious. Others included The Minories (or Montague Close), Salisbury Court, Fuller's Rents, Mitre Court, Baldwin's Gardens, The Clink (or Deadman's Place), The Mint and Stepney.

---

[7] *UMBS Online Ltd. v Serious Organised Crime Agency*, 2007.

[8] The term, 'Alsatia' had its origin in a seventeenth century play by Thomas Shadwell concerning the Rhineland province of the same name, long considered 'debatable ground' between France and Germany.

Though some of the tales concerning London's Alsatias are far fetched, they were very real nuisances in their day. By 1673 they were described as 'a reproach to ye Government, and look almost like petit rebellions'. An Act of 1697 sought to close them down, but it took some time before they all disappeared.

Recent research suggests that one of the most frightful procedures of the early law may have been based on nothing more than bad handwriting.

Death by calligraphy

During the witch frenzy of seventeenth century New England seventy year old Giles Corey was 'pressed' to death by order of the Salem magistrates. Suspected of witchcraft on the most ridiculous evidence the obstinate old man refused to agree to be tried by a jury at a time when such a trial could not take place without the consent of the accused.

In accordance with the common law, which the settlers had brought over with them from England, Corey was ordered to suffer the *peine forte et dure*. Under this, the prisoner was,

> ... sent to the Prison from whence he came, and put into a mean House, Stopped from Light, and there shall be laid upon the bare Ground without any Litter, Straw or other Covering, and without any Garment about him, saving something to cover his Privy Members and that he shall lie upon his Back, and his Head shall be covered, and his Feet bare, and that one of his Arms shall be drawn with a Cord to one side of the House, and the other Arm to the other side, and that his Legs shall be used in the same manner, and that upon his Body shall be laid so much Iron and Stone as he can bear, and more, and that the first Day after he shall have three Morsels of Barley Bread, without any Drink, and the second Day he shall drink so much as he can three times of the Water which is next the Prison Door, saving running Water, without

any Bread: and this shall be his Diet until be die. And he against whom this Judgment shall be given, forfeits to the King his Goods.[9]

Corey's last words are said to have been, 'More weight'.

The *peine forte et dure* had been in intermittent use in England for centuries. It was last invoked at Cambridge Assizes in 1741 and was finally done away with in 1772.

God alone knows how many unfortunates like Corey met their end in this grisly way. The irony is that the only legal authority for the *peine forte et dure* appears to have been a misreading of an Act of Parliament. The Statute of Westminster 1275 provided that felons who refused jury trial should be committed to 'a hard and strong prison' (*prison forte et dure*). The draftsman's bad handwriting led to these words being misread as *peine forte et dure* ('hard and strong penalty').[10]

Nations fearful of attack from their enemies will often resort to barbarous measures in their efforts to protect themselves. Though torture has never been a routine part of the English judicial system, it did enjoy a brief spell of popularity during the reign of the Tudors, no doubt in anticipation of the sensationalist television series of that name.

The only licensed torture chamber in London

For much of the sixteenth century England lived under threat of invasion from the Catholic powers. Though blown up out of all proportion by a few rascals seeking to profit from public fear, the threat was not entirely a Protestant fantasy. Jesuit priests were being sent into this country under-cover in large numbers. Their objective was not merely to offer consolation to their co-religionists (who were denied any lawful opportunity to take the mass), but also to prepare for

---

[9] Old Bailey Proceedings, 1721.
[10] Law Commission's report of July 2009.

a long hoped for invasion by France or Spain. Between 1540 and 1640, when the practice died out, eighty-one warrants were issued by the Privy Council authorizing the torture of suspects, mostly for political or religious crimes.

Queen Elizabeth was understandably concerned with the safety of her realm. When suspects were arrested she was determined that they should reveal all they knew about her enemies' plans. So much so that the rack, the manacles and the chamber of ease were known as 'our [that is the royal plural] Topcliffian customs'.[11] Elizabeth employed her very own torturer, one Richard Topcliffe who practised his trade from a 'stronge room' in his house in the grounds of Westminster Abbey, adjacent to the Gatehouse prison.

Topcliffe was a minor Lincolnshire landowner, who became a member of Gray's Inn and, subsequently, a Member of Parliament. His career as an interrogator began during the suppression of the northern rising of 1569. After that he began to be instructed by the Queen's Council or even by Elizabeth herself, to investigate various Catholic plots. In the case of the Jesuit priest, Robert Southwell, for example, Topcliffe was authorised to use torture short of death or maiming. On ten occasions the priest was manacled by the wrists with 'his feett standinge upon the grounde, & his hands But as highe as he can wratche [reach] against the wawle [wall]'

Topcliffe was an equal opportunity torturer, lavishing his attentions indiscriminately on prisoners of all classes and both sexes. Even Ben Jonson had a narrow escape when questioned about his suppressed play, *The Isle of Dogs*. He nearly came a cropper, however, when he raped a Catholic woman who had helped him arrest Southwell, but he managed to hush up the ensuing pregnancy by forcing her to marry one of his servants.

---

[11] We joke about these practices, but they were horrifyingly painful. The rack could leave its victim with permanently dislocated limbs, the manacles involved hanging the suspect from the wall until the flesh swelled causing intolerable pain. And the misnamed chamber of ease was a four foot square cell which made it impossible for its occupant to move.

After some difficulties with the Privy Council during which he himself was briefly imprisoned Topcliffe resumed his unpleasant occupation, but this time with more ordinary criminals. In 1604 he died peacefully in his bed at the age of 72.

Topcliffe's house is long gone and the Gatehouse prison was torn down in 1776. On its site stands the tall column which is the memorial to the Westminster scholars who fell in the Crimean war.

> *One of the last men to suffer judicial torture in this country was the Rev. Edmund Peacham. The report of his sufferings chills the blood.*

'Before torture, in torture, between torture, and after torture'

Peacham was the rector of the village of Hinton St George in Somerset. He strongly objected to the religious policies of King James I, notably his discrimination against Puritans and Presbyterians and made this clear in numerous pamphlets and books. He was arrested in 1615 for publishing a 'treasonable book' and asked twelve questions under torture in the presence of the Attorney General, Francis Bacon and others who had help draft them.

The cruelty yielded no results. As the torturers graphically reported,

> 'Upon these Interrogatories, Peacham this day was examined before torture, in torture, between torture, and after torture; notwithstanding, nothing could be drawn from him, he still persisting in his obstinate and insensible denials and former answers.'

Peacham was convicted of high treason and sentenced to death, but died of natural causes before sentence could be carried out.

To the shame of our age, torture as a tool of law enforcement seems to be making a come-back in the modern world, even in the 'civilized' West.

> It was only in the last century that the House of Lords was stripped of one of its ancient privileges. The last man to claim the privilege was Edward Southwell Russell, 26th Baron de Clifford, the Mr Toad of his day. Like his fictional counterpart, however, Lord Russell's motoring career was to end in tears.

Trial by his Peers

Douglas George Hopkins was driving on the Kingston Bypass on 15 August 1935 when he was involved in a head-on collision with Lord Russell's sports car, which at the time was on the wrong side of the road. Hopkins did not survive the accident and a coroner's jury unanimously held the Earl responsible. He was duly charged with manslaughter and dangerous driving, but it was only after he had been committed for trial to the Old Bailey that it was realized that, as a peer, Russell could not be tried there. Instead he had to be tried by his fellow members of the House of Lords.

Hereditary members of the House of Lords had always enjoyed a right to be tried by their peers for treason, felony and misprision of felony.[12] And it was a right which could not be waived. Russell's case threw the Parliamentary authorities into confusion. No one knew how such a trial should be organized as nothing like it had taken place since the second Earl Russell (also a motoring enthusiast, but no relative) had been convicted of bigamy in 1901. A select committee was hastily appointed to work out an appropriate procedure.

The trial took place in the Royal Gallery of the House of Lords under the chairmanship of the Lord Chancellor, Lord Hailsham, sitting in the capacity of Lord High Steward. The Lords themselves, attired in their full splendour, presented

---

[12] Misprision was the offence of failing to report a felony.

a stark contrast to the accused, who was in ordinary dress. It was a popular event with admission by ticket only. After some of those curious rituals so beloved of the English the accused knelt before the bar while the indictment was read. He answered by pleading Not Guilty.

Sir Henry Curtis Bennett, K.C., one of the great advocates of the day argued for Russell that Hopkins had been travelling at such excessive speed as to compel his client to switch lanes at the last moment to avoid a collision, only for the other vehicle to do the same. After retiring to consider their verdict, the Peers returned to court. Each rose in his place by turn and with a hand on his heart declared, 'Guilty upon my Honour,' or 'Not Guilty upon my Honour'. The 'Not Guiltys' had it and Russell was acquitted of manslaughter. The accompanying charge of dangerous driving was quietly dropped.

Russell, who had inherited his title when his father was killed in a road accident, decided to give up his cherished hobby of motor racing. He was the last Peer to be tried in this way: the archaic procedure was done away with in 1948.

1.2 THE SENTENCE OF THE COURT

Life was cheap in days gone by and penalties could be barbaric. Readers of a nervous disposition may wish to avert their eyes.

> *The Tudors could usually be relied upon to come up with imaginative methods of disposing of the condemned.*

A fate fit for a cook

Richard Roose was a cook in the household of the Bishop of Rochester. He was condemned to death by an Act of Parliament called an Attainder. It claimed that Roose did, 'caste a certeyne venym or poyson into a vessell replenysshed with yeste or barme stondyng in the Kechyn of the Reverende Father in God John, Bysshopp of Rochester at his place in Lamehyth Marsshe, wyth whych Yeste or Barme and other thynges convenyent porrage or gruell was forthwyth made for his famylye there beyng, whereby nat only the nombre of xvi persons of his said famylie whych dyd eate of that porrage were mortally enfected and poysoned and one of them that is to say, Benett Curwen gentylman thereof ys decessed, but also certeyne pore people which resorted to the sayde Bysshop's place and were there charytably fedde with the remayne of the saide porrage and other vytayles, were in lyke wyse infected, and one pore Woman of them, that is to saye, Alyce Tryppytt wydowe, is also thereof nowe deceased.'[13]

Roose had admitted to putting laxative in the meal as a joke, but King Henry VIII was not amused: he made an hour and a half address to the House of Lords urging that poisoning should be treated as high treason, punishable by boiling to death.

The sentence was duly carried out in Smithfield on 5 April 1531 where Roose was 'locked in a chaine and pulled up and downe with a gibbet at divers times till he was dede.'[14]

Only two other such sentences are known to have been carried out under the Act. In the same year, 1531, a maid-servant was boiled to death in the market-place at King's Lynn for poisoning her mistress. And in 1542 Margaret Davy, a 'maide', was 'boiled [alive] in Smithfielde for the poisoning of divers persons'.

This barbaric punishment was abolished as soon as Henry went to his death in 1547, its only memorial the phrase, 'getting into hot water'.

---

[13] 22 Henry VIII, c.9.
[14] The Chronicle of the Gray Friars of London.

In mediaeval days the worst crime known to the law was high treason or, as it was called, 'compassing or imagining' the death of the king. The punishment from the mid-fourteenth century on was to be hung, drawn and quartered. ('Drawing' in this context means eviscerating.) A Tudor chronicler recorded how the offenders were drawn, 'from the prison to the place of execution upon an hurdle or sled, where they are hanged till they be half dead, and then taken down, and quartered alive; after that, their members and bowels are cut from their bodies, and thrown into a fire, provided near hand and within their own sight, even for the same purpose.' The most skilful executioners were those who could keep the condemned man alive to witness the removal of his heart. At the end of the ceremony the parts of the body were distributed about the town or even the country for the purpose of discouraging others. Among those who suffered this dreadful fate were William Wallace, some of the regicides, the Jesuit priest, Edmund Campion, the Gunpowder plotters (but not Guy Fawkes, who cheated justice by throwing himself off the gallows and dying of strangulation) and the Blessed Oliver Plunkett. The oddest victim was Oliver Cromwell who was already dead at the time of his 'execution'.

One of the last to be hung, drawn and quartered was a Scottish spy convicted of passing naval secrets to the French.

The traitorous clerk

David Tyrie worked as a clerk in a naval office at Portsmouth. He was also a spy for the French. When caught, he offered to reveal the names of his accomplices, provided only that they would not be prosecuted. It was not a condition the government were prepared to accept.

Convicted at Winchester Assize of treason, Tyrie was sentenced to be hung, drawn and quartered. Despite a dramatic attempt led by the condemned man to dig through the three foot wall of his prison, he went to his death on 29 August

1782 on Southsea Common, Portsmouth. It was not a well organized event, as the local newspaper reported.

> '[Tyrie] conducted himself from the prison here to the place of execution, and during the whole of the preparation for his miserable dissolution, with the most singular composure and magnanimity. From the time he was put on the sledge, till be came to the gibbet, he continued in an unconcerned conversation with the gaoler, in which he expressed that he thought there were not three better, sounder, or honester hearts in the kingdom, than his own, which was just going to be burnt. ... When arrived at the place of execution, no halter was provided, upon which he smiled, and expressed astonishment as the inattention and neglect of his executioners; and indeed the business would have been retarded for some time, had not a rope and pulley been procured out of a lugger that lay under shore, during which time he read several passages in a bible he carried in his hand... After hanging exactly twenty-two minutes, he was lowered upon the sledge, and the sentence literally put in execution. His head was severed from his body, his heart taken out and burnt, his privities cut off, and his body quartered. He was then put into a coffin, and buried among the pebbles by the sea-side; but no sooner had the officers retired, but the sailors dug up the coffin, took out the body, and cut it in a thousand pieces, every one carrying away a piece of his body to shew their messmates on board. – A more dreadful, affecting execution was perhaps never seen.[15]

An Act of 1841 reduced the sentence for high treason to one of drawing (in the sense of being drawn to the gallows on a hurdle) and hanging until dead, followed by posthumous beheading and quartering. A further Act did away with the beheading and the quartering. After that, there really wasn't much left of the disgusting old sentence.

---

[15] *The Hampshire Chronicle*, 2 September 1782.

Some convicted prisoners were able to escape death by the curious custom of 'reading the neck verse'.

The neck verse

Ben Jonson had a quick temper. One day in 1598 the actor/dramatist killed another actor, Gabriel Spencer in a duel at what is now Hoxton. (The quarrel may have arisen out of a time the previous Summer when the two men were imprisoned together for taking part in a 'seditious' play.) Tried at the Old Bailey the following month, Jonson pleaded guilty to manslaughter. His goods and chattels were confiscated, but he avoided any further penalty by 'reading the neck-verse' and being branded on his left thumb with the letter 'T' for Tyburn. This strange privilege went back a long way.

In mediaeval times when clergymen, or 'clerks', as they were known, were able to escape execution for a felony by claiming what was known as benefit of clergy. Edward III extended this right to anyone who could read and understand Latin. By Jonson's day literacy was usually proved by the felon reciting the first verse of Psalm 51 in Latin:

> Miserere mei, Deus, secundum misericordiam tuam./Et secundum multitudinem miserationum tuarum, dele iniquitatem meam. ('Have mercy upon me, O God, according to Thy loving kindness: according unto the multitude of Thy tender mercies blot out my transgressions.').

For obvious reasons this was known as 'reading the neck verse'. If a judge had doubts about a convict's literacy, he could try to catch him out by requiring him to read another passage as well.

Henry VIII cut down on the concession by providing that certain offences should be 'unclergyable' and that benefit of clergy could be pleaded only once (at least, by laymen; the clergy were allowed to go on pleading it indefinitely), but the privilege continued to be abused. In 1575 it was confined to first-time offenders, who were allowed to escape death by being branded on the thumb and serving up to a year's imprisonment.

The reading requirement was done away with in 1706 and benefit of clergy privilege was abandoned altogether in 1827.

> *Just as high treason constituted disloyalty towards one's king, so petty treason was disloyalty towards one's lord or clerical superior, or, in the case of a woman, her husband. The punishment for men was to be hung, drawn and quartered. For reasons of modesty, it is said, women were burned at the stake instead. The last woman to suffer this dreadful punishment was Catherine Hayes.*

Burned at the stake

The terrible sufferings of Catherine Hayes led to the abandonment of burning at the stake.

Twenty three year old Catherine (known as Margaret) was a prostitute with an illegitimate child. After finding a job as a farmer's servant she managed to seduce his son, John, who was foolish enough to marry her. Two years later Catherine tired of country life and persuaded John to move with her to London where he became a coal merchant. The business prospered but Catherine wanted more and the two of them started to quarrel. Catherine took in two lodgers, her son, Thomas Billings who was a tailor, and Thomas Wood who was a butcher. Apparently finding her husband's attentions insufficient, Catherine bedded the two of them.

Deciding that three lovers were one too many, Catherine persuaded the two Thomas's to get rid of John. On 1 March 1725 the three of them took him out on the town and had a bet as to who could drink most. John is said to have drunk seven quarts of wine and spirits before he returned home and fell asleep. According to their pre-arranged plan, Billings hit John on the head with an axe while he was in a drunken stupor. It wasn't enough to kill him, so Wood stepped up and struck the fatal blow. At Catherine's suggestion the butcher, Wood cut the head off the corpse with a pocket knife in order to avoid identification and took it in a bucket to a wharf near the Horseferry where he ditched it in the water. The murderers had intended to smuggle out the rest of the body in a box which they had got hold of for that purpose, but even in its truncated state the box proved to be too short for the job, so Billings quartered the corpse and wrapped the remains in a blanket which the two men threw into a pond in Marylebone. Catherine rewarded them by dividing her husband's money between herself and her fellow murderers and gave his clothes to the two men.

The crime came to light in an unusual way. Instead of being carried away by the flow of water John's head had snagged on some obstruction and was noticed by a passer-by who took it to the authorities. It was preserved in spirits and displayed on a spike in the churchyard of St Margaret's, Westminster in the hope of it being identified. When it was the murderers were swiftly traced and arrested. All three were put on trial at the Old Bailey, Catherine for petty treason and her lovers for simple murder. The men pleaded guilty, but Catherine maintained that she had done no more than hold the candle for them. The jury were not impressed and all three were convicted and sentenced to death.

They were taken to the gallows at Tyburn on 9 May 1726, along with a number of other felons. The men travelled by tumbrel, while Catherine was drawn there by hurdle, as her sentence demanded. It must have been a poignant moment for the three killers when their route passed their house in Tyburn Road (now Oxford Street). Mass executions were always popular occasions and on this occasion, before the entertainment began, part of an overloaded grandstand collapsed, killing two men and wounding twelve others. Anxious not to miss the spectacle, more crowded onto the remaining part of the structure which was not strong enough to bear their weight. The predictable result only added to the death count

After the men had been turned off, as the saying went[16], it was Catherine's turn to die. Burning was never a pleasant fate, but her death was made particularly gruesome. According to a contemporary report, the terrified woman was,

> 'made fast to a stake, with a chain round her Waste, her feet on the ground, and an halter round her neck, the end whereof went through an hole made in the stake for that purpose: The fuel being placed round her, and lighted with a torch, she begg'd for the sake of Jesus, to be strangled first: whereupon the Executioner drew tight the halter, but the flame coming to his hand in the space of a second, he let it go, when she gave three dreadful shrieks; but the flames taking her on all sides, she was heard no more; and the Executioner throwing a piece of timber into the Fire, it broke her skull, when her brains came plentifully out; and in about an hour more she was entirely reduced to ashes.'[17]

Some reject the story of the executioner's carelessness, and put Catherine's cruel end down to the orders of the Sheriff who wanted to make an example of the husband murderer.

Catherine's grim story was to inspire Thackeray's first novel, *Catherine*, but death by fire had already been abolished before it was published.

From the seventeenth century on death became the sentence for an increasing number of offences. Even the un-sentimental Chief Justice Coke was moved:

'What a lamentable case it is to see so many Christian men and women strangled on that cursed tree of the gallows; insomuch as if in a large field a man might see together all the Christians that, but in one year, throughout England, came to that untimely and ignominious death, if there were any spark of grace or charity in him, it would make his heart bleed for pity and compassion.'[18]

---

[16] That is, turned off a ladder with the rope around their throats.
[17] The Weekly Journal or The British Gazetteer.
[18] Coke. *The Institutes*.

> *In the eighteenth century there were few activities that worried the land owning classes more than deer poaching and it wasn't long before that too was made a capital offence.*

The Waltham Blacks

In 1722 an Act of Parliament was passed, known as the Black Act, making it a felony, and thus punishable by death, to appear armed in a park or warren, or to hunt or steal deer with the face blackened or disguised.

The first to be prosecuted under the new Act were a gang of men who under their leader, 'King Orronoko' raided the Bishop of Winchester's park on Waltham Chase.

> 'Having provided themselves with pistols, and blacked their faces with gunpowder, they proceeded to their lawless depredations; and while the rest of the gang were killing of deer, Elliot went in search of a fawn; but while he was looking for it, the keeper and his assistants came up, and took him into custody. His associates were near enough to see what happened; and immediately coming to his assistance, a violent affray ensued, in which the keeper was shot by Henry Marshall, so that he died on the spot, and Elliot made his escape; but he was soon afterwards taken into custody, and lodged in the gaol of Guildford.'[19]

The Waltham Blacks, as they were known, were duly convicted and hanged at Tyburn. But the Black Act was only the beginning of a new policy of severity towards property crime. The Bloody Code, as the list of hanging offences came to be known, eventually extended to over 200 crimes, including damaging Westminster bridge, impersonating a Chelsea Pensioner, and 'strong evidence of malice' in a child.

---

[19] The Newgate Calendar.

Hung for a shilling

The most commonly charged capital offence was grand larceny, that is to say, the theft of goods worth one shilling or more. (In modern terms that would be about £200).

Like all arbitrary figures the one shilling rule led to injustice and anomaly and was often circumvented. A merciful prosecutor might charge the defendant with 'stealing £5, worth 10d'. And juries, often with judicial encouragement, gave the stolen property an implausibly low value in order to spare the prisoner's life. In practice, by one method or another the death sentence was not carried out in 70% of the cases for which it was prescribed by law.

Gradually the range of capital offences was reduced and an Act of 1823 did away with the offence of grand larceny. By 1861 only five crimes carried the death penalty.

Public executions were long regarded as a source of entertainment for Londoners, but all good things come to an end.

Street entertainment

Michael Barrett, 27, was the last man to be publicly executed in Britain. He was a Fenian (or Irish nationalists) who had been convicted for his part in the Clerkenwell bombing, an attempt to blow a hole in the House of Correction for the purpose of releasing two other Fenians from custody. Twelve people were killed in the blast and many others injured. Barrett's execution took place, as usual, in the street outside the Debtors' Door of Newgate prison, which stood on the site now occupied by the Central Criminal Court (or Old Bailey).

Executions had taken place at Newgate since 1783. Before that, they were in the village of Tyburn to the West of the City, near the present Marble Arch. So many went to their deaths there (on one occasion 24 simultaneously) that in Elizabethan times a unique three legged scaffold had to be erected for the purpose. It came to be known as Tyburn Tree.

The move was not welcomed by the mob at first. They had been accustomed to booing or cheering the condemned as they were drawn the length of Tyburn road (now Oxford Street), sometimes with a stop for refreshment on the way, but the new locale soon proved every bit as popular as the old. Indeed, so great were the crowds a that a tunnel had to be created between the prison and the nearby church of St Sepulchre's Without Newgate in order to allow the priest access to the condemned man.

The convicts themselves were led along a covered way between the prison and the court known as Birdcage Walk or Dead Man's Walk, under which many of them were buried. It is said that as soon as the first man began to climb the steps of the gallows there would be shouts of 'hats off' - not out of respect for the shortly to be deceased, but in order that those at the back could see better.

With entertainment went sustenance; in 1807 a pie-seller's stall overturned crushing 28 people to death. More refined fare was to be found at the *Magpie & Stump* public house, which commanded a good view of the spectacle. The *Ingoldsby Legends* describes how:

> The clock strikes Twelve – it is dark midnight –
> Yet the Magpie and Stump is one blaze of light.
> The parties are met;
> The tables are set ...

The pub's speciality was a 'hanging breakfast'.

Hangings were brought inside the prisons in 1868, not out of any sense of distaste, but to put an end to the pickpocketing and general disorder that had come to accompany them.

For centuries hanging by the neck was the commonest method of execution in England. It has an interesting history.

'Help the Poor Struggler'

In mediaeval times hanging consisted in the condemned being suspended by the neck from a tree or pole, sometimes after a stool had been knocked away from under him. Alternatively, he might be stood, noosed, on a cart. This process, known as the short drop, resulted in an unpleasant death by slow strangulation, unless the prisoner had friends who were able and willing to speed up the process by pulling on his legs.

The first step towards a more humane death was the brainchild of a former cobbler turned executioner, William Marwood who in 1872 proposed that, instead of relying on strangulation, the drop should be used to break the prisoner's neck, a technique which came to be known as the long drop. The advantage of this was that death could be instantaneous. But that was the ideal; many of the condemned still choked to death, while others fell so far that they were decapitated. These unhappy eventualities were avoided later in the century when tables were introduced for calculating a length of drop appropriate to the prisoner's height and weight.

The most proficient practitioner of the deadly art in modern times was Albert Pierrepoint, the landlord of the *Help the Poor Struggler* pub in Lancashire who was responsible in his spare time for the execution of over 400 criminals, one of them an habitué of his own pub. Others included William Joyce, John Haigh, Dereck Bentley, Timothy Evans and Ruth Ellis, as well as eleven of the SS warders at the Nazi concentration camps (for which purpose Pierrepoint was made a temporary Lieutenant Colonel.) After the second world war the public became increasingly uneasy about capital punishment, despite the fact that in 1949 a Royal Commission concluded that the swiftest, surest and least inhumane method was still the long drop.

Finally in 1965 capital punishment was temporarily replaced for most murders[20] by life imprisonment, a reform which was made permanent in 1969.

The French revolutionaries of 1789 were a bloodthirsty lot, but their concern to avoid unnecessary suffering to their many victims led to one of the most innovative methods of execution.

The mechanization of death

A pedestrian was robbed and murdered in the rue Bourbon-Villeneuve in Paris on the night of 14 October 1791. The robber, Nicolas Jacques Pelletier, was caught at the scene by a vigilant custodian (as the rudimentary policemen of the day were called). Brought to court and convicted, he was surprised not to be executed at once: his sentence was stayed while the National Assembly debated a change in the method of executing criminals.

Pre-revolutionary France had enjoyed (literally enjoyed: the spectacles were well attended by an appreciative audience) a variety of imaginative and usually excruciatingly painful methods of judicial execution, which varied according to the rank and crime of the offender. To replace these, an anatomy professor, Joseph-Ignace Guillotin proposed what he thought would be a more humane – and egalitarian – alternative. His 'guillotine', as it came to be called, was erected for the first time on a scaffolding outside the Hotel de Ville in Paris, and on 25 April, 1792 Pelletier had the dubious privilege of being the first person to try it out. It worked well, but after the event a contemporary reported that 'The people were not satisfied at all. ... Everything happened too fast. They dispersed with disappointment.'

Nevertheless, the guillotine continued to be the official method of execution in France, most notably during the Terror of 1793, when duplicates of the good doctor's invention

---

[20] Capital punishment was retained for a while for the crimes of treason, piracy and a few other rare crimes.

were sent to every major city in France in order to meet the growing demand. The guillotine was only retired in 1981 when the death penalty was abolished in France.

In fact, Dr Guillotin's invention was not novel, but an improved version of two British devices, the Halifax Gibbet and the Scottish Maiden.

The Halifax gibbet, as its name suggests, was a killing machine which was employed by the town of Halifax, Yorkshire. Since the thirteenth century the gibbet had been sited in the town's Market Place and was put to use on Saturdays. It consisted of a fifteen foot high wooden frame designed to drop an axe weighing seven pounds, twelve ounces on the victim's neck. The axe was raised by a rope attached to a horse. When it reached the top the rope was cut and the axe rattled down. Legend has it that the gibbet was invented by a 'feat [ie skilled] friar' as a means of execution without the need for direct human intervention.

The Halifax gibbet was last used on 19 April, 1650.

The Scottish guillotine, or Morton's Maiden as it came to be known, was inspired by the Halifax gibbet and brought to that country by the Regent, James Douglas, Fourth Earl of Morton. *The Holinshed Chronicles* recorded that the blade 'doth fall down with such violence, that if the neck of the transgressor were as big as that of a bull it should be cut in sunder at a stroke.' After it was installed the guillotine remained unused for so long that it acquired the name of The Maiden. Morton's guillotine lost its maidenhood in 1565. Between then and 1710 when it was permanently retired from service 120 people went to their deaths with its help in the Castlehill, Grassmarket and High Cross areas of Edinburgh. The device is now on display in the National Museum of Scotland.

The French guillotine was an improvement over its British counterparts by virtue of its blade, which was more efficient by being angled at 45 degrees to the horizontal. Contrary to legend, the inventor of the guillotine was not executed by his own device; Dr Guillotin lived until 1814 when he died of natural causes. The same cannot be said of James Douglas who fell victim to Morton's Maiden in 1581 for his part in the murder of Henry Stewart, Lord Darnley.

Whether the guillotine actually achieved its intended purpose of providing a relatively swift and painless method of execution is a matter of debate.

With the discovery of electricity it was inevitable that someone would realize its potential as a method of judicial execution, but should AC or DC current be chosen for the purpose? A lot of money rode on the answer to this question.

'Old Sparky'

The idea of the electric chair came from a resident of the city of Buffalo, New York, who was a member of a State committee charged with devising a more humane method of execution. (It is said that a chair was used instead of a table because the inventor was a dentist.) The first working model was built by two employees of the famous inventor, Thomas Edison. Edison was in the business of selling direct current and was anxious to demonstrate its advantages over the alternating current offered by his bitter rival, George Westinghouse.

In his campaign to popularise the use of the electric chair Edison 'executed' a number of animals, most notably Topsy the elephant whom he put down on Coney Island in 1903 after the beast had killed a number of men.

Edison won the war of 'electrocution' (a conflation of 'electricity' and 'execution') and on 6 August 1890 William Kemmler was the first person to die by that means. He had been convicted of murdering his common law wife with a hatchet. Just before his execution in New York's Auburn prison he told the officials, 'Take it easy and do it properly, I'm in no hurry.' He had his wish. When the switch was thrown it seemed to result in immediate death, but a few minutes later blood was seen flowing from Kemmler's nose and the switch was thrown for a second time. It took a further eight minutes of suffering before the murderer was finally pronounced dead. Afterwards, Westinghouse wryly commented that 'they would have done better using an axe'.

Electrocution nevertheless caught on rapidly in the eastern States of America, but its popularity is now declining in favour of lethal injection.

> Throughout history most sentences have not involved death. The whip, the stocks, community service and the fine have all played their part. In contemporary America the judges seem to enjoy greater latitude and imagination in the matter of sentencing than their English cousins.

'To make the punishment fit the crime'

Judge David Hostetler of Coshocton, Ohio once had the task of sentencing two men who had thrown beer bottles at a woman in a car. He gave them a choice between 60 days in prison or an hour of walking through the town centre in women's clothing, wigs and makeup. They chose the latter.

Painesville Municipal Court Judge Michael A. Cicconetti had to sentence a woman who had abandoned 35 kittens in a wood without food or water. Nine died and many others became ill. The judge asked the accused, 'How would you like to be dumped off at a metro park late at night, spend the night listening to the coyotes ..., listening to the raccoons around you in the dark night, and sit out there in the cold not knowing where you're going to get your next meal, not knowing when you are going to be rescued?' He then fitted his actions to his words by giving the woman a choice: either prison , or a donation to the Humane Society and a night alone in the woods. She chose the woods.

On another occasion the same judge ordered a man who shouted 'pigs' at police officers to stand on a street corner next to a 350 pound pig with a sign that read, 'This is not a police officer.'

Judge Ted Poe of the 228th Felony district court of Texas once placed an habitual thief on probation with the condition that he stand in front of a Kmart store with a sign that told of his crimes. Poe claims that the man never stole again and has since become a successful businessman grateful for the lesson he learned.

It is interesting to compare this case with the way in which an English thief was treated. The manager of an Essex flooring company caught one of his staff stealing, arrested the man and frog-marched him through the streets to the police station bearing a sign which read:

Thief.

I stole £845

on the way to the police station.

The thief was let off by the police with a caution. He then brought a civil action against his former employer for two years loss of earnings and 'distress', which the manager felt compelled to settle by agreeing to pay £5,000 in compensation and £8,000 in costs. (*The Times*, 16 February 2011.) At the time of writing the businessman is said to be on the verge of bankruptcy by virtue of these proceedings.

Some of the American judges reported above, and the English shop manager, may have 'gone over the top', but the outcome of the British case seems contrary to any sense of justice.

1.3 THE LONG ARM OF THE LAW

> Except where an offender is arrested at the scene of the crime the likeliest means of identifying him were, and still are, the informer. When an informant is prepared to abuse his position dreadful injustices can result. That was the case with England's most prolific – and villainous – informant, Titus Oates. Before he was finally exposed his lies sent some thirty five innocent men to the gallows.

The Perjurer

Titus Oates was the son of an Anglican clergyman. Expelled from school, he enrolled in Cambridge university but left without a degree and followed his father into the church. Father and son were later arrested for making a false accusation of sodomy. Titus escaped while awaiting trial and ran away to become a ship's chaplain. He in his turn was convicted of buggery, only escaping the rope by reading the neck verse (see above). After a pretended conversion to Catholicism Oates spent time 'studying' in two Jesuit Colleges before being expelled from both.

Back in London Oates met Israel Tonge, a one-time clergyman with a 'head, fill'd with all the Romish plots and conspiracies since the Reformation.' Together, the two men published forty-three anti-Catholic articles. Their major coup, however, was what came to be known as the Catholic Plot. Together, they managed to convince Parliament and society at large that there was a vast Jesuit plot to assassinate King Charles II - and his brother, James Duke of York too - unless he fell in with the plot. The purpose of the plot was said to be to invade Great Britain and massacre its Protestant inhabitants.

As soon as he heard of the 'plot' King Charles ordered an investigation. Oates had little difficulty in convincing the members of the Privy Council of the truth of his lie and they reacted with panic. Canon were placed around Westminster and Catholics were forbidden to come within ten miles of the capital. Oates was given a salary of £12 per week, began calling himself 'the Saviour of the Nation' and adopted the wholly unwarranted title of 'doctor'. Dressed in bishop's robes, he 'raced hither and thither, accompanied by soldiers, and enjoying complete power to imprison those he chose ... his greatest pleasure was to be feared by everyone and to harm as many as possible'. Hundreds of innocent people were locked up at his bidding and many of them hanged on his evidence, including a number of Jesuit priests and Oliver Plunkett, Archbishop of Armagh[21].

Oates went too far, however, when at the trial of the king's physician he accused the Queen of plotting to poison her husband. From the Bench Chief Justice Scroggs (who until then had accepted Oates' lies uncritically) poured scorn on the accusation, and the story of a plot began to unravel. One of Oates' principal accusations was of having been present at what he described as a secret Jesuit consult in London, but it soon became clear that on the day in question he had been in France and could not possibly have been at the supposed meeting. Oates reacted by pretending to have a bad memory and to be unwell, but it did not wash. He was arrested for calling the Duke of York a traitor and thrown into prison. Sentenced to a large fine for refusing to plead, he was brought before Lord Chief Justice Jeffreys a year later charged with perjury. His 'behaviour during the trial was very confident: many hott words pass'd between the chief justice and him', but in the end Oates was convicted. He was sentenced to life imprisonment, divested of his canonical garb and ordered to be brought to Westminster Hall with a paper on his head reading, 'Titus Oates convicted upon full evidence of two horrid perjuries'. To top it all, Jeffreys ordered that he should be whipped annually from Aldgate to Newgate. The whipping by the executioner, Jack Ketch is said to have been barbaric in its ferocity.

Oates' run of luck was restored, however, when after only three years in prison he was released by Parliament and given

---

[21] Plunkett was convicted at a show trial in London, there being no possibility of his being convicted by an Irish jury. He was the last English martyr and was made a saint in 1975.

a state apartment and a lavish allowance. After spells in and out of prison he was finally pensioned off by the sympathetic King William III. He married a wealthy widow and died in obscurity in 1705.

Of all the dodgy characters in this book it is difficult to think of anyone more unpleasant than Titus Oates.

Another famous villain who used the cloak of an informer to further his own ends was Jonathan Wild. His career was one of the most remarkable in criminal history.

The Thief-taker General

Tiring of his work as a Wolverhampton buckle maker, Wild left his home town and his wife and child for London. Shortly after, at the age of 27 he was arrested for debt. Instead of his downfall it proved to be his opportunity. While in debtors' prison Wild was so helpful to the authorities that he was let out from time to time to help trap thieves. Upon his release he set up home with a prostitute, Mary Milner, and together they carried on a brisk trade as robbers. Three years later Wild became an assistant to Charles Hitchen, a notorious villain who also functioned as a thief-taker, or man who sold thieves to the law. In time, Wild branched out on his own, eventually overtaking Hitchen to became the largest organizer of thieves in the City, with gangs in every part of London. He even gave up to the law any of his own men whom he wanted to be rid of.

It was a lucrative trade: the Justices paid Wild £40 for a highwayman or burglar, with a bonus of £100 if the offence took place within one hundred miles of London. It was said that no highwaymen worked in the London area without his permission. His most famous coup was arresting nearly a hundred members of a rival gang, thus at the same time pocketing the reward money and eliminating the competition. The now successful Wild abandoned Mary for a more up-market mistress and the pair lived together in luxury at a house in Old Bailey (the street, not the court). To make sure that they did not talk his staff were recruited from illegally returned transportees. As his business flourished he had to buy warehouses for his ill-gotten gains and even kept a sloop ready to whisk them away to Flanders or Holland.

In time Wild came to be seen by the authorities as someone who could keep a lid on crime and he was even consulted by the Privy Council. Inflated with a sense of his own importance, Wild began calling himself 'Thief-Taker General of Great Britain and Ireland' and carried a silver mounted staff as symbol of his 'rank'. The authorities finally realized what was going on and an Act of Parliament was passed to make it a capital offence to take a reward under the pretence of helping the owner recover stolen goods. But it did not stop Wild who believed that he would be protected by the magistrates who were making a tidy profit from his activities.

In the end it was Wild's relentless pursuit of the popular rogue, Jack Sheppard which lost him the goodwill of the crowd. One of Wild's own men went to the authorities and his warehouses were searched. He was arrested, convicted of the theft of 50 yards of lace and sentenced to death. On 24 May 1725, the morning set for his execution, Wild took a large dose of laudanum in an unsuccessful attempt to cheat justice. He was revived and taken, half conscious, by tumbrel through jeering mobs to Tyburn. His dead body was later sold for dissection and his skeleton may be seen in the Hunterian museum in Lincoln's Inn Fields.

As the *Newgate Calendar* commented, 'History can scarcely furnish an instance of such complicated villainy as was shown in the character of Jonathan Wild, who possessed abilities which, had they been properly cultivated, and directed into a right course, would have rendered him a respectable and useful member of society.'

Three years after his death Wild made a posthumous reappearance as Peachum in John Gay's *Beggar's Opera*.

It was with the Jonathan Wild scandal still in peoples' minds that two brothers were able to bring about real reforms in law enforcement.

The Fielding brothers - actually half brothers - were an extraordinary pair: the older was a famous novelist and England's first professional justice; the younger was his successor who built up the Bow Street Runners, England's first metropolitan police force. Between them they made Bow Street the hub of this country's law enforcement and the premiere magistrates' court, a role which it fulfilled until only recently.

The legend that was Bow Street

Henry Fielding was a general's son who married the daughter of a judge of the King's Bench. Shortage of money led him to the Middle Temple, but he soon realized that that his real talent was as a writer. In 1749 at the age of 42 Fielding published *The History of Tom Jones*, sometimes described as the first English novel. More importantly from our point of view, he was also appointed chief justice of the Bow Street court.

At that time London was policed by a clumsy system of 'thief-takers', who worked for a fee, part time 'constables' and the ineffective 'Charleys' (named after king Charles). In 1751 Fielding wrote a well considered analysis of the problem of crime in the City with proposals for reform. Determined to put his ideas into effect, he set up the Bow Street runners. Paid out of government funds, the Runners served writs, investigated crime and arrested suspects, at first in London, then all over the country. In effect, they were England's first national police force. Despite these achievements and his efforts in ridding the bench of corrupt justices, Henry Fielding never secured the judgeship he desired.

Upon Henry's death in 1754 John Fielding succeeded his brother as chief magistrate. (Before that he had served as an associate justice). Blinded by a clumsy surgeon after a naval accident at the age of nineteen, John's disability did little to limit his achievements. By the time 'the blind beak'[22] retired it was said that he could recognize over 3,000 criminals by their voices alone. He published a regular *Police Gazette* and was the first person to keep criminal records on a systematic basis. He died in 1780 after twenty six years on the bench.

In time, the Bow Street stipendiary magistrates, as they came to be called (now Deputy Judges), acquired a unique jurisdiction which extended beyond its geographical area to such places as the Epsom racecourse and British ships on the high seas. In later years, the chief magistrate also had the onerous task of interviewing in his chambers a queue of young soubrettes seeking licences to work abroad as entertainers.

The Bow Street Runners finally became redundant with the creation of the Metropolitan Police in 1829. Bow Street magistrates' court closed for the last time in 2006. Among those who had appeared in its dock were Casanova, Dr. Crippen, Oscar Wilde, Sir Roger Casement, William Joyce ('Lord Haw Haw'), the Kray twins, Jeffrey Archer and Jonathan Aitken, to name but a few.

Next door to the magistrates' court was the Bow Street police station. Like all other London police stations after 1861, Bow Street advertised its presence with a blue light. However, the light had to be removed after Queen Victoria complained that it reminded her, when visiting Covent Garden, of the blue room in which Prince Albert died. Thereafter, Bow Street police station was the only one in London to display a white light.

---

[22] The word, 'beak' is Eton College slang for a master.

> *Apart from Jonathan Wild few men have straddled both sides of the law as successfully as the Frenchman, Eugène François Vidocq.*

Vidocq

Most of what little we know of Vidocq's life is based on his unreliable ghost-written *Memoirs*. What is clear is that as a young man Vidocq was in and out of prison for petty crime until at the age of 21 he was given eight years hard labour for forging a pardon. After numerous escapes from and returns to prison he began working as a police informer, gaining the confidence of prisoners and infiltrating their gangs. He came to be relied upon by the authorities to such an extent that in 1811 he was allowed to set up a plainclothes unit within the French police entitled the *Brigade de la Sûreté* (Security brigade.) It was so successful that Napoleon converted it to the Sûreté National, with branches in Arras, Brest, Lyons, and Toulouse. The original eight detectives eventually swelled to 28, all of them former criminals. Vidocq was one of the first to use such novel methods of investigation as the comparison of bullet markings and the keeping of a card index of criminals. His success allowed him in 1817 to obtain a provisional pardon for his forgery conviction.

In 1828 Vidocq was forced by an intolerant superior to resign his post. He started up a paper factory and when this failed he established the world's first private detective agency, *Le Bureau des Renseignments* (Inquiries Bureau). In the end his cavalier attitude towards the law caused it to be closed down by the authorities and Vidocq went to prison for fraud.

The great detective died in 1857 at the age of 82, but his reputation was reflected in fiction for years after. The character of Jean Valjean in Victor Hugo's novel, *Les Misérables*, for example, was based partly on him, including the incident of raising a cart to save one of his workers.

> When law enforcement fails to work people may feel compelled to take the law into their own hands. One of the most notorious examples of modern day vigilantism is that of Bernhard Goetz, or as he became known:

'The Subway Vigilante'

For most of the 1980s crime on the New York subway was out of control, with passengers taking their lives in their hands. One day in December 1984 a thirty three year old electrical engineer by the name of Bernhard Hugo Goetz was travelling in a train when he was confronted by four young men from the Bronx intent on robbing him. All had criminal records and two were carrying sharpened screwdrivers. Goetz had been mugged by black teenagers before and suffered permanent injuries. This time he was prepared for them. When asked for money he drew an unlicensed revolver from his jacket and fired five shots in quick succession, hitting them all. After checking that noone else had been injured Goetz ran off, but surrendered to police nine days later after his identity had become known.

He frankly admitted: 'My intention was to murder them, to hurt them, to make them suffer as much as possible.' He admitted having said to one of the injured men, 'You don't look so bad. Here's another', before shooting him again. All the would-be robbers were seriously wounded, one of them becoming a paraplegic. Tried by an all white jury, Goetz was acquitted of attempted murder and first-degree assault, but convicted of carrying an unlicensed gun. Some of the jury exposed their prejudices by asking for his autograph. The sentence - of six months imprisonment with probation - was varied on appeal to one year's imprisonment without probation.

The most seriously wounded robber brought a civil suit against Goetz. When it came to trial eleven years later a Bronx jury comprising four blacks and two Hispanics found against him and awarded the plaintiff $18m in compensatory damages and $43m in punitive damages. The damages have never been paid.

Two of the robbers later went to prison for robbery. Exactly 27 years after the subway shooting another of them was found dead of a drugs overdose. He had just been released from a 25 year prison sentence for the rape of a pregnant woman.

Sometimes a crime does not need to be investigated because the offender owns up to his misdeeds. The consequences can be paradoxical, as a 2007 case from New Zealand demonstrates.

The Council that prosecuted itself

The City Council of Waitakere demolished a number of houses in order to build a car park, but discovered to their horror that they had failed to give themselves the building consents which were necessary in the case of a flood plain. In some cases the consents had been applied for, but not yet received. In others they had not even been applied for. The council decided on drastic action; they would prosecute themselves, along with the two removal firms involved.

When the case came to court the council pleaded guilty. Fining them a total of $4,800, with costs, Judge Paul Barber observed that the prosecution was 'appropriate'. A council official was quoted as having said, 'We are quite happy the council only got a small fine.'

The fines were paid into the Council's funds, apart from 10% which went to the court. The council's $3,000 costs were presumably met by the taxpayer, not the councillors.

Whether it is ever appropriate for a public body to prosecute itself is quite another matter. Normal principles of justice would prevent the same lawyers acting for both prosecution and defence. And what if the defendant had pleaded Not Guilty?

Chapter 2

THE ACCUSED

Just as actors famously prefer playing villains to heroes, so stories of the wicked tend to elbow out stories of the virtuous. We begin with a few villains who got their just desserts.

2.1 A GALLERY OF ROGUES (NOT ALL OF THEM LOVEABLE)

The English have always had a soft spot for a rogue, and there were few rogues more admired than Jack Sheppard.

The four escapes of 'Gentleman Jack'

Jack Sheppard had a quick wit and ready smile but it was his astonishing ability to get out of the strongest of gaols that made him so popular with the crowd.

Jack was born in poverty in Spitalfields, but 'prenticed to a carpenter with every hope of a promising career. While still in his early twenties, however, he was led astray by drink and a dissolute mistress. He first came to public attention after one of his accomplices was persuaded by the 'Thief-Taker

General', Jonathan Wild to betray him for receiving stolen goods. He was arrested and detained in the Roundhouse, the holding prison in the St Giles area of London. Within hours he had escaped. He had broken through a timber roof and lowered himself to the ground with the aid of a rope of knotted bedclothes before running off into the delighted crowd brandishing the manacles he was still wearing.

Arrested again the following month for pick-pocketing, Jack was banged up in the New Prison at Clerkenwell, where by a bit of luck he found himself in the same cell as his mistress (whom the guard assumed to be his wife). Within days, he had filed through his manacles, loosened a bar in the window of his cell and once again used his bedclothes to lower himself and his less than willowy mistress twenty five feet to the ground before escaping over the prison gate to freedom.

The next time Jack was not so lucky. Arrested at his mother's brandy shop, he was sent to the Old Bailey for trial. Two of the three charges were dismissed, but on the third he was convicted and sentenced to death. Returned to the New Prison as a condemned man, he waited until his gaolers went off drinking before loosening a spike in a hatch used by visitors and climbing through. He made his escape dressed in women's clothing that had been smuggled in to him surreptitiously by two friends.

Three months later, after a brief venture into highway robbery, Jack was arrested yet once more for theft and returned to the condemned cell at Newgate to await death. He was found to be in possession of files and was lodged in the strongest cell in the prison known as the Castle, stapled hand and foot to the floor. His stay there was interrupted by a visit to the Old Bailey in connection with charges against a former accomplice. After his erstwhile friend was convicted he launched himself at Jack across the court and managed to cut his throat badly with a clasp knife: it took three surgeons to close the wound.

When the warders entered Jack's cell two days later they were dismayed to discover it empty. He had managed to remove the handcuffs and, with the aid of a bent nail, released the lock securing the leg irons. He had then climbed up a chimney to the room above, from which he escaped across the roof of a neighbouring house. During the escape he had broken through a wall and six locked prison doors, all the while still wearing leg irons.

Drink proved to be Jack's downfall. When he was caught for the last time, he was not in a state to resist arrest and soon found himself once more in Newgate. This time there was to be no mistake: he was loaded with three hundred pounds of iron and watched day and night. By now, his celebrity was such that the King's painter visited him in prison to paint his portrait and the public paid to see him. Taken before Mr Justice Powis, Jack was offered a reduced sentence if he betrayed his associates; he refused and the judge confirmed the sentence of death.

Jack Sheppard's final attempt at escape was foiled when a warder searched him and found a knife with which he hoped to cut his bindings on the way to the gallows. Jack struggled to retain it and the warder was badly cut in the process. On 16 November 1724 Jack ended his days on Tyburn Tree[1] in the presence of a friendly crowd of about 200,000 who had come to see him off. He is said to have 'died with difficulty'. On the way to his death he had been permitted to stop off at the *City of Oxford* tavern in Tyburn Road (now Oxford Street) in order to drink a pint of sack. When he was cut down his body was handed to his friends, who carried it to another pub in Long Acre, presumably to share a last drink with the cadaver.

Appropriately for someone whose body is buried in the churchyard of the 'actors' church' at St Martin's-in-the-Fields, Sheppard's reputation was kept alive by the character of Macheath in John Gay's *Beggar's Opera* (1728). It was a remarkable tribute to a man whose criminal career had lasted no more than two years.

---

[1] Tyburn Tree was the popular name of the uniquely shaped gallows which stood near the present Marble Arch.

> With empty rural roads and no organised police force, the seventeenth century was the heyday of the highwayman. Many 'gentlemen of the road' acquired a legendary status even in their lifetime; sometimes it was deserved, sometimes not.

Two contrasting highwaymen

Claude Duvall (1643-1670) had the reputation of a gentleman highwayman who never resorted to violence.

Duvall was the son of a Normandy miller, though legend had it that he came from an impoverished noble family. Hired by a group of English royalists to tend their horses, he went to England after the Restoration as a footman to the Duke of Richmond, but soon found a more profitable career in robbery. Fashionably dressed and with an air of gallantry, Duvall plied his trade on the roads to the north of London. On one occasion, after holding up a coach, he danced with one of the lady occupants while playing on her flageolet[2]. He asked her husband for payment and accepted only £100 for the entertainment, well aware that the man had four times that amount on his person. But neither his gallantry nor widespread pleas for mercy prevented the twenty-seven years old Duvall from ending his days on Tyburn tree. Thousands turned up to see him off.

A contemporary memoir claimed that his tombstone bore the inscription:

> Here lies Du Vall. Reader, if Male thou art
> Look to thy purse: if female, to thy heart.

Sadly, like so much of Duvall's story, it is probably a fiction.

---
[2] A flageolet is a one handed pipe used for dancing. Presumably, he had brought it with him for the purpose.

A Gallery of Rogues (not all of them loveable)

Dick Turpin (1705 – 1739) is better known than Duvall, but for all the wrong reasons.

Born the son of an Essex innkeeper, Turpin became a butcher, augmenting his lawful income with cattle rustling. Upon being identified as a thief he ran away to join the infamous Gregory gang which specialized in robbery and burglary, occasionally using torture on their victims. From there, Turpin moved on to highway robbery, but when the law got too close he fled to York under an assumed name. Detained for having been involved in a trivial fracas, he wrote to his brother in law for help. By an extraordinary coincidence the schoolmaster who had taught him to read happened to be at the Post Office when his letter was received and recognized the handwriting of his former pupil. Turpin was hanged, not for murder or even robbery, but for stealing horses from Heckington Common. Before his death he confessed to the murder of one of his accomplices, for which he expressed regret, and of the Keeper of Epping Forest, for which he did not. Turpin at least went out in style wearing a new frock coat and shoes he had bought for the occasion.

The Turpin legend began shortly after his death and was given wings by the writings of the nineteenth century novelist, Harrison Ainsworth. Turpin never had a horse named Black Bess and his supposed ride to York in a day was in fact borrowed from another highwayman, John 'Swift Nick' Nevison, 'the glamorous highwayman' who in 1676 rode 190 miles from Gads Hill to York in about 15 hours in order to provide himself with an alibi for his felonious activities.

For all his supposed glamour, Nevison too ended up at the end of a the rope.

In the nineteenth century research into the fast growing science of anatomy depended on the availability of cadavers, but the only lawful source of these were the bodies of the hanged. When penal reforms reduced the number of capital crimes the supply of lawful cadavers began to dry up. It was at this point that private enterprise stepped in in the form of the grave robbers. So prevalent were the predations of the resurrectionists, as they came to be known, that Scottish churches began sprouting high walls and watch towers, with graves being protected by iron bars and night watchmen. Examples of the former can still be seen in some Edinburgh churches, such as St Cuthbert's at the foot of Lothian Road.

Most notable among the resurrectionists were two Irish navvies, whose names will forever be associated with their crime.

The Resurrectionists

William Burke and William Hare had come to Scotland to work on the Union canal.[3] Burke and his prostitute mistress, Helen McDougal, took lodgings at the home of Hare and his wife, Margaret in the sleazy area of West Port, Edinburgh. When another of Hare's lodgers, a pensioner by the name of Donald, died owing rent Hare recruited Burke to help him sell the dead man's body for £7.10s to a private anatomy lecturer, Professor Robert Knox for the purpose of dissection. They smuggled the body out of the house in a sack and concealed their crime by burying a coffin filled with bark.

Impressed at the commercial success of their efforts, the two men realized that they did not have to wait for the vagaries of mortality, but could hasten its actions by their own efforts. The plan they hit upon was to use their partners to lure men and women, often destitute, simple minded, or simply drunk, from nearby pubs to the lodging house upon

---

[3] The word, 'navvie' is an abbreviation of the term, 'inland navigator', or canal digger.

a promise of accommodation. Choosing their moment, the powerful Burke would hold the victim down while the violent simpleton Hare covered his nose and mouth. (Their method had the advantage of leaving the corpse relatively untouched.) Over a period of some twelve months the four of them did away with at least sixteen people in this manner, making a tidy income in the process.

Burke and Hare's murderous scheme came to light when one of the lodgers became inquisitive about the fate of a fellow tenant. The house was searched and the dead woman's body was found covered with straw at the foot of Burke's bed.

Burke and McDougal were put on trial for three sample counts of murder in the High Court of Justiciary. Hare and his wife escaped justice by agreeing to turn King's evidence. After a 24 hour trial which involved some 50 witnesses Burke was convicted and sentenced to be hanged. The charges against McDougal were found 'not proven'.

At the Lawnmarket, Edinburgh on 28 January 1829 Burke went to his death in the pouring rain before a crowd of some 20,000, chanting, 'Burke him, Burke him', a term which had come to mean stifle. Windows with a view of the scaffold had been sold for between five and twenty shillings each. Sir Walter Scott was among the crowd, an experience which was to inspire his story, *The Body Snatcher*. When Burke's body was cut down thousands came to view the naked corpse before it was publicly dissected. To this day his skeleton can be seem at Surgeon's Hall, Edinburgh, along with Burke's death mask and a piece of his tanned skin which had been made up into a wallet.

After the trial, Hare left for England, where he is thought to have died a beggar. His life mask turned up in Inverary gaol in 2009. Doctor Knox was never prosecuted because of the difficulty of proving that he knew how the corpses had died, but after his house had been attacked by a mob he thought it prudent to move to London, where he became anatomist to the London Cancer Hospital.

In 1832 the law was changed to provide a more abundant supply of corpses for medical purposes.

If Dr Knox flirted with the boundaries of medical ethics a very few medical practitioners have strayed well over the line. One of the most notorious of these was the man who will forever be known as Palmer the Poisoner.

'They hanged my sainted Billy'

William Palmer was the son of a rich timber merchant. Apprenticed to a firm of wholesale druggists, he was sacked for embezzlement. Another apprenticeship was terminated for sexual and financial misconduct. He then changed direction altogether, qualified as a doctor, and became a member of the Royal College of Surgeons, before going into general practice at Rugeley in Staffordshire. In 1847 Palmer married a pretty young heiress against her mother's wishes. Just over a year later the mother died while staying with the couple and, in accordance with the archaic marriage laws of the time, the good doctor scooped up her estate.

In 1852 Palmer gave up medicine in order to concentrate on his real love, the turf. But he had more ambition than success and soon had to seek the help of moneylenders. All this changed when his wife died, supposedly of the cholera epidemic then sweeping the country. He inherited her estate and at her grave cried through his tears, 'Take me O God. Take me with my darling treasure.' That night he seduced his dead wife's maid, who later gave birth to his illegitimate child. Palmer had insured his wife's life for £13,000, and had only paid one premium before she died. After using the insurance money to pay off his debts he continued to lose to the bookmakers and resorted to further loans at exorbitant rates of interest. He even forged his mother's name as an acceptor of new bills.

Palmer's brother, Walter was the next to die - shortly after William had insured his life. This time it was too much for the insurance company, which refused to pay up on the policy.

Palmer's downfall came three months after his wife's death when he attended the Shrewsbury Handicap accompanied by his friend, John Cook. Cook won a large sum of money and Palmer lost heavily, a fact which he tried to mitigate by fraudulently claiming his friend's winnings. Back at their hotel Cook began to feel ill and the two men returned to Rugely where they lodged at the Talbot Arms (now The Shrew inn). Cook's condition worsened and when a chambermaid sampled the broth Palmer had provided she too fell ill. Cook died in agony eight days later.

A post mortem examination found traces of the powerful poison, antimony in Cook's body, and an inquest jury returned a verdict of wilful murder, despite unsuccessful attempts by Palmer to bribe several witnesses. When the doctor was charged with Cook's murder the authorities felt that an impartial jury could not be found in Staffordshire, so Parliament was moved to pass an Act allowing the trial to be transferred to London.

The medical evidence was inconclusive at Palmer's trial, but the Attorney General, Sir Alexander Cockburn destroyed the defence witnesses in cross-examination and Lord Chief Justice Campbell summed up strongly in favour of conviction. Palmer was duly convicted and condemned to death. The charge of murdering his wife was not proceeded with.

At 8.00 a.m. on 14 June 1856 over 30,000 people waited all night in the pouring rain outside Stafford Gaol in order to watch the 31 year old doctor hang. When he stepped onto the gallows the condemned man eyed the trap suspiciously, asking the executioner, 'Are you sure it's safe?' Safe the gallows may have been, but they performed their function well. On learning of her son's death Palmer's mother is said to have cried out, 'They have hanged my saintly Billy.'[4]

Just before his death Palmer told the prison governor: 'Cook did not die from strychnine'. The statement contained an interesting implication by no means inconsistent with

---

[4] The phrase was used by Robert Graves as the title of a book which cast doubt on the conviction.

guilt. Some, like the poet, Robert Graves, have maintained Palmer's innocence, but present in court was a young barrister, James Fitzjames Stephens, later to become a distinguished judge. Stephens expressed his satisfaction that Palmer had had a very fair trial. As he pointed out, the jury were not told of the eleven other people, in addition to Cook, for whose death there was good reason to believe Palmer to have been responsible. They included his wife, the last four of his five legitimate children, his illegitimate child, two people to whom he owed money, his mother-in-law, and his brother.

Palmer's horse, *The Chicken*, on which he had lost so heavily, was bought by new owners, renamed *Vengeance* and won the Cesarewitch.

There is a delightful tale that Rugeley town council, upset at the bad publicity which the Palmer case had brought to their town, sent a deputation to the Prime Minister to seek approval to change its name. Lord Palmerston is said to have replied saying that he had no objections, provided they named it after him. Sadly, there is no truth in the story.

Lawyers too have been guilty of the most serious crime of all. One of them, Major Herbert Rowse Armstrong TD, MA, has the dubious distinction of being the only solicitor and the only justices' clerk to be hanged for murder.

'Excuse fingers'

It would be difficult to imagine anyone with a greater claim to middle class respectability than Herbert Rowse Armstrong. After gaining a law degree at Cambridge he qualified as a solicitor in 1895. During the Great War he served in the Royal Engineers, rising to the rank of Major, but was invalided out as a result of a head wound. After the war he lived with his wife and three children in the quiet village of Cusop Dingle in a valley crossed by Offa's Dyke. He had a law office in Hay-on-Wye and held the post of clerk to the Hay, Bredwardine and Paincastle Justices. A short, dapper man with a waxed moustache, Armstrong was also Master of the Freemasons' Lodge and a church-warden. At the age of fifty-two life seemed irreversibly calm and satisfying for this most upright and successful of men.

But all was not as it seemed. Armstrong's wife, Kitty was an unbalanced and domineering woman who kept her 5 foot husband firmly under her thumb. It was not a comfortable place to be. Events came to a head in 1920. Visiting London on business, Armstrong met and dined with a young woman he had known while in the army. During the meal he spoke to her of marriage. Shortly after his return, the solicitor redrafted his wife's will, leaving everything to himself. Kitty's mental state deteriorated thereafter and she had to be admitted to hospital for some four months.

On 22 February 1921, a month after she had been discharged from hospital Kitty died. There seemed to be no reason for concern at the time; heart disease was recorded on the death certificate, but she had also been suffering from rheumatism, nephritis and acute gastritis.

Now a widower, Major Armstrong's life proceeded along its usual quiet channels, except for a disagreement with Oswald Martin, another local solicitor who had been pressing him to repay a debt of £500 outstanding from a property transaction. The debt was eventually paid and the two men were seemingly reconciled. Nevertheless, Martin was surprised when in October 1921 Armstrong invited him to tea. During the meal his host picked up a scone and handed it to Martin, saying, 'Excuse fingers'. That night Martin was violently sick. He recovered, but it made him wonder about an anonymous present of chocolates which he had received earlier. When some of the sweets were eaten by a visitor to his home he too had become ill.

Kitty's doctor was struck by the fact that the symptoms that she had suffered before her death were similar to Martin's, another patient of his. A urine sample from Martin was found to contain 1/33 of a grain of arsenic and the doctor notified the Home Office of his suspicions. Armstrong was arrested and a search of his house revealed a quantity of the poison. The uneaten sweets were also found to contain arsenic. When Kitty's body was exhumed it too was found to contain the substance. Investigations revealed that only ten days before her death the Major had bought arsenic from a local chemist. He was charged with the murder of his wife and the attempted murder of his fellow solicitor.

The Notable British Trials series contains a delightful description of the committal proceedings:

> 'When Armstrong appeared before the magistrate at his own bench in Hay, his place as clerk was taken by his elderly colleague, the Clerk to the Bench at Talgarth, to whose office he had himself aspired already... It is said that there was a somewhat rich vein of comedy in the way he handled Armstrong in these proceedings. The prisoner himself, not to be outdone, offered to assist his elderly colleague, whose infirmity hampered him in the execution of his onerous duties.'

At the trial before Mr. Justice Darling at Hereford Assizes the prosecution was conducted by the Attorney-General who contended that Mrs Armstrong had been slowly poisoned by her husband over a long period. Sir Henry Curtis-Bennett KC for the defence sought to show that Armstrong, who was a keen gardener, had bought the arsenic for killing dandelions and that his wife had used it to commit suicide. This seemed unlikely in light of a nurse's evidence that on the day she died Kitty had said, 'I am not going to die, am I? Because I have everything to live for - my children and my husband'. Justice Darling asked Armstrong why, as he stated, he had made up some twenty small bags of arsenic to put into individual dandelion holes to kill weeds. Armstrong could give no satisfactory answer.

Armstrong was convicted and sentenced to death, but not everyone was happy with the verdict. There were problems with the evidence and problems with the conduct of the trial. The chemist from whom Armstrong had bought the arsenic was Martin's father-in-law and supposedly bore a grudge against the Major. The 73 year old judge was at the end of his career (he retired the following year) and his faculties may have been in decline. His decision to admit evidence of

Martin's death was questionable, though upheld in the Court of Appeal, and his proactive questioning of the defendant, which was probably conclusive in the jury's eyes, was felt by some to be pushing the boundaries of the judge's role. Despite all these criticisms, however, it is difficult to feel any real doubts about the outcome of the trial.

After an unsuccessful appeal Armstrong went to the gallows on 31 May, 1922 still protesting his innocence. An Englishman to the end, he was hanged in his best tweed suit.

The conviction in 1911 of one of Eliza Barrow's killers gave rise to one of the most dramatic moments in a criminal trial.

The Brotherhood

Forty-year-old Frederick Henry Seddon was a Superintendent of Collectors for an insurance company in north London. When off duty he spent much of his time devising schemes to make money. One of these involved a tenant of his, a 49 year old spinster by the name of Eliza Barrow. Seddon persuaded Eliza to make over her savings of £1,500 India Stock to himself in return for an annuity of £150 per year and remission of rent. These were followed by a gift of £200 and two properties in Camden. In August 1911 Seddon and his wife took Eliza on holiday with them to Southend. When they returned to London he sent his daughter Maggie to buy a three-penny packet of flypaper from the chemist's. Eliza died a month later. In his capacity as executor of Eliza's estate Seddon appropriated her residuary funds, which were intended to pay for the funeral, to himself. Eliza's cousin, who had hoped to inherit, became suspicious and an autopsy was ordered. It revealed the presence of two and a half grains of arsenic in the dead woman's body.

Seddon and his wife were arrested and put on trial at the Old Bailey for Eliza's murder. The Attorney-General, Sir Rufus Isaacs KC led for the Crown. For the defence, Sir Edward Marshall Hall KC suggested that Eliza's death had been brought about accidentally by her consumption of an arsenic containing medicine, while Seddon himself put forward the risible suggestion that Eliza might have drunk water from the flypaper dishes in her room.

Seddon was found Guilty of murder and his wife not guilty. When he kissed her in the dock she became hysterical and had to be removed from court. To understand what occurred immediately afterwards it is necessary to know that Masons call God 'the Great Architect' and that Seddon had been 'quite a light in the Masonic world', even though he had resigned from his lodges some years earlier.

Asked if he had anything to say why sentence of death should not be passed upon him, Seddon rehearsed his absurd defence at some length before dramatically ending, 'I declare before the Great Architect of the Universe, I am not guilty, my Lord.' According to some sources, the prisoner gave the First Degree Masonic sign, according to others, the Sign of Grief and Distress.

The judge, Mr Justice Bucknill, had been Provincial Grand Master of the Surrey Masons. He immediately fell silent, a silence which he maintained, save for the occasional sob, even after the 'black cap'[5] had been placed on his head. Finally in a broken voice he was heard to say, 'It is not for me to harrow your feelings'.

'It does not affect me,' said the prisoner; 'I have a clear conscience.'

'Try to make peace with your Maker', said the judge.

'I am at peace', replied Seddon.

'From what you have said,' Bucknill went on, 'you and I know we both belong to the same brotherhood, and it is all the more painful to me to have to say what I am saying. But our brotherhood does not encourage crime; on the contrary it condemns it. I pray you again to make your peace with the Great Architect of the Universe. Mercy - pray for it, ask for it...'

---

[5] Actually a square of black cloth which was placed over the wig.

Finally, he passed the only sentence allowed by law, death by hanging.

When one of England's most famous fraudsmen was convicted just over a century ago he was determined to escape his fate.

'I will not need that where I am going'

On 26 January 1904 James Whitaker Wright was sentenced to seven years penal servitude for commercial fraud by Mr Justice Bigham at the Royal Courts of Justice: it was a sentence he was not to serve.

Taken to an anteroom of the court while awaiting the prison van, Wright handed his watch to his solicitor, Sir George Lewis, saying (ambiguously as it turned out), 'I will not need this where I am going'. After visiting the lavatory the prisoner asked for a cigar which he puffed at once or twice before staggering and falling to the floor, dead. It turned out that, while in the lavatory, he had swallowed a tablet of cyanide of potassium which he had had in his pocket. Just for good measure he was also carrying a silver-plated revolver with six loaded chambers. Attitudes to court security were somewhat slack in those days.

The sixteen stone Wright was a man of humble origins who had made a fortune in America as a mining engineer. In 1881 at the age of 43 he returned to England where he lived in sumptuous splendour. He owned a Park Lane apartment with a drawing room which was a replica of the *Cabinet des Rois* of Louis XV and a racing yacht which he named *The Sybarita*, but his grandest property was in Surrey. Wright had bought two estates on the outskirts of Haslemere and combined them into one which he named Witley Park. Hills were levelled and the area was re-landscaped. The estate contained a vast lake, complete with a boathouse designed by Lutyens. Concealed beneath its waters were a billiards room and conservatory, both made of glass. A theatre, velodrome, private hospital and stabling for fifty horses completed the property. The development cost £1.85m, or about £114m in today's money.

Wright finally overstretched himself when he built the Bakerloo line of the London Underground and was forced to raise money by dubious means. His company boards were loaded with titled names, but when the economy collapsed his estate was found to be worth far less than it was valued at. When a warrant was issued for his arrest Wright hid in the ice house at Witley Park for a week before fleeing to New York by sea under a false identity. Arrested upon landing, he was extradited to England and began the journey that was to end in the lavatory of the Law Courts in the Strand.

Witley Park house burned down in 1952. The underwater rooms remain, however, eerily visible below the waters of the lake.

> Horatio Bottomley was an even more flamboyant fraudster than Whittaker Wright. He boasted that he had been through every court in the land except the divorce court; though why he escaped the last only his long suffering wife would have known.

'The soldiers' friend'

Born in Bethnal Green in 1860, Bottomley was orphaned at the age of four. He ran away from the orphanage to make his own way in the world, becoming, successively, a solicitor's clerk and court shorthand writer. Armed with a smattering, but useful, knowledge of the law, he set himself up in the publishing business where his talent for publicity was able to blossom.

Bottomley had a weakness for young women which he satisfied by packing his compliant wife off from time to time to a villa near Monte Carlo. In 1888 he founded the *Financial Times* which earned him a large fortune, but it was soon dissipated by his devotion to horse racing. (He twice won the Cesarewitch.) In 1889 he bought a house in rural Sussex where he could play the squire. The following year he was bankrupted and charged with conspiracy to defraud. He was acquitted after conducting a spirited defence of himself in court. Between 1901 and 1905 sixty seven writs and petitions for bankruptcy were served upon him. In 1906 he founded the journal, *John Bull* which proved to be another runaway success. In the same year he became Liberal MP for Hackney South, but had to resign after going bankrupt for the second time following a damaging series of civil actions arising out of his dubious financial schemes.

Bottomley was a magnetic speaker and during the Great War he toured the country as a recruiter for the army. At one event he declared, 'When the time comes I will not hesitate ... to insist upon the trial by court martial of every man who has taken advantage of his country's troubles to line his filthy pockets with gold at the expense of the State'. Bottomley created his hugely successful 'John Bull Victory Bonds' and pocketed much of the money contributed to them. In 1918 he re-entered Parliament as an independent MP.

Bottomley's final fall from grace occurred in 1922. After he had unsuccessfully prosecuted a former associate for criminal libel defaults of nearly half a million pounds came to light which had arisen from his various scams. Bottomley, now an alcoholic, was arrested for fraud, perjury and false accounting. In court he pointed to the sword of the figure of justice and, turning to the jury said, 'That sword would drop from its scabbard if you gave a verdict of guilty against me'. It didn't, and he was sentenced to seven years penal servitude. The prosecuting counsel, Travers Perkins KC later wrote of Bottomley's fall: 'the fact is that in those days (1914) he was a brilliant advocate and a clever lawyer, though completely unscrupulous in his methods ... In truth it was not I who floored Bottomley, it was drink. The man I met in 1922 was a drink-sodden creature whose brain would only be got to work by repeated doses of champagne'. It is said apocryphally that a visitor to Maidstone gaol, on seeing him working on a mail bag inquired, 'Sewing?' 'No, reaping', the prisoner replied.

Released after serving only five years of his sentence, Bottomley started yet another magazine which promised to reveal tortures in British gaols, but, as the Home Secretary remarked, the only torture he had suffered had been the gaol's failure to provide him with his favourite champagne.

There is no doubt of Bottomley's abilities, as an entrepreneur, orator and amateur lawyer. He was also a swindler on an industrial scale. In 1933 he died a pauper.

A former minister of the Crown staged his 'suicide' on 20 November 1974 by leaving a pile of clothes on a Miami beach. It was to lead to the exposure of his criminal, even treasonous background.

The real Reggie Perrin

John Thomson Stonehouse was born in 1925 the son of a Post Office engineer. He served as a pilot in the RAF, took a degree in economics and in 1957 was elected as Co-operative Party Member of Parliament for Wednesbury in the west Midlands. He served in Harold Wilson's Labour government as a junior minister of Aviation and as Postmaster General, but never attained Cabinet rank and left office when Labour were defeated in 1970.

Having failed to achieve his ambitions in politics, Stonehouse determined to succeed at business. The complex group of interlinked companies which he set up soon ran into difficulties. Realizing his position he cooked the books, lied to his accountants and stripped the companies of their remaining assets. He then applied for two false passports in dead men's names and left for a supposedly business trip to Florida. On hearing of his 'death' the House of Commons observed a minute's silence. They could have spent the time more profitably.

Armed with some £3m and leaving a wife and daughter behind him in England, Stonehouse fled to Australia where he planned to begin a new life with his former secretary, the beautiful Sheila Buckley. Using false names, he moved large sums of money between banks with a view to covering his tracks.

When the Australian police noticed that 'Donald Clive Mildoon' appeared to bear a strong resemblance to Stonehouse (and Lord Lucan too for good measure) he was arrested and deported to England. Released on bail in England, Stonehouse continued to attend the House of Commons and even went to the Labour Party conference. In August 1976 he was brought to trial on 18 counts of theft, fraud, deception and wasting police time. After a 68-day trial in which he conducted his own defence Stonehouse was convicted and sentenced to seven years' imprisonment. For her part in his schemes Ms Buckley received two years' imprisonment, suspended for two years. Stonehouse left prison three years later and married her. But not all of the story had yet come out.

The newly freed Stonehouse published several novels, one of them a mock autobiography portraying a spy caught in a 'honeytrap'.[6] It later came to light that he himself had been caught by just such a stratagem while in Czechoslovakia in the 1960s and had been recruited as a Soviet agent with the codename 'Kolon'. When the Prime Minister, Margaret Thatcher was told of this she had agreed that the former Labour Minister should not be prosecuted, but only because of the difficulties of using the Soviet source as a witness in court.

Stonehouse died of a heart attack in 1988. Part of his story was to become the inspiration for the television series, *The Fall and Rise of Reggie Perrin*.

2.2 GUILTY BUT INNOCENT (OR THE WRONGLY CONVICTED)

Over its fifteen years existence the Criminal Cases Review Commission has referred some 500 possible injustices back to the courts, of which 461 have resulted in the convictions being quashed. No such safeguard existed in the seventeenth century.

---

[6] A honeytrap is a stratagem whereby the target is put into a sexually compromising situation which can be used for purposes of blackmail.

> Sir Walter Raleigh has the dubious distinction of being beheaded fifteen years after he was sentenced to death. The trial at which he was convicted has gone down to history as one of the most horrifying examples of injustice in England.

Raleigh: tried once, sentenced twice

Raleigh, the poet, explorer and hero of Cadiz, had been a favourite at the court of Queen Elizabeth, but his position changed dramatically upon her death when King James VI of Scotland added to his titles that of James I of England. Raleigh was distrusted by the new King for his policy of rapprochement with Spain. Doubtful of Raleigh's loyalty and fearful of his power (he was formerly Elizabeth's Captain of the Guard), James had the adventurer stripped of his offices and in 1603 put on trial for treason. The excuse was his supposed involvement in a plot to dethrone the king and replace him by his relative, Arbella Stuart[7]. Convicted and condemned to a traitor's death, Raleigh's sentence was commuted to one of life imprisonment in the Tower of London, where his incarceration was relieved only by the comforts of tobacco (which he had brought back from the New World) and the writing of histories.

Thirteen years later King James, now short of funds, released Raleigh in order to allow him to mount an expedition to find the fabled treasures of El Dorado in what is today Guiana[8]. Raleigh failed and on the way home some of his men sacked a Spanish town against the king's express instructions. When he finally got back to England the death sentence, for which he had never been pardoned, was confirmed under pressure from Spain and the adventurer went to the block fifteen years after being sentenced to death.

---

[7] Arbella had secretly married without permission another potential claimant to the throne and was thrown into the Tower, from which she made an audacious escape. Caught at sea and returned to captivity, Arbella gradually lost her reason and eventually starved herself to death.

[8] El Dorado was a fabled 'lost' city of gold.

Raleigh's 1603 trial in the Great Hall of Winchester had been a travesty of justice. He had had no advance warning of the charges, the only evidence against him was the written confession of the main plotter, Lord Cobham, and had been twice withdrawn by its maker. It was also hearsay. Raleigh implored the court in his broad Devonshire accent: 'I have already often urged the producing of my Lord Cobham, but it is still denied me. I appeal now once more to your Lordships in this: my Lord Cobham is the only one that hath accused me, for all the treasons urged upon me are by reflection from him. It is now clear that he hath since retracted; therefore since his accusation is recalled by himself, let him now by word of mouth convict or condemn me.' The plea was rejected by Lord Chief Justice Popham (whose curious story is told below). Throughout the proceedings the prosecutor, Edward Coke, had adopted a bullying and abusive manner and twice lost his temper, shouting at the accused, 'Thou art a monster. Thou hast an English face, but a Spanish heart'.

Raleigh justifiably complained to the jury, 'if you yourselves would like to be hazarded in your lives, disabled in your posterities, - your lands, goods, and all you have confiscated, - your wives, children, and servants left crying to the world; if you would be content all this should befall you upon a trial by suspicions and presumptions, - upon an accusation not subscribed by your accuser, - without the open testimony of a single witness, then so judge me as you would yourselves be judged.' With a magnificent *coup de théâtre* he pulled out of his pocket a letter from Cobham which had been smuggled in to him in the Tower. When it was read out in court it proved to be a complete exoneration of the accused. There was consternation among the judges but they pulled themselves together sufficiently to send the jury out to bring in the inevitable verdict of Guilty.

One of Raleigh's judges confessed on his deathbed that 'the justice of England was never so depraved and injured as in the condemnation of Sir Walter Raleigh'. So blatantly unjust had the knight's trial been that it became the spur for a general reform of criminal procedure.

After his execution this poem was found in Raleigh's cell:

Even such is time, that takes in trust
Our youth, our joys, our all we have,
And pays us but with earth and dust;
Who, in the dark and silent grave,
When we have wandered all our ways,
Shuts up the story of our days;
But from this earth, this grave, this dust,
My God shall raise me up, I trust.

But the injustice of the courts was as nothing compared to that of Parliament, which had two sneaky ways of getting rid of people it disliked. They were called, respectively, impeachment and attainder. Neither involved a fair trial, and the Earl of Strafford had to suffer both.

'Put not your trust in Princes'

The execution of Sir Thomas Wentworth, 1st Earl of Strafford must rank among one of the worst betrayals by a king of a trusted servant.

After the defeat of the royal forces in the second Bishop's war King Charles I brought his friend, Wentworth back from Ireland (which he had successfully pacified in the usual bloody manner of the time) and made him Earl of Strafford and his chief adviser. At a critical moment in the King's relations with Parliament Strafford fell ill and Charles had no option but to recall its obstreperous Members. Well aware of their attitude toward 'Black Tom Tyrant', as some of them called Wentworth, Charles promised Strafford 'upon the word of a king, you shall not suffer in life, honour or fortune'.

As Charles feared, Parliament duly threw Strafford into the Tower of London and began impeachment proceedings against him for high treason. Impeachment was an ancient procedure which was Parliamant's equivalent to a trial, but without the safeguards of the ordinary courts of law.

Strafford's 'trial' began before the House of Lords in the Great Hall of Westminster Palace on 22 March 1641. His judges consisted of eighty peers with the proceeding managed by the leading Parliamentarian, John Pym.[9] The King and Queen were present as spectators. Despite the fact that 'he was ready to drop down in respect of his much sickness and weakness', Strafford made a spirited defence to each of the twenty six Articles with which he was charged, pointing out that the House had agreed that, standing alone, none of them amounted to treason.

The most damning evidence against the accused were some words addressed by Strafford in the Privy Council: 'You have an army in Ireland you may employ here to reduce this kingdom.' The kingdom he was referring to was almost certainly the kingdom of Scotland, but his enemies chose to construe it as a threat to use Irish troops against his own countrymen. Only one member of the Council, its former secretary the ageing Sir Henry Vane, was prepared to deny the prisoner's interpretation of what he had said; other members claimed that they could not remember or confirmed Strafford's own interpretation. As Strafford damningly observed, 'My Lord of Northumberland remembered no such thing; my Lord Marquis of Hamilton remembered no such thing; my Lord Treasurer remembered no such thing; my Lord Cottington is very well assured he said no such thing, for if he had, he should have taken offence at it himself, which he never did.' All Pym could say in answer was that 'the Earl of Strafford hath endeavoured, by his Words, Actions, and Counsels, to Subvert the Fundamental Laws of England and Ireland, and to introduce an Arbitrary and Tyrannical Government.' Strafford protested, 'My Lords. do we not live by laws and must we be punishable by them ere they be made?'

Parliament's case had effectively collapsed: its legal basis was rocky and Strafford's defence was strong. Realizing that sympathy was now swinging in the direction of the accused, Pym dropped the impeachment proceedings in favour of a

---

[9] Pym was a member of the Middle Temple, but was never called to the Bar.

bill of attainder, an archaic procedure that had been invented during the wars of the roses but which had long since fallen into disuse. This did not stop Parliament resurrecting it to allow the accused to be declared guilty without the tedious necessity of a trial.

The Bill was passed by both Houses. On Good Friday, 1641, still believing that he could still save his loyal servant, the King wrote to Strafford, declaring:

> 'The misfortune that is fallen upon you, being such that I must lay by the thought of employing you hereafter in my affairs, yet I cannot satisfy myself in honour or conscience without assuring you now, in the midst of your troubles, that, upon the word of a king, you shall not suffer in life, honour, or fortune.'

Charles pleaded with Parliament to substitute life imprisonment for death. He even sent soldiers to the Tower in an attempt to release his old servant. He had not reckoned with the strength of feeling in the country: Parliament and the mob were determined on Strafford's death. The judges advised the king that Strafford was guilty of treason and the church agreed that he had no option but to sign the death warrant.

In an act of amazing generosity Strafford released Charles from his promise. Nevertheless, on hearing that the king had signed the warrant he is said to have risen in his chair and exclaimed, 'O put not your trust in princes, nor in any child of man: for there is no help in them.'[10] On a sunny day in May, 1641 the head of the King's first minister was struck from his body at Tower Hill. Charles ruefully commented, 'My Lord of Strafford's condition is happier than mine.'

Ireland immediately rose in rebellion.

Eight years later Charles himself went to the block, no doubt regretting his betrayal of the only man who, had he been sent for earlier, might have saved him.

---

[10] Psalm 146, v. 3.

Possibly the greatest injustice ever perpetrated by a British court-martial was the trial of John Byng, Admiral of the Blue, who was sentenced to death for failing to win a battle. A Frenchman's comment on this disgraceful episode was to achieve immortality.

Shot for losing a battle

In 1756 the French sent a naval force to seize the British island of Minorca in the Mediterranean. England's response was to send a squadron of ships commanded by Admiral Byng with orders to relieve the island, a task for which they were wholly unequipped. When the two forces met on 20 May many of Byng's ships were damaged and his officers killed. After a council of war he decided not to renew the attack the next day, having regard to the small prospects of success and the fact that failure might endanger the even more important island of Gibraltar. The country was shocked at the loss of Minorca and upon returning to England the government immediately had Byng arrested and put on trial before a court-martial. Determined to secure his conviction, the Admiralty published a mutilated version of his despatch which put his actions in the worst possible light.

But there was worse.

Despite being acquitted of 'cowardice' and 'disaffection' the only remaining ground for conviction was 'negligence', but the record of the court martial reveals not the slightest evidence of a finding of negligence. The Admiral was nevertheless convicted and sentenced to death. Despite a plea for leniency from the court-martial and the Prime Minister, and an unprecedented request for mercy from the commander of the French fleet, Byng was shot on 14 March 1757 on the quarterdeck of a ship he had once commanded.

Byng's tragic death led to Voltaire's well known remark: 'Dans ce pays-ci il est bon de tuer de temps en temps un amiral pour encourager les autres' ['In this country (England) it is good to kill an admiral from time to time to encourage the others'.]

Less well known is the epitaph on Byng's monument in his village church of All Saints church, Bedford. Probably composed by the great Dr Johnson, it is dedicated:

> *To the Perpetual Disgrace of Public Justice, the Hon. John Byng, Esq., Admiral of the Blue,*
>
> *fell a Martyr to Political Persecution, March 14th, in the year MDCCLVII;*
>
> *when Bravery and Loyalty were insufficient Securities*
>
> *for the Life and Honour of a Naval Officer.*

The almost unbelievably tragic story of Tilly Matthews and the Air Loom Gang began in the House of Commons, moved to a magistrates' court and ended in a lunatic asylum.

The Air Loom Gang

On 28 January 1797 the Home Secretary, Lord Liverpool was making a statement in Parliament about the government's delicate negotiations with France (with which country England was effectively at war) when he was suddenly interrupted by a shout of 'Treason!' from the public gallery. It came from a thirty year old London tea merchant by the name of James Tilly Matthews.

Arrested and asked to explain himself, Matthews told a far-fetched yarn about how he had been involved in secret peace negotiations with the French on behalf of the British government, and of having been arrested, abandoned by his English masters and cast into a Paris dungeon. The implausibility of this story was confirmed by an even less likely tale which Matthews then embarked upon. According to this, his mind was being controlled by a mysterious gang through the medium of rays emitted from a machine called an Air Loom which ran on a mixture of revolting substances. It was enough for the Bow Street magistrate to declare him a dangerous lunatic and Matthews soon found himself locked in Bethlem asylum in Moorfields, more commonly known as Bedlam.

Bedlam's resident apothecary was a man by the name of John Haslam who was prepared to listen to Matthew's wanderings. The Air Loom, his patient told him, was in a basement cellar by London Wall ministered by Jacobin revolutionaries intent on maintaining the war between Britain and France. Their leader was named 'Bill the King' (who was never known to smile). His second-in-command was 'Jack the Schoolmaster'. Other colourful characters included The Glove Woman and Sir Archy. The Loom was an immensely complicated machine, using a combination of Leyden jars and windmill sails to emit rays controlling a magnet which had been implanted in Matthews' brain. It had settings with bizarre names such as 'fluid locking', 'stone making', 'lobster-cracking' and 'brain-saying'. Matthews even produced a detailed technical drawing of the strange device.

But no one believed him and Matthews remained confined a mental patient. Thirteen years later his family, believing him to be better, took out a writ of habeas corpus to seek his release. Despite written reports from two doctors certifying him to be sane the Commissioners in Lunacy resisted the application on the basis of a long report from Haslam to the contrary. But the authorities' trump card was a letter from Lord Liverpool asking that Matthews should continue to be detained - strangely, at His Lordship's expense, 'together with the Expenses of his funeral in case he dies there'. The family's application was rejected by Lord Chief Justice, Lord Ellenborough.

Years passed and the authorities decided to hold a competition for the re-building of Bethlem hospital. Matthews, a man experienced in architectural drawing and engraving, entered the competition with a magnificent set of plans embodying enlightened and thoughtful design features. In the end none of the entries was accepted, but Matthews was awarded a prize of £30 for his 'labour and abilities'.

A second application for Matthews' release was made in 1814, with no better result than the first. By that date, however, he had been moved to a private asylum in Hackney where he was treated as entirely sane. He became a trusted inmate and assisted in the management of the institution until his death there the following year.

Meanwhile, the House of Commons received a report from its Committee of Mad Houses in England. This revealed that Haslam, frustrated at Matthews' refusal to admit his madness, had been in the habit of chaining his patient up (a practice of which he had publicly expressed disapproval). His dismissal from office was a belated measure of justice for the now deceased Matthews.

But the real irony was that the tea merchant, a man of strong Republican sympathies, *had* been involved in secret negotiations between London and Paris with the aim of preventing war between the two countries. He *had* drafted peace proposals and submitted them to the governments of the two nations. And he *had* indeed met Pitt, Lord Liverpool and other dignitaries, not once, but on several occasions. When at the height of the Terror the moderate Girondists with whom Matthews had been negotiating lost power to the Jacobins he had been arrested on suspicion of being an English agent and imprisoned in France for three years. The brutal conditions of his confinement had unhinged his mind.

Matthews' mistake was in writing to ministers threatening to expose how he had been betrayed. They repudiated their former agent and refused to assist him in his hour of need. For the rest of his life he was effectively a political prisoner in his own land.

Matthews' Air Loom is now recognized as the first identifiable example of what is known as an 'influencing engine' a device common to the imagination of schizophrenics.[11]

> When a country is in the grip of what is now called institutional racism the most frightful injustices can go unnoticed. The conviction for treason of a Captain in the French army is a case in point. It began with a simple error, was compounded by prejudice and sealed by forgery. Even when the truth came to light the French authorities refused to recognize what was arguably the greatest personal injustice of the nineteenth century.

'J'Accuse!'

The story began in 1894 when a handwritten letter (the *bordereau*, or memorandum) was surreptitiously removed from a waste-basket in the German embassy in Paris by French military intelligence. Signed only by the letter 'D', it contained an offer to provide information about French artillery to the German military attaché.

Bertillon, the famous handwriting expert, examined the document and concluded that 'D' was Alfred Dreyfus, a 35 year old artillery officer serving on the General Staff. Dreyfus, who was of Alsatian Jewish descent and thus already half guilty in French eyes, was arrested and tried in secret by a military court. The evidence against him was weak, but a Major Hubert Henry testified 'on his honour' that he had received information from a source he refused to disclose that Dreyfus was, indeed, the traitor. On the basis of this wholly inadequate evidence Dreyfus was convicted of treason on 5 January 1895 and sentenced to military degradation followed by transportation and solitary confinement for life. At a ceremony in the Champ de Mars in Paris attended by thousands of hostile spectators the epaulettes of the proud artillery officer were torn from his shoulders and his sword

---

[11] The full story of the Air Loom may be found in Mike Jay's *The Air Loom Gang*, Bantam Books, 2004.

broken, while all the time he protested his innocence. Afterwards, he was shipped to Devil's Island, France's feared penal colony off the coast of French Guiana.

Nearly a year later another incriminating document was retrieved from a German embassy waste basket, this time a telegram known as a *petit bleu* by virtue of the colour of its paper. Its wording suggested that the spy was in fact a Major Ferdinand Walsin-Esterhazy. Esterhazy was put on trial but acquitted after the same Major Henry produced a forged document which appeared once again to incriminate Dreyfus.

The first to expose Esterhazy and to challenge the Henry forgery was the chief of army intelligence, Lt Col Georges Picquart. For this act of perception he was arrested and spent time in prison before being exonerated.

In 1897 the famous novelist Émile Zola stunned France by protesting against Dreyfus' treatment in an open letter to the President of the Republic entitled *J'Accuse* ('I Accuse'). The author was prosecuted for criminal libel and convicted, but fled to England before he could be sentenced. Nine months later the forged *bordereau* was conclusively traced to Henry. He was arrested, but slit his throat before he could be tried. After his death 350 Catholic clergy sponsored a monument in his honour.

By 1899 the evidence in Dreyfus' favour was mounting and Esterhazy fled to England. When a re-trial was ordered the court decided to sit in secret. Unbelievably, after a month of hearings Dreyfus was found guilty of treason once again, though his sentence was reduced to one of ten years imprisonment on 'extenuating circumstances' of an unspecified nature! Dreyfus was immediately released because he had already served the ten years. A few days later he was given a Presidential pardon. Eventually, in 1906 Dreyfus' conviction was overturned by the *Cours de Cassation*, France's supreme court. He was reinstated in the army and went on to give distinguished service on the Western Front which led to his being awarded the Légion d'Honour.

Zola was not around to welcome the outcome. He had died in 1902 of carbon monoxide poisoning caused by a blocked chimney. There are credible grounds for suspecting that he may have been murdered. It is notable that nearly all the characters in this tragedy were anti-Semites, from Bertillon, Henry and Esterhazy, to the judges, ministers and clergy concerned and, ironically, Picquart.

To this day Esterhazy remains an enigma. Formerly an officer in French counter-intelligence, he seems to have been a spy for the Germans, but may also have been a counter-spy for the French - which would explain his being pensioned off after the Dreyfus affair. Apparently considering the pension to be insufficient reward for his services Esterhazy swindled his cousin out of a large sum of money. Sentenced to three years imprisonment for the crime, he fled to England, where he spent his remaining years in Harpenden writing anti-Semitic articles under an assumed name.

The case of John Henry George Lee is remarkable for two reasons; not only was he convicted of a murder he probably did not commit; the circumstances of his 'execution' proved to be of a wholly exceptional nature.

The man they couldn't hang

In the early hours of 15 November, 1884 Miss Emma Keyse was found dead in the living room of her beachside house, 'The Glen' in Babbacombe, Devon. Her throat had been slit almost to the bone, the side of her head had been smashed in and attempts had been made to burn the body with newspapers and paraffin.

Sixty-eight year old Miss Keyse had in her youth been a lady-in-waiting to the future Queen Victoria. She lived alone in her house with her servants Jane and Eliza Neck, and Elizabeth Harris the cook. Elizabeth's step brother, John, sometimes known as John Babbacombe Lee, acted as a groundsman and occasional butler to Miss Keyse.

The twenty year old Lee had a shady history. He had briefly worked for Miss Keyse as a boy, but left to become a sailor. Discharged from the sea as an invalid, he went to work in hotels. During this period he served a six month prison sentence for stealing silverware from his employer. But Miss Keyse had a high opinion of the young man and took him back into her service. He broke this trust shortly before the murder, when he stole a guitar belonging to Miss Keyse and sold it to a shop in Torquay. For some reason, possibly his relationship with Elizabeth, he was not dismissed, though his wages were reduced.

When the fire started on the night of the murder Lee had rescued Jane Neck, but he soon came under suspicion. He had a bloody hand which he claimed to have cut while breaking a window to let out smoke. The hatchet which he used to break down a rafter was found to fit the wound in Miss Keyse's head. And an almost empty paraffin can bearing bloodspots was found in the pantry in which he slept. He was arrested and charged with murder and arson.

Lee pleaded Not Guilty at his trial at Exeter Assizes. At first he was represented by a local solicitor, Reginald Templer who had volunteered for the task despite the fact that he was a friend of the dead woman. Templer showed signs of mental instability (he was to die in a sanatorium two years later) and was replaced by his younger brother, the local MP. That was not a good choice either: he failed to cross examine some of the prosecution witnesses and called none for the defence. Lee himself was unable to give evidence because of the archaic laws of the day. Despite the absence of any credible motive, he was found guilty and sentenced to death. Before he left the dock the judge, Mr Justice Manisty, commented on his calmness. Lee replied, 'The reason I am so calm, is that I trust in the Lord, and he knows that I am innocent.'

Awaiting execution, Lee wrote to his sister, 'It must be some very hard hearted persons to let me die for nothing ... they have not told six words of truth, that is the servants, and that lovely stepsister, who carries her character with her.'

At eight o'clock on the morning of 23 February, 1885 Lee was taken from the condemned cell at Exeter gaol to the newly-erected scaffold. It was a collapsible design which could be moved from prison to prison as the need demanded. Despite the fact that it was a wet morning James Berry, the hangman, was confident of his equipment, having checked it only two days before.

Berry put the noose around Lee's neck and placed a black hood on his head, but when he pulled the lever the mechanism jammed. The executioner and some of the officials stamped on the boards to get them to move, but without success.

This failure was a not entirely unheard-of occurrence and a carpenter was called to adjust the mechanism. Twenty minutes later after it had been tested and found to work properly Lee was back on the scaffold, the lever was pulled again, but again the trap failed to open. The condemned man was taken back to the cells a second time while the carpenter planed the edge of the trap. When on the third attempt the trap still failed to open Lee showed signs of fainting and the prison surgeon stepped in: 'You may experiment as much as you like on a sack of flour,' he said, 'but you shall not experiment on this man any longer.' When the facts were reported to the Home Secretary, Sir William Harcourt, he commuted Lee's sentence to one of life imprisonment. 'It would', he said, 'shock the feeling of anyone if a man had twice to pay the pangs of imminent death.'

It was never discovered why the trap failed. Some said that it was because of the rain or because it was tested with a different number of people standing on it. Whatever the case, the debacle led to the adoption of an improved design of trap.

Twenty two years later in 1907 Lee was released from prison. He later married and fathered two children, but disappeared just before the birth of the second. There is some evidence that he left for America in 1911, where he is thought to have lived until his death in 1945. But did he kill Miss Keyse?

The prosecution claimed that he had been the only man in the house that night, yet Lee told his solicitors that Reginald Templer was there as well. Many years later a local newspaper reported that Templer had been having an affair with Elizabeth, Lee's attractive step sister, who was to give birth to an illegitimate child six months after the murder. Another paper reported that Elizabeth, who had joined the Salvation Army, had made a deathbed confession which exonerated Lee.

Assuming that Lee was not the murderer, the most likely scenario is that Elizabeth and her lover, Templer were having a noisy late night party below stairs at which drink flowed freely. It woke Miss Keyse, who discovered the couple, possibly in compromising circumstances, and the infuriated and tipsy Templer struck her, causing her death. At his sister's entreaty Lee may have made a clumsy attempt to cover up the crime by faking a fire.

To this day no one can be sure of Lee's innocence, but there can be little doubt of the injustice of his conviction and sentence.

There was a time when an accused could appeal against his conviction for crime only on a point of law and not on the facts of the case. The need for change was brought home by a number of scandalous convictions, most notably the cases of George Edalji and Adolf Beck.

The great injustice done to Edalji only came to light by the efforts of an amateur sleuth.

The amateur sleuth

Shapurji Edalji was the vicar of St Mark's Church in Great Wyrley, Staffordshire. He was a Parsee turned Christian who had married an Englishwoman, an arrangement which did not find favour with many of his parishioners. The couple had three children, the eldest being a boy, George. In 1888 and again in 1892, when George was 16, the Edaljis received anonymous letters of a threatening, abusive and scurrilous nature, and were harassed in various ways. The chief constable suspected that George was at the bottom of it all, but could not prove it.

George was a studious grammar school lad who went on to study law. After taking articles he became a solicitor with offices in Birmingham, while still living at home in Great Wyrley in his spare time he wrote *'Railway Law for "The Man in the Train"'*. By 1903, fifteen years after the anonymous letters, George, might have been pardoned for thinking his troubles were behind him, when sheep, cows and horses in the Great Wyrley area were attacked at night in their fields, with shallow slits being cut along their stomachs. Six constables were assigned to watch out for the attacker, but without success. Local rumour had it that the mutilations were of a ritual nature of a type associated with an alien religion and police received an anonymous letter accusing George of the crimes. The vicarage was searched and a pair of muddy shoes and other clothing were discovered bearing what seemed to be traces of blood and horse hair. George was arrested and charged with killing a pit pony (the eighth and most recent of the atrocities) and with writing a threatening letter. Put on trial, George denied the accusations vigorously. Despite the vicar's evidence that his son slept with him in a locked room which he could not have left without being detected George was convicted and sentenced by an inexperienced chairman of quarter sessions to seven years penal servitude.

When the atrocities continued the police put them down to copycat crimes. But doubts began to grow about George's conviction. Three years later, as a result of representations from a former chief justice of the Bahamas, George was released from prison, though he was not pardoned and had to report regularly to the police.

As a result of an article which George had written for the press a Scottish General Practitioner with a taste for mysteries decided to look into the case. After examining the evidence he noted that the 'blood' on George's razor was merely rust, that the mud found on his clothes was of a different type from that found at the scene of the crime and that the horse hair came from a piece of animal hide wrapped around the clothes by the police. He also discovered that the handwriting 'expert' the police had used had given misleading evidence in the Adolf Beck case (see below).

The GP was also an experienced eye doctor, and when he saw George reading he noticed that he,

> 'held the paper so close to his eyes and rather sideways, proving not only a high degree of myopia but marked astigmatism. The idea of such a man scouring fields at night and assaulting cattle while avoiding the watching police was ludicrous to anyone who can imagine what the world looks like to eyes with myopia of eight dioptres.'

As a result of these discoveries George was given a free pardon for the livestock mutilations. However, a Home Office investigation of the case concluded that he was nevertheless the author of the anonymous letters. As a result he was refused a re-trial and received no compensation. The Law Society took a more generous view and readmitted George to the roll of solicitors. In 1934 a farm labourer confessed to having been a member of the gang which wrote the anonymous letters.

The doctor's methods might justifiably be compared with those of the fictional detective, Sherlock Holmes; which is not surprising since the doctor was in fact Sir Arthur Conan Doyle.

George Edalji's sorry fate was the result of racial prejudice and poor policing. But the person ultimately responsible for what happened to George was the wicked individual who committed these atrocities in the first place.

Adolf Beck was the victim of an equally great injustice, not once but twice.

'Sir, I know you'

In December 1895 a young woman named Ottilie Meissonier went up to a smartly dressed man waiting at the door of her apartment building in London's Victoria district and said, 'Sir. I know you.' The man was one, Adolf Beck. When Ottilie called him a thief Beck panicked and ran, followed hard by his accuser. When the two of them came across a policeman Beck complained that he was being chased by a prostitute. An indignant Ottilie told the officer that Beck, using the name 'Lord Willoughby', had conned her into giving him some of her jewellery three weeks before.

The police believed Ottilie and charged Beck with fourteen offences of fraud and theft. They had good reason for doing so. At his trial at the Old Bailey a police officer firmly and unequivocally identified Beck as 'John Smith', a man he had seen convicted of theft eighteen years before. 'There is no doubt whatever - I know quite well what is at stake on my answer and I say without doubt he is the man.' Ottilie and twelve of 'Smith's' other victims gave equally firm evidence that Beck was the fraudster who had approached them describing himself as 'Lord Willoughby', or some such name, and conned them into parting with cash or valuables. 'Willoughby's' modus operandi was to charm his victims into agreeing to become his housekeeper/mistress with the opportunity of enjoying the good life and living on his yacht. On the pretext that he needed some new clothes but had no ready change he got the women to give him cash in exchange for a cheque. At the same time, he offered to buy them a better ring and took one of theirs 'as a sample of finger size'. 'Lord Willoughby' then absconded with the cash and the ring, never to return; and, of course, his cheque bounced. The prosecution also produced expert evidence to the effect that certain incriminating documents were in Beck's handwriting.

Beck's defence was that he could not have been 'Willoughby' as he had been in Peru at the time 'Smith' was convicted and he offered to prove it, but was not allowed to do so. By an extraordinary coincidence, the Common Serjeant (or judge), Sir Forrest Fulton, who was trying the case, had as a barrister prosecuted 'Smith', and he refused to allow the witnesses to be cross-examined on his past. 'The question whether the prisoner was or was not the man convicted in 1877 was not admissible', he ruled, 'upon the ground that it related to another and distinct issue, and one calculated to mislead the jury.' Effectively deprived of his only defence, Beck was convicted and sentenced to seven years penal servitude. While he was in prison it was discovered that 'Smith', unlike Beck, was a circumcised Jew. The judge was consulted, but advised the Home Office that this fact alone was insufficient to overturn the 'clear' evidence of Beck's guilt.

Beck served his full sentence, but his sorrows were not at an end. In 1904, three years after his release from prison, yet another woman came forward to identify him as 'Lord Willoughby'. When yet more women turned up with similar tales Beck was arrested for a second time and to his dismay charged with these new offences. At his second trial Beck passionately declared, 'Before God, my maker, I am absolutely innocent of every charge brought against me. I have not spoken to or seen any of these women before they were set against me by the detectives.' It cut no ice and he was convicted once again. Fate, however, was about to come to Beck's aid. While Beck was in custody awaiting sentence two sisters went to the police to report that they had just been defrauded by 'Lord Willoughby'. At this point a police officer realised that a prisoner at Tottenham Court Road police station bore a strong resemblance to Beck; upon inquiry he turned out to be the real 'John Smith'.

Confronted with the true conman, 'Lord Willoughby's' victims had to concede they had been wrong in identifying Beck, the handwriting expert retracted his evidence, and Beck was freed, pardoned and compensated for his pains. An inquiry by the Master of the Rolls exonerated the police, but severely criticized both the judge and the Home Office.

In 1907 a new court was established with jurisdiction to hear appeals on the facts as well as on the law. Two years later the by now impoverished Beck died of pleurisy.

When a young American teacher agreed to put himself forward as the defendant in a test case concerning the teaching of evolution in schools he had no idea how significant the proceedings were to become.

The confrontation on the lawn

In early twentieth century America idea of evolution, or the gradual development of species by inherited changes, was anathema to the people of the Bible Belt[12] and laws were passed to prevent the pernicious doctrine being taught to their children. In 1926 John Thomas Scopes was convicted of teaching evolution contrary to a Tennessee statute. It was a cause célèbre in its time, but not everything was as it seemed.

Scopes was a 24 year old science teacher and football coach at the High School in the quiet town of Dayton, Tennessee. At his trial the prosecution was led by William Jennings Bryan, a lawyer, national politician and renowned preacher who had come close to being elected President of the United States. The defence was dominated by Clarence Darrow, an outstanding advocate of firm liberal sympathies. The high point of the proceedings was 'the confrontation on the lawn', so-called because the hearing had been adjourned to the open air out of fears that the courthouse would collapse because of the weight of the many spectators who had crowded into the building from all over the United States.

The case became known as 'the monkey trial' because of the way both sides misused it as a platform for their views concerning Darwin's theory of evolution (which, strictly speaking, was not in issue at the trial). Putting the evolutionary case, Darrow said with his usual eloquence,

---

[12] The Bible Belt is that part of south-east and south central America which is home to a large number of fundamentalist Christians.

'If today you can take a thing like evolution and make it a crime to teach it in the public school, tomorrow you can make it a crime to teach it in the private schools, and the next year you can make it a crime to teach it to the hustings or in the church. At the next session you may ban books and the newspapers. Soon you may set Catholic against Protestant and Protestant against Protestant, and try to foist your own religion upon the minds of men. If you can do one you can do the other. Ignorance and fanaticism is ever busy and needs feeding... After a while, Your Honour, it is the setting of man against man and creed against creed until with flying banners and beating drums we are marching backward to the glorious ages of the sixteenth century when bigots lighted fagots to burn the men who dared to bring any intelligence and enlightenment and culture to the human mind.'

To which Bryan replied,

'...[the evolutionists] cannot find a single species that came from another, and yet they demand that we allow them to teach this stuff to our children, that they may come home with their imaginary family tree and scoff at their mother's and father's Bible... (T)hey do not explain the great riddle of the universe -they do not deal with the problems of life - they do not teach the great science of how to live... They shut God out of the world.'

In the end Scopes was convicted and ordered to pay a small fine, which was later overturned on a technicality.

The proceedings were subsequently made into a film, 'Inherit the Wind', starring Spencer Tracy, Gene Kelly and Frederic March. Though widely admired as a work of art, the movie seriously traduced the actions and motives of those involved. The real life Darrow was not rejected by the townsfolk in the way portrayed on screen and Bryan's views were nowhere as fundamentalist as the film made out. Despite the fevered atmosphere that surrounded it, the trial was in fact a collusive action designed to settle a contested interpretation of the law. The fact that it turned into a debate on 'evolution versus religion' was down to a weak judge who failed to control the advocates appearing before him.

And it later turned out that Scopes never actually taught evolution.

But there is more: the biology book which was at the heart of the prosecution was not the rational tract its libertarian supporters assumed. As well as teaching evolution it also inveighed against the perpetuation of inferior stock and condemned intermarriage with the 'low and degenerate' races, themes later to be taken up by Nazi Germany.

Those who denied the theory of evolution were proud to call themselves creationists. Many years later, after a number of adverse court rulings, creationism was re-branded as the 'theory' of 'intelligent design'. Despite a recent decision of the American courts that 'intelligent design is not science and cannot uncouple itself from its creationist, and thus religious, antecedents', 'intelligent design' is still very much alive, both in the United States and in the United Kingdom.

As a distinguished American lawyer chillingly commented, 'The Scopes trial may not be an anachronism. It may be a portent'.[13]

One of the most controversial trials of post-war Britain concerned two young men accused of the murder of a police officer. Not only were doubts expressed concerning their conviction, the man who fired the fatal shot escaped with a sentence of imprisonment while his co-defendant went to his death on the gallows.

'Let him have it, Chris'

On the evening of 2 November 1952 police were called to a confectionary warehouse in Croydon after two men had been seen attempting to break in. When they arrived they found 16 year old Christopher Craig and 19 year old Derek Bentley on the roof. Craig was carrying a Colt .45 revolver which he had adapted to allow different calibre rounds to be used in it.

---

[13] Alan M. Derschowitz. *America on Trial.*

Bentley was armed with a sheath knife and a spiked knuckle duster. When a Detective Sergeant Fairfax climbed up and seized Bentley Craig began taunting the police. Bentley managed to break away and shouted, 'Let him have it, Chris'. Craig then fired his revolver, hitting Fairfax in the shoulder. The officer nevertheless managed to re-arrest Bentley who offered no further resistance. When police reinforcements arrived, a PC Sidney Miles was the first to bravely jump onto the roof, only to be fatally shot in the head by Craig. After exhausting his ammunition Craig jumped off the roof, injuring his spine.

At their trial before Lord Chief Justice Lord Goddard both Craig and Bentley pleaded Not Guilty. Craig claimed that in firing the shot he intended only to frighten the officers (a claim that the Court of Appeal was later to dismiss as improbable). Bentley's defence was that he had not incited Craig to fire the gun and that he had not been party to its use. Indeed, he had not even known that Craig had a gun until the first shot was fired.

The prosecution maintained that Bentley's words 'Let him have it, Chris' were an encouragement to his friend to 'shoot the officer'. The defence were in a dilemma: to suggest that the words had the alternative, though deeply implausible, meaning of 'hand over the gun' would only confirm that Bentley knew that Craig possessed the weapon, which they were denying. In the end they claimed that these words had not been said at all, or that, if they had, that they did not bear that meaning. After a strong summing up by Goddard, in favour of conviction the jury returned a finding of Guilty. Because of Craig's age the only possible sentence was for him to be detained at Her Majesty's pleasure, which meant until the Home Secretary authorised his release. For an adult like Bentley, however, the only sentence allowed by law was death by hanging. Despite the jury's recommendation for mercy the judge advised the Home Secretary that he saw no reason why Bentley should not die. Although the 19 year old was not 'feeble-minded' within the meaning of the law the medical report revealed that he was of low intelligence. Nevertheless, the Home Secretary confirmed the death sentence and Bentley went to the gallows in Wandsworth prison.

Craig was released from prison in 1962.

The case caused a furore at the time not only because of the disparity of the sentences but also because of Lord Goddard's conduct of the trial.

Forty one years after his death Bentley was granted a posthumous royal pardon. Five years later his conviction for murder was set aside by the Court of Appeal. Goddard's summing up to the jury came in for heavy criticism. It was, the Court said, over-weighted in favour of conviction. 'Such a direction by such a judge must in our view have driven the jury to conclude that they had little choice but to convict; at the lowest, it may have done so.' They concluded,

> 'It is with genuine diffidence that the members of this court direct criticism towards a trial judge widely recognised as one of the outstanding criminal judges of this century. But we cannot escape the duty of decision. In our judgment the summing up in this case was such as to deny the appellant that fair trial which is the birthright of every British citizen.'

We shall never know how the jury would have decided in Bentley's case had they been properly instructed.

The criminal law has its limitations, as the case of the American 'Book Bandit' demonstrates.

The book thief

For most of his life Stephen Blumberg of Ottumwa, Iowa had been a book thief on an industrial scale. And he did it for pleasure, not gain. He was finally caught in 1990 after his long-term associate in crime turned government informer for reward. When Blumberg's three-storey house was searched it was found to be crammed from floor to ceiling with more than 90 tons of literature comprising 20,000 rare books and

10,000 manuscripts stolen from 140 or more universities in 45 American states and Canada. The FBI had to hire a forty foot tractor trailer to remove them. Another 11,000 books were returned to Blumberg's father because it could not be proved that they were stolen. The house also held a large collection of stolen stained-glass and 50,000 antique brass doorknobs.

'The Book Bandit', as he had become known, was charged with interstate transportation and possession of 19 tons of rare books and manuscripts valued at approximately $20,000,000. His plea of not guilty by reason of insanity was rejected, despite the fact that from a young age Blumberg had been receiving treatment for paranoid schizophrenia and other mental disorders. He was convicted and sentenced to 71 months in prison, fined $200,000 and ordered not to enter any library. His appeal to Federal Court was dismissed.

Blumberg, who enjoyed the benefits of a generous family trust, was a bibliomane, but it was not his first love: as a boy his obsession had been collecting antique fixtures from condemned houses. When he turned to books he was prepared to do whatever was necessary to get them, crawling through ventilation ducts and lift shafts by night, by-passing alarms and security guards. His greatest coup was in 1980 when he stole the faculty ID card of an associate professor of psychology at the University of Minnesota and used it in universities all over the country. His practice was to select the book he wanted, remove its markings by licking off the labels, and replace them with fake markings from another library before walking out. Once, he even ate a rubber stamp in order not to be caught. He sought to justify his thefts by saying that he was saving the books from destruction.

Part of the reason Blumberg got away with his depredations for so long was that at that time libraries, on discovering a theft, refused to publicize the fact for fear of ridicule and would not co–operate with police lest it advertise their lack of security. It took a campus police officer at Washington State University to bring Blumberg to book (as it were).

Blumberg was released from prison in 1995. In 2004 he

was put on probation for burglary. Later the same year he was arrested again for a similar offence.

Blumberg never married and his house was a tip: a friend's wife felt she had to disinfect any chair she sat on. A former associate described how, 'It was his habit to read constantly through the night, cat-napping, waking, reading, dozing, waking, reading again, never fully sleeping.' Although he was smart and determined in pursuit of his obsession Blumberg clearly did not possess the moral constraints that prevent the rest of us from such extremes of anti-social behaviour. Obviously, something has to be done about people like him simply in order to protect society, but it cannot be right to punish him as if he had full responsibility for his actions.

2.3 THOSE WHO GOT AWAY (OR THE WRONGLY ACQUITTED)

It has been said that,

> 'Throughout the web of the English criminal law one golden thread is always to be seen - that it is the duty of the prosecution to prove the prisoner's guilt subject to ... the defence of insanity and subject also to any statutory exception.'

No one can read the facts of the case in which these oft quoted words were first spoken without an uneasy feeling that the trial failed to do justice to the victim.

The Golden Thread

On 22 November 1934, Reginald Woolmington, a 21-year-old farm labourer, shot dead his 17 year old wife Violet.

Woolmington had been married for only three months when he learned that his bride intended to leave him. He stole a double-barrelled shotgun and cartridges from his employer, sawed off the barrel and threw it in a brook. In the words of one of his judges, he then,

'... got a piece of wire flex which he attached to the gun so that he could suspend it from his shoulder underneath his coat and so went off to the house where his wife was living. He knocked at the door, went into the kitchen and asked her "Are you coming back? ' She made no answer. She came into the parlour and on his asking her whether she would come back she replied she was going into service. He then, so he says, threatened he would shoot himself and went on to show her the gun and brought it across his waist, when it somehow went off and his wife fell down and he went out of the house.'

When Woolmington was arrested, a note was found in his pocket which read, 'It is agonies to carry on any longer. I have kept true hoping she would return this is the only way out. They ruined me and I'll have my revenge. May God forgive me for doing this but it is the Best thing. ... Her mother is no good on this earth but have no more cartridges only 2, one for her and one for me. I am of a sound mind now. Forgive me for all trouble caused.'

At his trial at Bristol Assizes Mr Justice Swift ruled, wrongly but understandably, that the case was so strong against the accused that the onus was on him to show that the shooting was accidental. It was enough for the conviction to be quashed by the Appeal Committee of the House of Lords, with Lord Sankey coining for the first time the mantra reproduced at the head of this section.

Whether justice was done for Violet is another matter.

This case illustrates forcefully how, despite newspaper headlines such as 'X CLEARED ON APPEAL' the overturning of a conviction on appeal is a long way from a declaration of the defendant's innocence.

One of America's first Vice Presidents was successful in escaping, first a charge of murder and, later, a charge of treason. His story illustrates how events outside the courtroom can influence the outcome of legal proceedings.

The Heights of Weehawken

On 11 July 1894 a duel took place on a rocky ledge known as the Heights of Weehawken, New Jersey, a popular site for such events. What exactly happened is still a matter of debate, but one of the bullets struck home and the injured man died the following day. So ended the life of one of America's Founding Fathers and the reputation of another.

The survivor of the duel was Aaron Burr, his victim, Alexander Hamilton. Hamilton was America's first Secretary of the Treasury. Burr was a brilliant attorney who had distinguished himself as a soldier in the revolutionary war. In 1800 Thomas Jefferson and Burr both ran for the office of President. The two men tied in electoral votes and when Jefferson was voted the winner by Congress he appointed Burr as his Vice President. But when Burr ran for the governorship of New York, he found himself vilified by Jefferson and his supporter, Hamilton as 'a man of irregular and insatiable ambition ... who ought not to be trusted with the reins of government'. Hamilton went too far when at a dinner party he declared that he could express a 'still more despicable opinion'. Burr demanded an apology or denial and when it was not forthcoming challenged Hamilton to the fatal duel.

A New York coroner's jury recommended that Burr be indicted for murder, but as the duel had taken place outside New York State he could be charged only under an anti-duelling statute. Whatever the law, duelling between gentlemen was at the time tolerated to such an extent that Burr was never brought to trial. The saga then moved to New Jersey where he was indicted for murder by a grand jury, but got off this charge too when the indictment was quashed on a technicality.

When the publicity died down Burr returned to Washington to complete his term of office as Vice President. Three years later he was to be indicted again, this time for an even more serious offence.

'King' of Mexico?

By 1807 large parts of Spanish controlled Mexico had been settled by Americans and tensions were developing between the two countries which America's President Jefferson was anxious to dispel.

Aaron Burr had other plans. Anticipating a popular revolt by the American settlers against the Spanish, he had leased 40,000 acres of land in the Texas part of Mexico. A clue to what he intended to do with this is apparent from a letter Burr wrote to the British minister to his country at a time when Anglo American relations were distinctly rocky. He offered in exchange for cash to separate 'the western part of the United States from that which lies between the Atlantic and the mountains.' Burr planned nothing less than a take-over of Mexico, possibly with himself as king. Following secret negotiations with General James Wilkinson, Governor of the recently created Louisiana Territory, Burr raised a pitiably small group of volunteers, using the island of Blennerhassett on the Ohio river as his base. But the plot was reported to the President and a warrant was issued for the former Vice President's arrest. Wilkinson, no doubt fearful for his own safety, did a swift *volte face* and rushed troops in to frustrate his old friend's plans.

Burr's 'army' swiftly melted away and he agreed to surrender to government forces. He was charged with treason as respects the plan to separate the western from the eastern states, and with the 'high misdemeanour' of sending a military expedition against territories of a friendly power, namely Spain. His trial took place on 3 August 1807 in the Virginia Circuit Court before John Marshall, chief justice of the US Supreme Court. President Jefferson was convinced that Marshall, his distant cousin and political foe, was biased in favour of the accused, and consequently ignored the court's order to produce documents Burr had asked for. Wilkinson was called to give evidence against the accused, but the effect of his testimony was weakened when he had to admit that an incriminating letter from Burr which he had produced had been doctored.

It made little difference to the outcome. Even before the prosecution had completed their case the chief justice ruled against them. The Constitution required an overt act for treason and not merely an intention to commit treason, and the evidence, he held, did not establish that Burr had actually levied war. Faced with this ruling, the jury reluctantly returned a verdict of Not Guilty. On the remaining count - of attacking Spain – Marshall gave a similar opinion and Burr walked free.[14] Jefferson, who had been determined to see Burr convicted, protested, 'It now appears we have no law but the will of the judge.'

Acquitted or not, Burr's career was at an end. He left the country to wander aimlessly around Europe. Five years later he returned to America to resume his law practice under a false name. Burr's actual intentions at the time of the Mexican adventure are still a mystery, but shortly before his death in 1836 at the age of 80 he learned that the Texan revolution against the Spanish had begun. 'There! You see?', he said, 'I was right! I was only thirty years too soon. What was treason in me thirty years ago, is patriotism now'.

Burr's extraordinary character was summed up by yet another of the Founding Fathers, John Quincy Adams, who wrote,

> 'He lived and died a man of he world – brave, generous, hospitable and courteous, but ambitious, rapacious, faithless and intriguing. His character raised him within a hair's breadth of a gibbet and a halter for treason, and left him for the last thirty years of his life a blasted monument of Shakespeare's vaulting ambition.'

Murder in the Palace

King George V died at Sandringham House on 20 January 1936. The official cause was a coronary thrombosis and lung cancer: the reality was different.

---

[14] After the trial the infuriated prosecution managed to get Burr committed to an Ohio court on the lesser charge, but he was never indicted on that committal.

Nearly half a century later it emerged that, shortly after composing the famous bulletin which reported that 'the King's life is slipping peacefully to its close', the King's physician, Sir Bertrand Dawson had hastened his comatose patient's end by injecting a lethal mixture of cocaine and morphine into his jugular vein. The doctor's notes recorded:

> 'At about 11 o'clock [at night] it was evident that the last stage might endure for many hours, unknown to the patient but little comporting with the dignity and serenity which he so richly merited and which demanded a brief final scene. Hours of waiting just for the mechanical end when all that is really life has departed only exhausts the onlookers and keeps them so strained that they cannot avail themselves of the solace of thought, communion or prayer.'

If this alone had been the reason for Dawson's conduct it might have been understandable, given the attitudes of the time. However, the doctor's notes indicate a further motive, namely that news of the King's death should be announced 'in the morning papers rather than the less appropriate evening journals'.

The royal stamp collector may not have been our most outstanding monarch, but he was not a bad one. In any event he did not deserve to be murdered just in order to be kept off the front page of the *Evening News*.

> *Some people have, quite literally, got away with murder – and got good publicity out of it too. Here's what happened to two young women in 1920s Chicago. They were strangers who only met in prison, but fate was to link their names for ever.*

The two flappers

A young cabaret singer, Belva Gaertner was arrested in 1924 for the murder of her married lover, Walter Law. Law had been found dead in the front seat of her car with a bottle of gin beside him, along with a gun from which three shots had been fired. When Belva's apartment was searched by police it was found to be strewn with blood-soaked clothing. Arrested, she said that she had been out drinking with Law and could not remember what happened. In court she ran the defence that Law might have killed himself.

Just over a fortnight later in a quite unconnected incident a laundry worker, the titian haired beauty, Beulah Annan shot her lover, Harry Kalstedt. When her husband, a night worker, returned to the apartment she told him she had murdered an intruder in self defence. She was more forthcoming with the police, saying that she and Harry had had a drunken argument and that she had shot him in the back while he was putting on his coat. Her story changed yet again in court, where she claimed that Harry had become angry when she told him she was pregnant. He reached for the gun, there was a struggle and she got to it first. The public were fascinated by the detail that, as her lover lay dying, Beulah drank cocktails while the Hula Lou foxtrot played on the Victrola (an early form of gramophone).

In prison the two young flappers posed for press photographs together. Garish publicity surrounded their trials, helped by the lively coverage of a young *Chicago Tribune* journalist, Maureen Watkins who quoted Belva as saying, 'Gin and guns - either one is bad enough, but together they get you in a dickens of a mess, don't they?'

Both women were acquitted at separate trials. (One can only wonder what effect the girls' glamorous appearances had on the all male juries.) They could not have imagined that their sordid tales would still be in the headlines in the next millennium.

Maureen Watkins left journalism for the Yale School of Drama, where she wrote a play, *Chicago* loosely based on the murders. In the play Beulah became "Roxie"; Belva, "Velma", while a real Mob attorney and another lawyer were combined in the character, 'Billy Flynn'. In time the story became a Bob Fosse musical and, subsequently, a movie.

> *Ruth Ellis was the last woman to be judicially executed in England. She was properly convicted according to the law at the time and as recently as 2003 the Court of Appeal refused to upset her conviction, but did she deserve to die?*

The bleached blonde

Ruth Ellis was a woman with a past. While still in her teens, she had had a son by a married French Canadian soldier who promptly decamped to his native country. She became in turn a nightclub hostess, nude model and part time prostitute. In 1950 at the age of 24 she had an illegal abortion. Later the same year she married one of the patrons of her club, a dentist, and moved with him to Southampton. He turned out to be a violent drunk and when Ruth gave birth to a daughter he refused to acknowledge the child as his. She left him to return to London where she became the manageress of a night club. Among her lovers were two of her customers, David Blakely, a wealthy racing driver and former bomber pilot, and his friend, Desmond Cussen, a businessman.

Blakely, though well aware of Ruth's relations with Cusson, was violently jealous and once punched her in the stomach while she was pregnant, causing a miscarriage. She in turn suspected him of having an affair with a friend's nanny. Drink played a large part in their relationship. Once, when police were called to Cusson's flat they discovered Ruth covered in bruises. She had been badly beaten by Blakely who in turn claimed that she had tried to stab him.

The couple continued to row and Blakely went to stay with friends in an attempt to evade Ruth. When she rang the friends they denied he was with them so Ruth went round to their flat and made a scene, leaving only when they called the police. Two days later on Easter Sunday 1955 Ruth lay in wait for Blakely outside a Hampstead public house. She was armed with a .38 Smith and Wesson revolver. When Blakely appeared and refused to speak to her she fired a shot at him and then followed him round a parked car, firing a second shot. As he collapsed onto the pavement she emptied the remaining four bullets into his dying body, slightly injuring a passer-by. After the killing Ruth appeared mesmerised until she asked a passer by to call the police. When a constable arrived she told him, 'I am guilty. I am a little confused.'

At her trial at The Old Bailey Ruth pleaded Not Guilty to the charge of murder. Smartly dressed in a black two-piece suit with astrakhan collar and cuffs and white blouse, her hair freshly dyed a platinum blonde, she gave the impression of being cold and detached. Christmas Humphreys QC for the Crown asked her only one question in cross examination: 'When you fired the revolver at close range into the body of David Blakely, what did you intend to do?' She replied, 'It was obvious that when I shot him I intended to kill him'. Despite the representations of her counsel, Melford Stevenson QC, the judge, Mr. Justice Havers ruled that there was 'insufficient material, even upon a view of the evidence most favourable to the accused, to support a verdict of manslaughter on the grounds of provocation.' The jury retired only briefly before finding Ruth Guilty of murder. When the verdict was announced she muttered, 'Thank-you'. Havers passed the only sentence allowed by law. Ruth refused to appeal or to apply for clemency.

After the trial the judge wrote privately to the Home Secretary, Gwilym Lloyd George asking him to exercise the prerogative of mercy; his plea was refused. The general public took an unfavourable view of Ruth, based probably on her appearance as the 'blonde killer'. A few were more sympathetic: petitions were organized on her behalf and on the day of her execution a crowd of about five hundred stood in silence outside the prison. The prison governor received a hoax call saying that a reprieve was on the way, but nothing could stop the inevitable. Albert Pierrepoint, the hangman, later wrote to Ruth's sister, 'She died as brave as any man and she never spoke a single word'. Christmas Humphreys paid for her funeral.

At the time of her arrest Ruth claimed that she had been given the gun by an American serviceman as security for a nightclub debt, and that she had taken a taxi to the pub. Just before her execution her solicitor, Victor Mishcon came to see her in the condemned cell. She told him, 'You won't hear anything from me that says I didn't kill David. I did kill him. And whatever the circumstances you as a lawyer will appreciate that it's a life for a life. Isn't that just?' She added that Cusson had given her the revolver and had driven her to the pub. A prison officer who was present at the time heard it somewhat differently; according to him, Ruth told Mishcon that she had asked for the gun.

Much later, Ruth's sister claimed that Ruth had been raped by her father as a child and that she was addicted to antidepressants. Post-mortem representations on her behalf have concentrated either on her state of mind following her abortion or on a far fetched conspiracy theory, centring on the role of Desmond Cusson. The more critical have pointed out that she went to kill her lover with premeditation and with apparent disregard for the fate of her children.

In 2003 the Criminal Cases Review Commission referred Ruth's case to the Court of Appeal on the ground that she was suffering from post-miscarriage depression at the time of the killing. The reference was dismissed as being without merit. The court even criticized the decision to refer.

Ruth certainly had a fair trial and was properly convicted according to the law. She accepted her guilt and repeatedly insisted that it should be 'a life for a life'. Ruth went to the gallows as a result of a mandatory law and a Home Secretary fearful of thwarting the public's demand for vengeance. Nevertheless, her death by hanging still leaves a bad taste in the mouth of anyone who looks into it.

Ruth's son committed suicide in 1952. George Ellis did the same in 1958.

One expects bad behaviour from rebellious young men, but not from the police and the courts which have to deal with them.

'The Chicago Seven'

America's role in the Vietnam war led to bitter internal division in that country. One of its more eccentric manifestations were the Yippies, or members of the Youth International Party. (The term, 'Yippie' was coined to describe a merger of hippie sub-culture with Leftish politics.) The only mark they left on history was a drug crazed 'Festival of Life' aimed to disrupt the 1968 Democratic National Convention in Chicago. Predictably, the demonstration swiftly turned into a riot and had to be dispersed by a body of police whose unrestrained violence against what was seen as the counter-culture only served to increase the disorder.

A Grand Jury indicted eight protesters and eight policemen for a variety of offences. At their trial the hippies, by now known as the Chicago Eight, did all they could by way of disrespect and vulgarity to provoke the obviously intolerant Federal Judge Julius J. Hoffman – and succeeded beyond their expectations. Not merely the defendants but their counsel also were cited repeatedly by Hoffman for contempt of court. One of them, the 'Black Panther', Bobby Seale, was so abusive that the judge ordered him to be handcuffed to his chair and gagged. When he continued to protest violently Judge Hoffman declared a mistrial in his case and sentenced him to four years imprisonment for contempt of court.

And then there were seven.

At the end of the chaotic four month trial two of the defendants were cleared of all charges. The rest were convicted of crossing State lines with intent to incite a riot, but acquitted of conspiracy to incite a riot. 'Conspiracy?', Abbie Hoffman famously remarked. 'Hell, we couldn't agree on lunch.' They were each sentenced to five years imprisonment and a fine.

The convictions were reversed on appeal because of the 74 year old Judge's 'deprecatory and often antagonistic attitude toward the defense'. The appeal court also condemned Hoffman's refusal to allow inquiry into the cultural biases of potential jurors and the bugging by the FBI of the offices of the defence attorneys. Five of the accused were re-tried, convicted and sentenced once again to prison, this time suspended. None of the police officers charged in connection with the riots was convicted, an outcome which probably represented society's prevailing disgust toward the rioters.

Of the Chicago Seven, the mop haired, bi-polar Abbie Hoffman went into hiding to avoid drugs charges. He later became a comedian and died of an overdose of barbiturates and alcohol in 1989. Jerry Rubin became a stockbroker and was killed in a road accident. Tom Heyden married Jane Fonda and became a member of the California State Assembly. John Froines opted for a career in public health. Rennie Davis became a venture capitalist and a lecturer in meditation. And Lee Weiner, 'the quiet defendant', taught sociology and worked for AIDS research. Only David Dellinger pursued his radical path for the rest of his life. During Bobby Seale's prison term for contempt he was accused of the murder of a fellow prisoner but was acquitted when the jury failed to agree on a verdict. He left the Party in 1974 after a violent disagreement and went on to write a cookbook and advertise Ben & Jerry's ice cream.

The acquittal of the American football star and movie actor, OJ Simpson for a double murder put an end to one of the most bizarre trials in twentieth century America, but not to' O.J.'s remarkable career in court.

'O. J.', or justice will out

Orenthal J. ['O.J.'] Simpson was an outstanding football player of his generation. A handsome young black American, he went on to become a minor movie star, appearing in such films as *The Towering Inferno* and the *Naked Gun*.

It was a sensation, therefore, when in 1994 'O.J.' was seen by millions on live television driving his car at low speed across the expressways of Los Angeles followed by police. He had failed to answer bail after being arrested for the brutal murders of his ex-wife, Nicole and her friend, Ronald Goldman, and it was his failure to answer bail that had led to the Keystone Cops low speed chase. When he finally surrendered 'O.J.' was kept in custody until his trial began.

The prosecution had a strong case, but it was fatally weakened by the perjured evidence of a racially prejudiced police detective that not even the antics of defence counsel could offset. Judge Lance Ito's control of his court also left much to be desired and in the end Simpson walked free on both charges. Usually an acquittal is the end of the matter, but this one proved to be only the beginning of a bizarre series of events.

Two years later the families of the deceased sued 'O.J.' in civil court for wrongful death. This time the proceedings were held in private, the police officer in the criminal trial was not called to give evidence and the hearing was conducted with scrupulous care. The jury found for the plaintiffs and ordered Simpson to pay over $8.5 million in compensatory damages, together with punitive damages of $25 million. The money was not paid.

In 2006 Simpson took the extraordinary step of writing a book entitled 'IF I DID IT'. It purported to be the murderer's account of the deaths of Nicole and Ronald. Widespread disgust followed which led the publisher to withdraw the book at the last minute. The following year a Florida bankruptcy court awarded the rights in the book to the Goldman family in partial satisfaction of the unpaid civil judgment. It was finally published under the revised title, 'IF I DID IT. THE CONFESSIONS OF THE MURDERER', with the word 'IF' in letters almost too small to read.

In 2008, just when it seemed that the 'O.J.' story could get no more surprising, Simpson was found guilty of conspiracy, kidnapping, assault with a deadly weapon and robbery. He and a number of his friends had entered a Las Vegas hotel and stolen at gunpoint various sports memorabilia which Simpson claimed were his. He was convicted and sentenced to a total of 33 years imprisonment with the possibility of parole after 9 years. The sentences were upheld on appeal.

The conviction took place 13 years to the day after Simpson's acquittal for the murder of his wife and her friend.

2.4 UNSOLVED MYSTERIES

Everyone loves a mystery, but many of the cases which come to court do not end tidily.

When the wife of the man seeking to woo England's Queen died in mysterious circumstances suspicion naturally fell on her husband, but was he guilty of her murder? The facts came out in the coroner's inquest, but its conclusion was lost, not to be rediscovered until over four centuries later.

The death of Amy Robsart

On 8 September 1560 twenty eight year old Amy Robsart was found dead at the foot of the stairs in her house, Cumnor Place in the village of Cumnor in Oxfordshire.

Amy Robsart was the wife of the powerful Lord Robert Dudley, Master of the Horse - and suitor - to Queen Elizabeth. His role at court, combined with Elizabeth's jealous nature, meant that he had little time to spare for his wife. In fact, Amy had not seen him for over a year. It was to lead to rumours of foul play, rumours which were compounded three centuries later by Sir Walter Scott in his novel, *Kenilworth* in which Dudley's steward is portrayed as the assassin. A coroner's inquest was held, but its report was lost in the National Archives and only came to light in 2008. (It had been filed in the wrong year!) So how did poor Amy die?

On the day of her death Amy had risen early. She was in an angry mood and impulsively told her servants to take themselves off to Abingdon fair, which suggests that if her death was murder it was not premeditated. Dudley heard the news the next day at Windsor Castle and immediately wrote to his steward, Thomas Blount, asking him to use all 'means you can possible for the learning of the truth' about Amy's death and instructing him to demand an inquest. Blount reported that Amy's behaviour had been odd and that 'truly the tales I do hear of her maketh me to think she had a strange mind in her.'

There are reports that Amy had been suffering from depression and that she had 'a malady in one of her breasts', which raises the possibilities that her death could have been the accidental stumble of a woman in a distressed state of mind, or even suicide by someone fearing a slow and painful end from disease.

The coroner's verdict when it finally came to light was that Amy, 'being alone in a certain chamber ... *accidentally* fell precipitously down' the adjoining stairs 'to the very bottom of the same'. (Emphasis added.) She had sustained two 'dynts', or wounds, on her head, one 'of the depth of a quarter of a thumb', the other 'of the depth of two thumbs'. Her neck was broken, 'on account of which ... the same Lady Amy then and there died instantly'. The verdict was death by 'misfortune', which on the facts of the case seems the most likely explanation.

Cumnor Place was pulled down in 1910.

Sir Thomas Overbury's grisly death in the Tower of London was one of the most notorious scandals in the history of the English court. His suspected murderers were convicted and sentenced to death, but the truth is still far from clear.

The Overbury mystery

Overbury had long been the friend and adviser of Robert Carr, Earl of Somerset, the 'Favourite' of King James I. But when Carr decided to marry his mistress, Lady Frances Essex (who at the time was already married to another) Overbury, no doubt fearful of his own position, did what he could to frustrate Carr's ambition. The infuriated Earl responded by tricking his old friend into defying the king who reacted by committing Overbury into the Tower of London. He was still there nearly five months later when he died in agony after a long illness. Three years on, after Carr had achieved his ambition of marrying Francis, evidence came to light which resulted in husband and wife both being charged with Overbury's murder. She pleaded Guilty; her husband denied the charge and was put on trial before the House of Lords.

The prosecutor, Francis Bacon planned the conduct of the case with unexampled care. According to Andrew Amos, a nineteenth century professor of laws, it was 'perhaps the most remarkable specimen, in ancient or modern trials, of the Genius of Order presiding over a systematic arrangement of evidence'. Despite a brave defence Somerset was convicted and, like his wife, sentenced to death. Lord and lady were pardoned by the indulgent king, while the 'small fry' who had assisted them went to their deaths on the scaffold. In those days it paid to be 'noble'.

Frances had certainly tried to poison Overbury, as she admitted to the court, but there is reason to believe that her poisons were not the cause of his death. And Carr, while certainly guilty of tricking his old friend into the Tower, had probably been convicted unjustly.[15]

It can be all too easy for the unscrupulous to build a case against an innocent man, and difficult for him to prove his innocence from a prison cell. Allegations against England's most famous diarist caused him to be imprisoned in the Tower. It could have ended his career, even his life, but for his persistent efforts to get at the truth. This strange story began with the case of the murdered magistrate.

---

[15] At least this is the contention of the present writer in his book, *Passion, Poison and Power*, Wildy, Simmonds and Hill, 2010.

Pepys in the Tower

On 12 October 1678 Sir Edmund Berry Godfrey, a Westminster Justice, was found dead in a ditch in Primrose Hill. He had been strangled and run through with his own sword.

Samuel Pepys, the diarist and Secretary to the Admiralty, was also a justice of the peace in Kent and in that capacity received reports of a 'Colonel' John Scott who had been seen hanging around Gravesend seeking passage across the Channel. Wondering if this could be Godfrey's assassin, Pepys had the stranger's lodgings searched. They were found to contain a secret paper on the cost and strength of the Navy which Pepys himself had written and submitted to Parliament. He immediately issued a warrant for Scott's arrest.

Scott was in fact no colonel but a thoroughgoing rogue and fraudster with a murky past. Born in Kent and brought up in America, Scott had run into difficulties with the Dutch authorities on Long Island and with the English in Connecticut and New York, and had been labelled as 'born to work mischief'. At one time or another he had been involved in fraud, kidnap and the theft of jewels. When the authorities got on his trail he fled to England where he insinuated himself into court circles, even undertaking a treasonable mission to the French king on behalf of the Duke of Buckingham.

At the time of Godfrey's death the country was in the grip of the so-called 'Catholic Plot', a supposed conspiracy to kill the King and massacre the English Protestants. Though accepted as true by many in high places, the 'plot' was in fact a lie dreamed up by the villainous Titus Oates (see above) who, a month before, had made a sworn deposition before the magistrate. To cover his tracks he claimed that Godfrey had been murdered because he knew too much about the affair.

Pepys had powerful political enemies, most notably Anthony Ashley-Cooper, first Earl of Shaftsbury, who were quite happy to use the services of 'Colonel' Scott in their efforts to destroy him. Ten days after the discovery of the justice's body an information was laid before the authorities claiming that Pepys' clerk, Samuel Atkins had been involved in Godfrey's death. The clerk was arrested and put on trial, but was acquitted when Pepys provided an alibi for him. But Pepys' enemies did not give up easily. On 20 May, 1679, William Harbord, M.P. reported to the House of Commons from the Committee of Enquiry into the Miscarriages of the Navy 'some miscarriages of Sir Anthony Deane and Mr. Pepys relating to Piracy &c.'

Pepys and his friend, Deane were suspected of passing secret information to the French, piracy, and in Pepys' case, being a Catholic. Credence was added to this allegation by the fact that Pepys' patron, the Duke of York had publicly converted to Catholicism. The plotters put it about that Pepys had done the same, but in private. The two men were arrested and thrown into the Tower and Pepys was forced to resign from office. It was all poppycock: though loyal to his Catholic monarch, Pepys was a staunch Protestant. Nevertheless, the two men would have been aware that, if convicted before Chief Justice Scroggs, they would, like so many others before them, undoubtedly have been sentenced to be hung, drawn and quartered.

The resourceful Pepys wasn't the man to take this lying down and from his cell in the Tower he used private investigators, his trusty Sam and a network of friends to build a case for his defence. As the truth gradually came to light Pepys and Deane were released on bail, but this did not stop Pepys' efforts to clear himself. Concealed in a closet, he overheard some of Scott's 'horrendous revelations'. 'If an angel from heaven had recorded this,' Pepys said afterwards, 'I would not have believed it.' Proceedings against the two men were finally dropped when Scott refused to acknowledge the truth of his original deposition.

Shaftesbury made an ill conceived attempt to assassinate the king and had to flee the country. Exposed and wanted for the murder of a hackney-carriage driver, Scott fled the country, only to continue his predatory activities abroad until Pepys' enemies persuaded William III to pardon him and allow him the title, gentleman.

To this day no one can be sure who killed Justice Godfrey, or why.[16]

Everyone knows of the French revolutionary, Jean-Paul Marat who was stabbed to death in his bath by Charlotte Corday. But is it possible that he could have been the same man who over a decade before was convicted of theft from one of Britain's most famous museums?

Orthodox opinion indignantly rejects the suggestion, but the truth is not entirely clear cut.

The museum thief

This is how the *Newgate Calendar* recorded the crime and its punishment:

'Peter Le Maitre was a French teacher at Oxford, and, being supposed a man of industry and good morals, he was indulged with free admission to the Ashmolean Museum. Thither he frequently went, and appeared very studious over the rare books and other valuable curiosities there deposited. He was left alone to his researches. At one of such times he stole two medals, and at another he secreted himself until the doors (without the keeper's suspecting anyone was there) were locked for the night. When all had retired he came from his lurking-place and broke open the cabinet where the medals were locked up, and possessed himself of its contents; then he wrenched a bar from a window and, unsuspected, made his escape.

He was advertised and described, and by this means apprehended in Ireland. He had first fled to Norwich, where he sold a variety of gold chains and various valuable coins. ... [Put on trial at the Oxford Assizes on 6 March 1777 before

---

[16] For a full account of Scott's activities see *'The Plot Against Pepys'* by James Long and Ben Long, Faber and Faber, 2007.

Baron Eyre] He had little to offer in his defence and, on the clearest evidence, the jury found him guilty. Upon argument it was found that no punishment adequate to the crime could be inflicted; and Monsieur Le Maitre paid the penalty of his offence by five years' hard labour at ballast-heaving on the River Thames.'

The first suggestion that Le Maître was the same man as the French revolutionary, Jean-Paul Marat was made sixteen years after the event, in 1793.[17] To this day it is a bone of contention among scholars.

The problem with sorting truth from fiction is complicated by the fact that our knowledge of Marat's life in England has been described by his biographer as 'very fragmentary and in most cases obviously false'. So far as can be ascertained, Jean-Paul Marat the revolutionary was born in 1743 and left home at the age of sixteen to find work abroad. After studying medicine in Paris without gaining any qualification he travelled to London around 1767, where he began calling himself 'doctor'. From London he moved to Newcastle upon Tyne where he practised both as a veterinary surgeon and a doctor. In 1774 at the age of thirty Marat published, in English, his revolutionary tract, *'The Chains of Slavery'*. 'At a time,' he wrote, 'when the French had no country, I was anxious to contribute to the triumph of liberty in a country which seemed its last asylum.' The authorities took umbrage at the *Chains* and Marat had to flee England to Holland, returning later via Edinburgh. The following year he is known to have received an honorary degree in medicine from St Andrew's University for his essay on 'gleets', or gonorrhoea.

A paper by Marat on a rare eye disease was published in London in 1776, (though this does not mean that he was in the capital at that time). In any event he is known to have been in Paris in the Summer of 1777 where he published further medical papers. But it is what the historical Marat was up to the year before that which has given rise to so much

---

[17] In an article in *The London Star* of 4 March 1793. A similar suggestion was made by the Rev. W. Turner writing as 'V. F.' in the Unitarian *Monthly Repository* of 1813.

controversy. Is it possible that the revolutionary was the same man as the common criminal? It seems unlikely, but yet ...

The name of the man convicted at Oxford is officially recorded as 'John Peter Le Maitre, alias Le Maire, and La Mair'. For convenience he will be called Le Maître hereafter. He is said to have been a tutor in modern languages at Warrington Academy, a well known school for Dissenters in what was then Lancashire.[18] Here he was described as 'a native of France ... being invited here by a gentleman of this college to teach the French language'. After leaving Warrington he went to Oxford posing as a French barber under an assumed name. It was here that he committed the museum theft.

By contrast, the records of the Oxford Assizes describe the accused as 'a native of Switzerland'. He is said to have 'harangued the court for a considerable time on his own situation (with considerable ability and no small degree of confidence)'. The court took the view that it was the duty of the accused to prove that he had come about the coins honestly. He could not do this and was convicted and sentenced to five years on the Woolwich hulks, where he was employed de-silting the Thames. About a year after his conviction Le Maître is said to have escaped from custody and fled abroad. (There was indeed a mass escape from the hulks in April 1777.)

Fans of the revolutionary Marat – and amazingly there are some even today – dismiss the Oxford story as a piece of Jacobin slander and point to the fact that the revolutionary Marat was appointed physician to the guards of the Comte d'Artois in a document dated 24 June 1777 at a time when Le Maître was on the run from the hulks.

Supporters of the Le Maître story counter this with a number of arguments. The revolutionary's initials were the same as those of the felon's. His name was originally spelled 'Mara' (one of the aliases of the Oxford thief) and only acquired the final 't' when he left for France as a young man. It has also been observed that 'it is odd that Le Maître's Christian

---

[18] The Academy's records do not mention anyone of this name, but they are incomplete.

names, John Peter should have been those of Marat's younger brother, and Henry Peter, the names given by Le Maître to his child, those of Marat's elder brother.'[19] And it may be noted that, while Le Maître was described as a Swiss barber, Neuchâtel, the place of Marat's birth, is in what today we call Switzerland. Marat's father had been a barber at a time when 'barbers' were also surgeons. Furthermore, the description of Le Maître in the Oxford 'wanted' notice as 'short and slender' corresponds with the known descriptions of Marat. Marat suffered from chronic dermatitis, which is usually put down to his time hiding in the Paris sewers. Might it not equally be blamed on his time working in the foul river Thames? And, of course, there is the fluency with which Le Maître is said to have addressed the Oxford Assize, a fluency which would not have been out of place in the politician, Marat.

As an intriguing footnote it should be noted, for what it is worth, that the name of one of the conspirators in the 'pop-gun' plot of a few years after the Oxford Assizes (see below) is recorded as John Peter Le Maitre, 'a native of [the French speaking island of] Jersey'.

The otherwise unremarkable murder of a twenty year old girl is notable for two reasons. Her alleged murderer walked free from court after claiming a form of trial which had been unused since mediaeval times. And over a century and a half later her sad end was to be eerily replicated.

The Whit Monday murders

At 6.30 am on 27 May 1817 a woman's clothing and a bloody shoe were found beside a flooded sandpit in the village of Erdington near Birmingham. When the pit was dragged 20 year old Mary Ashford's lifeless body was recovered from

---

[19] JM Thompson in *The English Historical Review*, XLIX, 1934, pp 55-71. It is the best review of the literature that the present writer has come across.

the water: she appeared to have been raped and forcibly drowned.

The night before, Mary had gone to an 'annual club feast and dance' at a local pub, leaving it at 11 pm along with Abraham Thornton, the village Lothario, her friend, Hannah Cox and Benjamin Carter. Mary and Abraham left the other two and went to the house of Hannah's mother where she changed back out of her party frock into her work clothes. She left there at about 4am. It was the last time she was seen alive.

Upon being arrested, Thornton's undershirt was found to be blood-stained. Told of Mary's death, he said 'I cannot believe she is murdered; why, I was with her until four o'clock this morning.' At the dance he had been heard to boast that he been intimate with Mary's sister 'and I will have connection with her though it cost me my life.' When t his was put to him he admitted having had sex with Mary the night before, but claimed that it was with her consent.

Thornton was tried for murder at Warwick Assizes. He claimed that he had waited for Mary to come out of her friend's house. When she failed to do so he had left for home. His alibi was confirmed by three witnesses who gave evidence under oath. The bloodstains were passed of as Mary's menstrual blood. The judge summed up strongly in Thornton's favour and it took the jury only six minutes to declare him Not Guilty.

Mary's brother, William was horrified at the outcome of the trial and turned to his solicitor for advice. As a long shot the solicitor suggested that his client resort to an archaic procedure known as an appeal of murder. It had been used in mediaeval times to resolve property disputes, but began dying out in the fourteenth century. By 1817 the practice was regarded by most lawyers as extinct. Nevertheless when William applied to the Secretary of State for a warrant to take Thornton into custody the warrant was granted and the case removed to the Court of King's Bench. In court, Thornton pleaded, 'Not Guilty', adding, 'and I am ready to defend the same with my body'. Handed two 'gauntlets' by his counsel, he put one on and threw the other onto the floor, thereby challenging William to trial by combat.[20] Naturally, Thornton resisted the move, but after several days of argument the Court held that,

> 'in an Appeal of Murder, the defendant was indeed entitled to prove his case by his body. As abhorrent as the idea of single-combat might be to a modern enlightened society, the procedure had never been abolished by Parliament.'

By the ancient law Thornton could be deprived of his right to battle if it was sufficiently obvious that he was the guilty man. After hearing argument on the point the court decided that it was not sufficiently obvious and adjourned the trial to allow William to decide whether to accept the challenge. In a letter to his clerk William's solicitor described his client as a 'stripling', expressing his fear that 'our poor little Knight will never be able to contend the Battle with his brutish opponent'. After reflecting on his chances in a fight with the sturdily built bricklayer William prudently withdrew his appeal of murder and Thornton walked free.

His fate was not an enviable one.

> 'Shunned by all who knew him, his very name became an object of terror, and he soon afterwards attempted to proceed to America; but the sailors of the vessel in which he was about to embark refused to go to sea with a character on board who, according to their fancy, was likely to produce so much ill-luck to the voyage; and he was compelled to conceal himself until another opportunity was afforded him to make good his escape.'[21]

Trial by combat was abolished the following year.

There was an eerie footnote to Mary's death. Over a century and a half later on 27 May 1975, the same day of the year that Mary's body had been found, the body of another 20 year old single woman by the name of Barbara Forrest

---

[20] The hand-made 'gauntlet' was in fact a home made leather mitten with a trailing feather attached.
[21] *The Newgate Calendar.*

was discovered. It was in a ditch only a few hundred yards from the site where Mary's body was found. Both girls were partially clothed. Both had been raped and strangled. Both had worked at the same location. Both had been out with a boyfriend the night before (Mary to a pub dance, Barbara to a pub crawl). Both deaths occurred on Whit Monday.

But there was more. Just as in Mary's case, a man by the name of Thornton who had been seen with the dead girl on the night of her death was arrested for her murder. Just as with his namesake, blood was found on his clothes. Just as in Mary's case, Thornton was tried for murder and acquitted on the judge's direction.

But then, coincidences happen.

The guilt of a young heiress convicted of poisoning her husband remains controversial to this day.

The Maybrick poisoning case

Florence Chandler, the strawberry blonde daughter of an American banker, met James Maybrick, an English cotton broker, on a voyage from New York to Liverpool in 1881. She was eighteen and he was forty two. They fell in love and married later that year in the fashionable St James's church, Piccadilly. In time the couple were blessed with two children. Some six years later Florence discovered that James had fathered five more children by another woman, two of them since they had been married. Shortly after, she herself began an affair with a younger man. When James got to hear of this there was a blazing row which ended by Florence agreeing to break off her affair and James agreeing to pay off her debts.

A few weeks later James fell ill. He was treated by doctors for acute dyspepsia, but died shortly after on 11 May 1889. James' brother was suspicious and a search of the house revealed seventy grains of arsenic, some of it marked, 'Poison for cats'. James' body was exhumed and found to contain less than half a grain of arsenic. The coroner's inquest determined that James had died from 'an irritant poison' administered by Florence.

At Florence's trial for murder at St George's Hall, Liverpool the prosecution called evidence of her having purchased flypapers containing arsenic. It was her intention, they claimed, to administer it to her husband in a meat juice bottle. A nurse gave evidence of Florence having tampered with the bottle. She also produced a letter which Florence had written to her lover, the terms of which, the prosecution claimed, were suggestive of her guilt. At that time arsenic was widely self-administered as a medicine. In anticipation of this being run as a possible defence, the prosecution called medical evidence to the effect that James was not an habitual consumer of arsenic. Defence counsel did indeed run the defence that the arsenic in her husband's body had been self-administered as a cure for gastro-enteritis. This was born out by three witnesses from America who testified that the dead man was a long time sufferer from acute dyspepsia for which he had taken the then fashionable remedy of arsenic. A chemist confirmed that Maybrick had been buying white arsenic for eighteen months and that at his death he was taking a third of a grain of the poison a day.

According to the law of the time Florence was unable to give sworn evidence in her own defence. Instead, she made an unsworn statement to the court, admitting having extracted arsenic from the flypapers, but claimed that she only did so in order to make a face bleach (a common practice of the time). The jury did not believe her and she was convicted and sentenced to death. The weak and conflicting evidence against Florence resulted in a public outcry. There was an additional cause for concern: the judge, Mr Justice James Fitzjames Stephen, though an outstanding criminal lawyer, was going into a decline, and his summing up to the jury lacked a proper grasp of the evidence. (He retired from the Bench two years later and in 1893 was admitted to a mental asylum.)

After reviewing the case at length the Home Secretary concluded that 'the evidence leads clearly to the conclusion that

Mrs Maybrick administered poison to her husband with intent to murder, yet it does not wholly exclude a reasonable doubt whether his death was in fact caused by the administration of arsenic'. He accordingly commuted the sentence to one of penal servitude for life. It was a curiously unsatisfactory compromise. As Florence's counsel observed, she was 'to suffer imprisonment on the assumption of [the Home Secretary] that she had committed an offence, for which she was never tried ... and of which she has never been adjudged guilty'.

Despite strenuous efforts on her behalf Florence was not released from prison until 1904. She died in America at the age of 79, alone except for her cats.

Florence's conviction was controversial, but life is seldom straightforward. In 1926 a former chief constable of Liverpool disclosed in his autobiography that a chemist had told him that Florence had twice bought 'a large quantity' of powdered arsenic from him just before her husband's death.

There is yet a further bizarre footnote to this case. In 1992 a Liverpool scrap dealer produced a diary purporting to have been written by James Maybrick which 'admitted' that he had been Jack the Ripper. The Ripper murders had, indeed, ceased at about the time of Maybrick's death and there were a number of features about the diary which convinced some of its authenticity. Others are less gullible.

Chapter 3

GOING TO LAW

From the point of view of the man or woman in the public gallery civil actions lack much of the drama which can surround a criminal trial, certainly in the days when a finding of Guilty usually meant a visit to Jack Ketch[1]. But this is not always the case.

3.1 'PUBLISH AND BE DAMNED'

Of the two leading cases on the law of negligence, one English and one American, the first has never given up its full story and the second arose from such a curious combination of circumstances as to lighten the heart of anyone who comes across it. Let's begin with the famous snail.

The snail in the ginger beer bottle

The story as presented to a Scottish court was that a Mrs. May Donoghue and her forever-to-be-unidentified woman friend went to the Wellmeadow Café in Paisley on the evening

---

[1] Jack Ketch was a seventeenth century executioner who gave his name to subsequent executioners for many years.

of Sunday, 26 August 1928. They ordered ice cream and ginger beer (a tempting combination, you might think) and the owner, Mr Minchella, brought them two slabs of ice cream in a glass and an opaque bottle of ginger beer, part of which he poured into the tumbler. Mrs. Donoghue drank some of the liquid, but as her friend began to pour out some more from the bottle she noticed the decomposed remains of a snail emerging with the liquid.

Mrs Donoghue brought an action for damages against David Stevenson, an aerated water manufacturer, in respect of the gastroenteritis and the severe shock which she had suffered as a result of the incident. The trial judge found that there was a case to answer but was overruled by the Scottish Inner House (or appeal court). Mrs Donoghue then petitioned the Appeal Committee of the House of Lords, the highest court in the land. It upheld her appeal by a majority. One of the court's members, Lord Atkin, memorably expressed their reasoning as follows,

> 'The rule that you are to love your neighbour becomes in law you must not injure your neighbour; and the lawyer's question: Who is my neighbour? receives a restricted reply. You must take reasonable care to avoid acts or omissions which you can reasonably foresee would be likely to injure your neighbour. Who, then, in law, is my neighbour? The answer seems to be - persons who are so closely and directly affected by my act that I ought reasonably to have them in contemplation as being so affected when I am directing my mind to the acts or omissions that are called in question.'

Lord Atkin's question was a conscious echo of the words of 'a certain lawyer' who was said to have asked Jesus, 'Who is my neighbour?' Jesus answered by telling him a parable in which the lawyer comes to realize that the neighbour of the man who fell among thieves was 'the good Samaritan' at a time when Samaritans were a despised caste.[2]

Atkin's decision in *Donoghue v Stevenson*, as the case is known, effectively created the modern law of negligence. It

---

[2] Luke 10:29.

is not generally realized, however, that this leading case was never tried on its facts. The argument was heard on what is called a demurrer, a procedure in which the court's role is limited to testing the legal principle involved on the basis of the facts *as they were alleged*, not as they were admitted or found by a court. Sadly, Mrs Stevenson died after judgment had been given and her executors settled the case. The extraordinary result therefore is that we will never know whether the famous bottle contained ginger beer or some other beverage (in that part of the world 'ginger beer' referred to any fizzy drink), whether the creature in the bottle was a snail or a slug, or even whether it existed at all.

The Wellmeadow café is long gone; in its place is a public seat and a small memorial to the most well known case in the law of tort.

Farce on the tracks

A case which is as well known to American law students as *Donoghue v Stevenson* is to English is that of *Palgraf v Long Island Railway Co.* (1928). The facts, as summarized by Chief Judge Benjamin Cardoza in the New York Court of Appeals, consisted of an unusual sequence of events:

> '[Mrs Helen Palsgraf, the] Plaintiff was standing on a platform of defendant's railroad after buying a ticket to go to Rockaway Beach. A train stopped at the station, bound for another place. Two men ran forward to catch it. One of the men reached the platform of the car without mishap, though the train was already moving. The other man, carrying a package, jumped aboard the car, but seemed unsteady as if about to fall. A guard on the car, who had held the door open, reached forward to help him in, and another guard on the platform pushed him from behind. In this act, the package was dislodged, and fell upon the rails. It was a package of small size, about fifteen inches long, and was covered by a newspaper. In fact it contained fireworks, but there was nothing in its appearance to give notice of its contents. The fireworks when they fell exploded. The shock of the

explosion threw down some scales at the other end of the platform, many feet away. The scales struck the plaintiff, causing injuries for which she sues [the railroad].'

The Court overturned the finding for the plaintiff, holding that there was no way the railway guard could have anticipated the injury to Mrs Palgraf.

The Carbolic Smoke Ball

Perhaps the most famous advertisement in the law of tort (or civil wrong) appeared in the *Pall Mall Gazette* of 13 November, 1891. It read:

> '£100 reward will be paid by the Carbolic Smoke Ball Company to any person who contracts the increasing epidemic influenza colds, or any disease caused by taking cold, after having used the ball three times daily for two weeks, according to the printed directions supplied with each ball. £1000 is deposited with the Alliance Bank, Regent Street showing our sincerity in the matter. During the last epidemic of influenza many thousand carbolic smoke balls were sold as preventives against this disease, and in no ascertained case was the disease contracted by those using the carbolic smoke ball. One carbolic smoke ball will last a family several months, making it the cheapest remedy in the world at the price, 10s. post free. The ball can be refilled at a cost of 5s. ...'

The 'last epidemic of influenza' referred to the Russian pandemic of 1889-90.

The 'smoke ball' consisted of a rubber ball filled with carbolic acid, or phenol, to which a tube was attached for insertion in the nose. One of its purchasers was a Mrs Louisa Carlill. Having used the device for two months without success, she claimed her reward. When the company failed to come up with the £100 her lawyer husband took the case to court and won. The company's appeal was rejected by the Court of Appeal in a decision known to every law student as *Carlill v Carbolic Smoke Ball Company*. (For the curious, the principle which the case decided was that an advertisement offering a reward can constitute a binding contract as soon as the terms of the offer are satisfied.)

Having lost their action, the company ingeniously tried to turn it to their advantage, announcing that, 'Many thousand Carbolic Smoke Balls were sold on these advertisements, but only three people claimed the reward of £100.' It was a brave try, but it did not stop the company going bust four years later.

Mrs Carlill died in 1942.

Of influenza.

The question of when an offer can give rise to a contract came up again in 1999 in quite another context.

A disappointing prize

Cathy McGowan was a video shop manager who entered a radio competition for a Renault Clio car. She correctly identified a scrambled version of Geri Halliwell's pop record *Look at Me*, but when she went to Radio Buxton to collect her prize she was dismayed to receive only a 4" long model car.

When Cathy turned to the courts for relief the radio station claimed that their offer was just a prank. Judge James Orrell disagreed: 'Looking at the transcript of the broadcast, there was not even a hint that the car would be a toy.' He held that the radio station had established a legal contract to supply a proper car and ordered it to pay £8,000 in damages to Miss McGowan.

But this is a line of reasoning that can only be pushed so far.

Only a few years earlier Pepsi Cola had run a marketing campaign in America under the name, 'Pepsi Stuff'. A random number of points was displayed on the twist-off caps of Pepsi bottles which could be redeemed in exchange for promotional 'stuff', such as T-shirts, hats and so on. In a television commercial promoting the campaign a student was shown arriving at school in a Jet fighter with the words 'HARRIER FIGHTER JET: 7,000,000 POINTS' displayed on the screen. A student by the name of John Leonard saw the ads and began collecting Pepsi caps. In time he presented Pepsi with the seven million points and asked for the Harrier in return.

Pepsi declined to honour the request, claiming that the use of a helicopter in the advertisement was a joke. The student took the case to the US District Court for the Southern District of New York, where Judge Kimba M. Wood ruled against him, holding that, '... no objective person could reasonably have concluded that the commercial actually offered consumers a Harrier jet.'[3]

One can only wonder what condition the student's digestive system was in after he had finished acquiring 7,000,000 Pepsi points.

A railway company got a shock when a coroner's jury ordered it to pay damages under a legal rule that was thought to have been dead for centuries.

Deodand

A publican and his wife were travelling by stagecoach from Portsmouth to London in 1808 when it overturned on the highway. He was badly bruised but his wife was more seriously injured and died in hospital a month later. He sought damages for the loss of her 'comfort, fellowship, and assistance'.

Rejecting the publican's claim, the Lord Chief Justice, Lord Ellenborough held – quite rightly as the law then stood - that in a civil Court the death of a human being could not be complained of as an injury. The publican could not sue for

---

[3] *Leonard v. Pepsico, Inc.* 1996.

his wife's death or for any suffering it might have caused him, only for the physical injuries he himself had suffered. This came to be known as the rule in *Baker v Bolton*. The logic of the rule was that a careless driver would be better off financially killing, rather than merely injuring, his victim.

But human beings are endlessly ingenious and an unexpected consequence of this decision was that coroner's juries began to resurrect an ancient remedy under which any object that caused a death could be awarded to the relatives of the deceased in compensation. It was called deodand, or 'Deo damdum' ('giving to God').

Deodand had originally been limited to moving objects like horses and carts, thus giving rise to the old saying:

> 'Whatever moved to do the deed
> Is deodand and forfeited.'

In time deodand was extended to any object that brought about someone's death. But no one had reckoned on the invention of the railways and the appalling accidents to which they could give rise.

The implications of this were brought vividly home following an incident on Christmas Eve, 1841 when a Great Western train was derailed in Sonning Cutting near Reading, resulting in the deaths of nine passengers and injuries to many more. The coroner's jury found that 'great blame attached to the company in placing the passenger trucks so near the engine' and that 'great neglect had occurred in not employing a sufficient watch when it was most necessarily required'. They ordered the railway company to pay £1,100 to the lord of Sonning manor or forfeit the engine, tender and carriages. The order of deodand was later quashed on technicalities.

Deodand and the rule in *Baker v Bolton* were both abolished five years later.

> *We should not forget that pirates had contracts too, though there is no record of any of them going to law to enforce their rights.*

The pirates' code

Just like the crews of merchant ships, pirates had to abide by their ship's articles. As you would expect, many of the rules were common to all pirate ships, as for example those governing the division of the spoils, compensation for loss of limbs and the prohibition of gambling, fighting or misuse of firearms.

Other rules were could be more individual, not to say idiosyncratic.

The articles of Edward Low and George Lowther, for example, demanded,

- Good Quarters to be given when Craved.

According to Captain John Phillips' Code,

- If any Man shall offer to run away, or keep any Secret from the Company, he shall be marooned with one Bottle of Powder, one Bottle of Water, one small Arm, and Shot. [Presumably the 'shot' refers to the contents of a musket, not the fate of the pirate.]

- If any Man shall steal any Thing in the Company, or game, to the Value of a Piece of Eight he shall be marooned or shot.

- If at any time you meet with a prudent [ie virtuous] Woman, that Man that offers to meddle with her, without her Consent, shall suffer present Death.

And the Code of the infamous Bartholomew ('Black') Roberts wisely required,

- No boy or woman to be allowed amongst them. If any man were to be found seducing any of the latter sex, and carried her to sea, disguised, he was to suffer death; (so that when any fell into their hands, as it chanced in the *Onslow*[4], they put a sentinel immediately over her to prevent ill consequences from so dangerous an instrument of division and quarrel; but then here lies the roguery; they contend who shall be sentinel, which happens generally to one of the greatest bullies, who, to secure the lady's virtue, will let none lie with her but himself.

- The musicians [musicians?] to have rest on the Sabbath Day, but the other six days and nights, none without special favour.

The Codes paint a colourful picture of life under the skull and cross bones, with its gallant swordsmen, disguised doxies and, above all, chamber orchestras. It would be interesting to know if today's Somali pirates have anything similar.

Someone who had more experience than most of the libel laws – from both sides – was Winston Churchill. Two of the cases in which he was involved concerned the former lover of Oscar Wilde.

Churchill v. Douglas

Lord Alfred Douglas was the son of the violent, almost deranged Marquis of Queensbury. He was a talented poet who, like his father, was, 'totally spoiled, reckless, insolent and, when thwarted, fiercely vindictive.'[5] According to his biographer, H. Montgomery Hyde, the notoriety from the Oscar Wilde scandal had left Douglas, now in his early fifties, 'a man with a permanent chip on his shoulder, aggressive,

---

[4] The frigate, *Onslow* had been seized by Roberts in 1721.
[5] Richard Ellman, *Oscar Wilde*, Vintage Books, 1998.

quarrelsome and apt to take offence easily.' In the 1920s he somehow got it into his head that Winston Churchill, the former First Lord of the Admiralty but now a back bencher, was a paid agent of an international Jewish conspiracy. He persuaded himself that Churchill had been bribed by his friend, the Jewish banker, Sir Ernest Cassel to write an unduly pessimistic communiqué on the great sea battle of Jutland with a view to manipulating the price of German shares on the New York Stock Exchange to the benefit of his Jewish friends. In fact, the memorandum had been prepared by Churchill at the request of the government and its thrust had been that the battle was at worst a draw.

Another of Douglas' fantasies was that Churchill had arranged the death of Field Marshall Lord Kitchener when HMS Hampshire, the warship on which he was crossing the channel, sank after hitting a mine. This improbable 'murder', Douglas saw as yet another Jewish conspiracy designed, he believed, to prevent Kitchener from reaching Russia and thus ending the (Jewish inspired) Bolshevik revolution.

No one would have bothered if Douglas had kept these odd notions to himself, but he was unwise enough in 1923 to use his anti-Semitic journal, *Plain English* to ventilate them to the world. *The Morning Post* newspaper responded by attacking Douglas for inventing 'vile insults against the Jews'. Douglas took offence and sued the paper for damages.

At the trial for libel before Mr Justice Salter Douglas realized that he was not in a position to prove his allegations so he fell back on claiming that he had sources for each of them and had acted in good faith. Seemingly as a result of an error by Churchill's counsel the jury found in Douglas' favour on the ground that he had not published the stories in 'reckless disregard of the truth'. They indicated their view of the allegations, however, by awarding Douglas only one farthing in damages. The judge followed suit by refusing Douglas his costs, even though he had technically won.

Later the same year Douglas repeated his claims at a public meeting, following this up by distributing some 30,000 pamphlets repeating the libels. It was the last straw. Douglas was arrested and charged with criminal libel.[6]

At his trial Douglas disregarded his counsel's advice and sought to prove the truth of his allegations against Churchill, which, of course, he could not. He also made a fool of himself by complaining to the judge, Mr Justice Avery that in an earlier trial of one of his friends the judge in that case (Mr. Justice Darling) had been put up by the government in order to secure a conviction. He complained, 'I have not been allowed to put my case before the court at all. I have been treated grossly unfairly. Every time I tried to present my case to the jury I have been prevented from doing so. I have never been able to tell the jury why I did it or where I got the information, and everything has been stopped. It is the most abominable piece of unfairness I have seen in my life.'

In his charge to the jury, Avery described Douglas' article as a diatribe of vituperative abuse against politicians in general and Churchill in particular. It took them only eight minutes to find him guilty and he was sentenced to six months imprisonment, two of which he spent in the prison hospital.

There is an uplifting postscript to this sordid tale. Nearly two decades after his libel trials Douglas wrote a poem in fulsome praise of Churchill, now Britain's wartime Prime Minister. It was published in the *Daily Mail*:

> Not that of old I loved you over-much
> Or followed your quick changes with great glee
> While through rough paths or harsh hostility
> You fought your way, using a sword or crutch
> To serve occasion. Yours it was to clutch
> And lose again. Lacking the charity
> Which looks behind the mask, I did not see
> The imminent shadow of "the Winston touch."
> Axe for embedded evil's cancerous roots,

---

[6]Criminal libel was a somewhat vague and unsatisfactory offence which was abolished in 2010.

> When all the world was one vast funeral pyre,
> Like genie smoke you rose, a giant form
> Clothed with the Addisonian attributes[7]
> Of God-directed angel. Like your sire
> You rode the whirlwind and out-stormed the storm.

Douglas' nephew sent an advance copy of the poem to Churchill. The great man replied with characteristic generosity, 'Tell [him] from me that Time Ends All Things'.

Civil litigation is not for the faint hearted; and for that reason it is normally unwise to embark upon it without legal representation. An heroic exception to this rule occurred in what became known as the Maclibel case.

The longest British litigation

In 1986 the London branch of the pressure group, *Greenpeace* distributed leaflets accusing the fast food chain, McDonald's of encouraging litter, mistreating animals and workers and destroying the rain forests.

The company served writs for libel on five volunteers of the group demanding that they retract their claims and apologize. Two of them refused to submit and their cases went to trial. They were Helen Steele, a part-time bar-worker, and David Morris, an unemployed postman.

It was a mammoth trial: fifty nine witnesses gave evidence for the defendants, seventy one for McDonald's. Nearly three years after the evidence was concluded Mr Justice Bell, delivered a lengthy judgment, in which he held that a number of the defendants' claims were untrue. These included the claim that McDonald's food was unhealthy, that the company was responsible for starvation in the Third World and for providing bad working conditions. On the other hand some of

---

[7] A reference to Joseph Addison, the eighteenth century essayist.

his findings were favourable to the defendants, such as that McDonald's had pretended to a positive nutritional benefit which their food did not match, had exploited children in its advertising, and had paid their employees badly. Because of the proved libels Steele and Morris were ordered to pay £60,000 in damages to the plaintiffs. This figure was later reduced by the Court of Appeal to £40,000 and the House of Lords refused to hear any further appeal. McDonalds treated it for what it was, a technical victory for them, but it was a temporary one.

During the proceedings Steele and Morris had received £40,000 in public donations, but it was totally inadequate to pay for their legal representation, even with the sporadic assistance of some pro bono lawyers. They accordingly took their case to the European Court of Human Rights which held that, having regard to the parties' resources in such a complex case, the laws of the United Kingdom had not struck the correct balance between the need to protect the applicants' rights to freedom of expression and the need to protect McDonald rights and reputation. The court ordered the UK government to pay the defendants £57,000 in compensation.

No one can fail to admire Steele and Morris for their skill and determination in successfully resisting a civil suit brought by a powerful multi-national corporation in what was probably the longest civil action in this country.

Judges can sometimes be faced with problems of comprehension in court.

'Shizzle my nizzle'

A band known as the Ant'ill Mob sued another band, Heartless Crew, alleging that they disparaged the plaintiff's copyright for its 2001 hit song, *Burnin* by remixing the song, using lyrics which they claimed referred to drugs and violence.

'The nub of the original complaint,' said Mr Justice Lewison, was 'that the words of the rap ... contained references to violence and drugs. This led to the faintly surreal experience of three gentlemen in horsehair wigs examining the meaning of such phrases as "mish mish man" and "shizzle (or sizzle) my nizzle". He went on, 'A search on the Internet discovered the Urban Dictionary which gave some definitions of "shizzle my nizzle" (and variants) none of which referred to drugs. Some definitions carried sexual connotations. The most popular definitions were definitions of the phrase "fo' shizzle my nizzle" and indicated that it meant "for sure". There were no entries for "sizzle my nizzle" or for "mish mish man"'

The judge concluded that the words of the lyric, though 'in a form of English, were for practical purposes a foreign language'. The parties could not decipher all of them or even agree as to what they meant. Counsel submitted that the evidence, not being the evidence of an expert, was inadmissible. 'I think that he is right,' said the judge, 'although the occasions on which an expert drug dealer might be called to give evidence in the Chancery Division are likely to be rare.'

The claim was dismissed in its entirety.[8]

It was the daunting task of Mr Justice Gray to determine in the course of a libel action whether a historian allowed his admiration of Adolf Hitler to influence his academic judgements. The outcome, coupled with the judge's comments on the plaintiff's integrity, destroyed the reputation of a major historian of the Nazi era.

'Yes, mein Führer'

The British historian, David Irving filed a suit in 1996 claiming that he had been libelled in a book entitled *'Denying the Holocaust - The Growing Assault on Truth and Memory'*. The defendants were the book's author, Deborah Lipstadt, an American professor of Jewish and Holocaust studies, and her

---

[8] *Confetti Records (a firm) & Ors v Warner Music UK Ltd t/a East West Records*, 2003.

publishers, Penguins. Mr Irving, who represented himself, had two main complaints. The book had described him as a Holocaust denier, whereas, he alleged, the gas chambers were a myth and there was thus no Holocaust to deny. Even more importantly for his reputation, the book suggested that Irving had falsified evidence and distorted documentary sources. The defendants took the bold step of claiming that their allegations were true. By agreement, the case was heard by Mr Justice Grey without a jury.

Irving had lived in Germany and spoke the language well. As an historian of the Nazi era, he was well regarded, even among other historians, such as the distinguished military historian, the John (later, Sir John) Keegan OBE, FRSL. But, like other critics, Keegan disapproved of Irving's views and detected in his writings an unhealthy admiration for the Third Reich.

Richard Evans, professor of modern history at Cambridge was the principal defence witness. He spent some two years researching the defence. His evidence ranged widely from the events of 'Kristallnacht' in 1938 to various deportations and massacres of Jews, and what exactly went on at Auschwitz concentration camp. The defendants pointed to Irving's book about the bombing of Dresden in support of their contention that he distorted and twisted historical facts in order to make them conform to his own political ideology. In the witness box Evans was challenged by Irving on almost every point.

Mr Justice Grey had a difficult furrow to plough. He had to assess the evidence concerning highly controversial historical events without forming any conclusion as to what had actually happened; his role was confined to deciding the issues between the parties, in particular whether Irving had provided an accurate narrative of past events.

The judge delivered his 333 page judgment in April 2000, nearly four years after the writ had been filed. He accepted that as a military historian Irving had much to commend him. He possessed 'an unparalleled knowledge' of world war II and a 'remarkable' command of the documents. He was able and intelligent and had discovered much new material.

However, the judge concluded that Irving displayed all the characteristics of a Holocaust denier and was an anti-semite and a racist who associated regularly with extremist and neo-Nazi organisations and individuals. As to his treatment of the evidence, he declared that:

> 'Irving has for his own ideological reasons persistently and deliberately misrepresented and manipulated historical evidence; that for the same reasons he has portrayed Hitler in an unwarrantedly favourable light, principally in relation to his attitude towards and responsibility for the treatment of the Jews; that he is an active Holocaust denier; that he is anti-Semitic and racist, and that he associates with right-wing extremists who promote neo-Nazism. ... therefore the defence of justification succeeds. ... It follows that there must be judgment for the Defendants.'

For an historian it was a damning indictment.

Irving's application for leave to appeal was dismissed by the Court of Appeal. He was ordered to pay Penguin's costs, which were in the region of £2m, and when he failed to pay he was bankrupted.

One of the most extraordinary incidents in this extraordinary trial was when Irving, replying to a question from the judge, was heard to answer, 'Yes, mein Führer'.

The courtroom collapsed with laughter.

3.2 MARTIANS IN COURT

The strangest of people sometimes appear before the courts as litigants, but few as odd as the following.

Satan immune from suit

A plaintiff in a Pennsylvania court in 1971 prayed for leave to file a complaint against Satan and his staff.

Gerald Mayo alleged (1) that Satan had on numerous occasions caused the plaintiff misery and unwarranted threats, all against his will; (2) that Satan had placed deliberate obstacles in his path that caused his downfall; and (3) that Satan had deprived him of his constitutional rights.

Yes, the application was obviously daft, but how should the judge deal with it?

Judge Gerald J. Weber was up to the task. He announced with his tongue in his cheek that he had discovered 'an unofficial account of a trial in New Hampshire' where the defendant filed an action of mortgage foreclosure as plaintiff. The defendant in that action, he said, was represented by the pre-eminent advocate of that day, and raised the defence that the plaintiff was a foreign prince with no standing to sue in an American Court. 'This defense was overcome by overwhelming evidence to the contrary.' (In fact, there was no such case; the judge was referring to the plot of Stephen Vincent Benet's short story, *The Devil and Daniel Webster*.) 'Whether or not this would raise an estoppel in the present case,' the judge went on, 'we are unable to determine at this time.'

If such action were to be allowed, he said, 'we would also face the question of whether it may be maintained as a class action. It appears to meet the requirement ... that the class is so numerous that joinder of all members is impracticable'. (The judge was probably referring to the Book of Luke, 8.30 which records Satan as saying that his name was Legion because many devils were entered into him.)

Finally, Judge Weber noted that 'the plaintiff has failed to include with his complaint the required form of instructions for the United States Marshal for directions as to service of process.'

The action was dismissed.[9]

---

[9] *United States ex rel. Gerald Mayo v. Satan and His Staff*, 1971.

Martians in court

A Mr Rene Joly brought suit in the Ontario Superior Court of Justice in 1999 against numerous defendants, including the CIA and President Bill Clinton. He alleged that they had 'conspired with the American government in its attempts to eliminate him and have otherwise taken various steps to interfere with his ability to establish himself and live freely as a Martian.'

After observing that Mr Joly 'presented himself as polite, articulate, intelligent and appeared to understand completely the issues before the Court and the consequences should I grant the relief sought', Judge Epstein, held that,

> 'Neither pleading discloses a cause of action. While conspiracy to do harm to someone is the basis of many actions in this Court there is a fundamental flaw in the position of Mr. Joly. Rule 1.03 defines plaintiff as "a person who commences an action". The *New Shorter Oxford English Dictionary* defines person as "an individual human being". Section 29 of the Interpretation Act provides that a person includes a corporation. It follows that if the plaintiff is not a person in that he is neither a human being nor a corporation, he cannot be a plaintiff as contemplated by the Rules of Civil Procedure. The entire basis of Mr. Joly's actions is that he is a Martian, not a human being. There is certainly no suggestion that he is a corporation. I conclude therefore, that Mr. Joly, on his pleading as drafted, has no status before the Court.'[10]

Sometimes it really is not easy being green.

3.3 WEIRD WILLS

'Let's choose executors and talk of wills'.

Richard II in Shakespeare's play of that name

---
[10] *Joly v Pelletier et al*, 1999.

Few human activities are as capable of giving as much innocent pleasure as the making of wills.

There are countless examples of probate lawyers whose testamentary efforts proved to be less than satisfactory, but for sheer negligence we must look to a Lord Chancellor, no less.

The absent minded Chancellor

Lord St Leonards (formerly Sir Edward Sugden) was a brilliant lawyer and former Lord Chancellor who in his time had been responsible for many reforms of the law, notably in relation to wills.

At the time of his death at the age of 93 St Leonards was believed to have made at least two wills and eight codicils which he kept in a locked box in his house. You can guess what is coming. When the box was opened it was found to contain six codicils, but no will. Fortunately, his daughter and secretary, Charlotte, was able to recollect the contents of this complex document because her father was accustomed to read it to her every night. Once, when she froze in the witness box the noise of counsel pouring her a glass of water is said to have reminded her of her father's habit of serving sherry as he read aloud.

In a step which was unusual, perhaps unique, in testamentary law Probate was granted in respect of a will which existed only in a witness's recollection, despite the fact that the witness was an interested party.

It later came to light that St Leonards was also accustomed to dictating his wills and codicils while wandering around the garden in his dressing gown. At his request he had been buried in that very same garment. Some have speculated that the missing will might still be in one of its pockets.[11]

---

[11] *Sugden v. Lord St. Leonards*, 1876.

The rhyming will

John Hedges' will was proved in the Prerogative Court of Canterbury in 1737.[12] It was unexceptional save for the fact that it was written wholly in rhyme. After the usual preliminaries it read:

> 'Because I foresaw/That my brethren-in-law,
> If I did not take care,/Would come in for their share;
> Which I no wise intended,/Till their manners are mended.
> And of that, God knows, there's no sign;/I therefore enjoin,
> And do strictly command,/As witness my hand.
> That nought I have got./Shall go into hotch-pot;
> But I give and devise./As much as in me lies,
> To the son of my mother,/My own dear brother,
> To have and to hold./All my silver and gold,
> As the affectionate pledges/Of his brother, John Hedges.'

'Hotchpot', by the way, refers to property in a common fund designed so that everyone should get equal shares. It comes from an old French term for pudding.

3.4 SCANDAL!

Though scandalous behaviour is, fortunately, not a crime it seems to crop up frequently in litigation.

---

[12] The executors of a will have to 'prove' it in the High Court in order to establish their right to administer the estate.

The greatest scandal at the French court came to light as a result of a laboratory explosion. It all began with an unhappily married young woman.

The Affair of the Poisons

Marie-Madeleine-Marguerite d'Aubray, Marquise de Brinvilliers was just 21 years old in 1651 when her father gave her in marriage to an army officer. It wasn't the happiest of alliances, and when her husband unwisely invited a fellow officer, the young Godin de Sainte-Croix, into his house his wife soon began an openly scandalous affair with their guest. Her father intervened to obtain a *lettre de cachet* (or sealed warrant) and had the lover thrown into the Bastille. Sainte Croix's incarceration proved to have its advantages, for in that grim prison he acquired from an Italian alchemist knowledge of various 'inheritance powders.' (They were probably a mixture of arsenic, lead and belladonna). Upon his release Saint Croix passed his knowledge on to his mistress. It was to be the foundation of an amazing career.

The Marquise immediately realized the potential of the knowledge. She was too prudent to use it untried so she administered it first, disguised in sweets, to the dying patients in the Hotel-Dieu, or hospital for the destitute. The patients' accelerated and agonising deaths gave cause for puzzlement among the authorities but satisfied the Marquise, who began administering the poison surreptitiously to her father. When he fell ill with stomach pains, she nursed him solicitously until he died several months later. To the frustration of the Marquise, however, the fortune went wholly to her older brother.

In order to get close to him she placed a rogue called La Chaussée in her brother's household as a valet. After several unsuccessful attempts La Chaussée finally succeeded in poisoning his master, an achievement which the Marquise promptly went on to repeat with her younger brother, thus allowing her to scoop up the whole of the family fortune. She then took a new lover, a 32 year old seminarian by the name of Jean-Baptiste Briancourt, to whom she revealed her poisonous arts.

In time the Marquise was deserted by both her lovers. When Briancourt died from a laboratory explosion a casket was found in his house containing letters and powders. The police tested the powders on dogs with fatal results and the letters were found to incriminate La Chaussée and his mistress. The Marquise fled abroad before she could be arrested, but La Chausée was put to the water torture.[13] He confessed all and was condemned to death by being broken on the wheel. After a while the Marquise returned to France, entering a convent at Liége where she thought she would be safe. She was wrong: a fake priest tricked her out of the building and she was promptly arrested.

A full written confession was found on the Marquise. She claimed to have written it in a fever and it took the court two and a half months deliberation before they agreed to receive it in evidence. The confession was more than enough to convict her. The young woman's icy demeanour in court had chilled her judges and she was condemned to be decapitated by a sword after first suffering the water torture. As a final indignity the court ordered her dead body to be burned at the stake.

During her trial the Marquise had repeatedly protested, 'Half the people I know - people of quality – are involved in this kind of thing and I could drag them down with me should I decide to talk.' To everyone's horror the claim proved to be true.

The affair of the poisons

The King, Louis XIV of France was horrified at what had come out at the trial of the Marquise de Brinvilliers (see the previous entry). He ordered his chief of police, Nicolas de La

---

[13] It was a nasty business: don't ask.

Reynie, to investigate the underworld of poisoners, witches and fortune-tellers which surrounded the king's court, and resurrected an old institution for the purpose of dealing with them. It was known as the Chambre Ardente (illuminated court) because of its lack of windows. La Reynie carried out his investigations thoroughly and exposed an extraordinary state of affairs which came to be known as *L'affaire des poisons*.

At the heart of the affaire was Catherine Deshayes Monvoisin, known as La Voisin. The wife of an unsuccessful jeweller, La Voison was an abortionist and a self-proclaimed witch with a clientele of rich court women. Her boast was that 'nothing is impossible to me'. Under questioning, she made widespread accusations against ladies of the court and many arrests followed.

The gravity of the affaire moved up significantly when the King's mistress, Athénais, Marquise de Montespan, was accused of having used La Voisin to obtain love philtres to retain the royal passion, and of attempting to poison various people, including her young rival, Mlle. de Fontanges, even the King himself. Wild stories flew around, like that of the defrocked priest who was supposed to have performed a Black Mass using the naked body of an unidentified noblewoman (widely assumed to be the king's mistress) as an altar upon which to sacrifice babies.

La Voisin was convicted of witchcraft and burned at the stake on 22 February 1689.

Although the charges against the King's mistress were never proved, they were allegations too far for Louis. He closed the Chambre Ardente and suspended all further investigations. He expelled his mistress from court but arranged for her to enjoy a comfortable retirement. The sixty or so suspects still imprisoned awaiting trial were not so lucky. They were dispersed to some of the strongest prisons in France where they were kept in solitary confinement for the rest of their lives, forbidden on pain of whipping to speak, even to their gaolers.

There is no doubt that some of the accused were poisoners and that some believed themselves to be witches, but most were no more than silly superstitious society women caught up in the poisonous fashion of the day.

> *There is no reason why the marriages of kings and queens should be any more successful than those of their subjects, but when their matrimonial affairs are washed in public they are bound to give rise to embarrassment all round.*

The 'delicate investigation'

George, Prince of Wales married his first cousin, Princess Caroline of Brunswick in 1795. Their subsequent divorce was to be one of the most scandalous in royal history.

It was not a marriage made in heaven. He was fat and already married,[14] she was a stranger both to discretion and to personal hygiene. He spent their first night together drunk in the bedchamber grate and the rest of his honeymoon in the arms of his mistress. The couple separated the following year after the birth of their daughter Charlotte. Caroline went on to adopt a number of other children, one of whom was rumoured to be her son. This gave rise to an allegation of adultery, and an all male commission of inquiry was set up chaired by the Prime Minister, Lord Grenville with the task of conducting a 'delicate investigation'. It found no evidence of misconduct on Caroline's part, but the situation did not improve and in 1814 she was persuaded to live in Italy by the offer of a substantial allowance. Once there, rumours soon started circulating to the effect that she was consorting with a member of her household. The evidence was considered insufficient to warrant an ecclesiastical divorce, so three commissioners were sent to Milan, where she was living at the time, in a fruitless effort to obtain proof of adultery.

When George's father, the old king, died in 1821 Caroline rushed back to England to claim her rights as Queen. Her

---

[14] The 'marriage' to Lady Fitzherbert was constitutionally illegal, but this did not unduly concern George who declared her to be his only true wife.

furious husband postponed his coronation and persuaded the House of Lords to introduce a bill of pains and penalties which would end his marriage and strip his wife of the title, Queen. The procedure had the advantage – to him - of denying her the opportunity of attacking her husband's own dubious morals. Caroline attended the second reading of the bill in the House of Lords. Although it was, effectively, her trial she was not allowed to give evidence. Lord Eldon presided on the Woolsack with the Lord Chief Justice and twelve other judges in attendance to offer legal advice.

The Attorney General, Robert Gifford made what was generally judged to be a weak speech for 'the prosecution', but the details of Caroline's conduct that emerged horrified many who until then had been her supporters. Notwithstanding the unexplained absence of a 'prosecution' witness and the advocacy of the great Henry Brougham KC the bill scraped through. Because of George's unpopularity in the country, however, the prime minister refused to send it to the Commons. Caroline's remaining supporters organized a thanksgiving service in St Paul's Cathedral, at which psalm 140 was read: 'Deliver me, O Lord, from the evil man'.

When the day arrived for George to be crowned King Caroline was instructed not to attend the ceremony, but went to Westminster Abbey anyway. Turned away from the main entrance at bayonet point, she tried to enter by a side door, but was persuaded not to do so. A fortnight later she died from an intestinal obstruction and her body was returned to Brunswick, more with relief than gratitude.

A few months before Caroline's death Napoleon died on St Helena. There is an apocryphal tale that George, on being told that 'Your greatest enemy is dead', replied, 'Is she, by God'.

The scandal is remembered in a notable piece of doggerel which hit the public mood of the time:

> Most gracious Queen, we thee implore
> To go away and sin no more.
> But if that effort be too great,

To go away at any rate.

Caroline Sheridan married a wrong'un who used the archaic laws of his day to maintain his rights as a husband. Her reaction gives the lie to the idea that all Victorian women were content to live under archaic and oppressive laws.

The poet, the prig and the Prime Minister

Caroline was the beautiful granddaughter of the playwright, Richard Brinsley Sheridan, but the penniless background of this 'passionate and self-willed child' made it difficult to find her a suitable husband. In the end, however, she was married off at the age of nineteen to George Chapple Norton, a barrister and MP with the reputation of being dull, mean and alcoholic. Caroline used her influence to secure the post of Metropolitan Stipendiary Magistrate for George at a generous salary, but it did nothing to improve their relations. The opposite political affiliations of the couple's families did not help: hers were Whig; his Tory. Caroline reacted to her loveless marriage by taking up the writing of verse, for which she had a talent. (Even in 1939 an example of her work was still included in the *Oxford Book of English Verse*; her most well known line, 'Not dead, but gone before'.) George predictably resented her success.

The next few years were a story of violent quarrels and separations - over money and the custody of their three children. Unhappy at home, Caroline threw herself into the literary world, attracting the attentions of the Prime Minister, William Lamb, First Viscount Melbourne. His own marriage was not a success and he was looking for comfort elsewhere, Caroline being merely one of the objects of his attentions. George took every opportunity to cash in on his wife's acquaintance, but when Melbourne got fed up with his attempts to obtain patronage the barrister began leaking stories to the press suggesting that the Prime Minister was having an affair with his wife.

Scandal! 139

On returning from a holiday with her family in 1835 Caroline found herself locked out of her house. It was the last straw and the couple agreed to separate, but this did not put an end to her problems. George claimed his wife's literary income as his own, which as a husband he was then entitled to do; she responded by running up bills in his name. Nor could the couple agree over the custody of their children. It came to a head when George exercised his right to take the children to Scotland with him and refused to tell Caroline where they were. He also demanded £1,400 from Melbourne and, when it was not forthcoming, brought an action against the Prime Minister for 'criminal conversation' (as adultery was then charmingly known) with his wife. It was the necessary first step to obtaining a divorce by Act of Parliament. More important to George, however, was the £10,000 in damages which he sought from Melbourne as co-respondent.

Norton's evidence at the trial consisted solely of letters and the testimony of disgruntled servants who had been bribed by his brother to give evidence on his behalf. (By the peculiar rules of the day Caroline herself was debarred from giving evidence.) After a nine day hearing Norton's petition was dismissed without Melbourne having to give evidence. Nevertheless, Caroline's reputation was ruined and Melbourne nearly forced to resign, though he kept on seeing Caroline.

There was one person who benefited from the trial, however, the court reporter. Some six months after it had ended Charles Dickens published an episode of The Pickwick Papers in which Mr Pickwick was sued for breach of promise of marriage by a Mrs Bardell. The report of this fictional case echoed in a number of ways the characters and some of the evidence in Lord Melbourne's trial.

Despite Norton's defeat in court, he still had the power to deny his wife access to her children. It was too much for Caroline; she approached Thomas Talfourd MP and serjeant-at-law who agreed to introduce a bill to give mothers the right to appeal to the Court of Chancery for custody of her children under seven years of age, with rights of access to older children. The bill was passed in the Commons but rejected by the Lords. Caroline then threw herself into writing a flurry of pseudonymous pamphlets urging reform of the law, with copies sent to every Member of Parliament. The result was the Custody of Infants Act 1839, which gave effect to her proposals.

In 1848 Caroline agreed to her husband's suggestion that, in exchange for a life mortgage on a trust fund which had been settled on her she would be provided with an annual allowance of £500 and an undertaking never to interfere in her affairs. Melbourne died in 1849 leaving her an allowance of £2,000 a year. Added to a legacy from her mother, Caroline was now financially comfortable. Norton now thought fit to break his agreement by claiming, as he was entitled under the law, that his agreement to pay an allowance to his wife was binding in honour only. On her lawyers' advice Caroline refused to pay a bill and referred it to her husband. He took her to court. Despite the fact that his behaviour towards her throughout the proceedings was so disgraceful as to alienate all present he won on a technicality and Caroline had to pay the bill.

It was like a red rag to a bull. Caroline immediately decided to change the law under which she had been so badly misused. She began by privately publishing an account of her own experiences entitled *English Laws for Women in the Nineteenth Century*, followed by *A Letter to the Queen on Lord Cranworth's Marriage and Divorce Bill*. The result was an Act of 1857 which allowed married women to inherit property and take court action on their own behalf. Although much still remained to be done, the foundations for an equitable law of marriage were now well and truly laid.

When George died in 1875 Caroline married an old friend. Sadly, she died three months later.

> Sir Charles Wentworth Dilke, second baronet, was tipped at one time to succeed Gladstone as leader of the Liberal party. Called to the bar at the Middle Temple, he never practised, but turned to politics, in time becoming President of the Local Government Board. Unfortunately, his extra-mural activities destroyed his reputation and he became a man with a future which never materialized.

Somewhat too Liberal?

As with many energetic men, Charles Dilke managed to combine a busy career in politics with wide cultural interests, an exotic lifestyle and an active and imaginative sex life. Dilke's relationships were particularly complex, so pay attention.

Before his second marriage in 1884 Dilke had been the lover of a married woman, Mrs. Ellen Smith. The affair continued even after his first marriage. Ellen had a daughter, Virginia, who married a Mr Donald Crawford MP in 1882. Charles Dilkes' brother, Ashton later married Virginia's sister.

In 1885 Virginia 'confessed' to her husband, Crawford – and later repeated publicly - that Dilke had seduced her the year she was married and had continued an affair with her on and off for over two years. She also claimed, correctly, that Dilke had had a number of other lovers, including his maid, Sarah.

Crawford was furious and brought an action for divorce.

The Crawford divorce case was heard in a crowded courtroom on 12 February 1886 before the Hon. Mr Justice Butt, with Dilke being cited as co-respondent. The evidence against Virginia consisted almost entirely of her 'confession'. She was by law unable to go into the witness box and Dilke took the same course on legal advice. It was a bad decision. Virginia's adultery was found proved, but the petition against Dilke was dismissed, two conclusions which, the judge frankly acknowledged, appeared to be inconsistent. He sought to justify the result by declaring: 'It would be monstrous if a person in Sir Charles Dilke's position could be convicted on charges of that nature on the statement of a person not on oath, the truth of whose story he had no opportunity of testing by cross-examination.' Nevertheless, as the *Oxford Dictionary of National Biography* puts it, 'The verdict appeared to be the perverse one that Mrs Crawford had committed adultery with Dilke, but that he had not done so with her.'[15]

In an attempt to restore his reputation Dilke persuaded the Queen's Proctor to intervene to show cause why the decree nisi should not be made absolute. Strangely for a lawyer, he appears to have overlooked the fact that, because he had been dismissed from the earlier proceedings, he had no legal standing in the new action except as a witness. Denied legal representation and without the opportunity to address the court as a litigant, Dilke suffered a wounding cross-examination before the decree absolute was granted. As a result of the scandalous nature of the allegations (which included what today's redtops would describe as 'three in a bed romps with a housemaid') Dilke's reputation was in tatters and he never received the advancement he might otherwise have expected.

The general opinion among historians today is that Virginia was lying, possibly to distract her husband from another, real liaison.

Investigative journalism has always been beset with dangers, as a respected nineteenth century journalist discovered to his cost.

'The Maiden Tribute of Modern Babylon'

There was consternation when the crusading editorial director of the respected evening newspaper, *The Pall Mall*

---

[15] Roy Jenkins, 'Dilke, Sir Charles Wentworth, second baronet (1843–1911)', Oxford Dictionary of National Biography, Oxford University Press, 2004.

Gazette appeared at the Old Bailey in 1885 along with three other men charged with the abduction and indecent assault of young women.

William Thomas ('W.T.') Stead was a man with a mission. The son of a Congregationalist minister and supporter of the Salvation Army, he was disturbed by rumours of the abuse of young women in London's sexual underworld and decided to bring the scandal to light. He diligently set about reproducing the abuse in a way designed not to be harmful to the girl in question and published the fruits of his labours in an article entitled, 'The Maiden Tribute of Modern Babylon'. It accused one 'well-known member of Parliament [as being] ready to supply... 100 maids at £25 each' and 'unscrupulous medical men' of certifying, for a price, the girls as virgin, thus increasing their merchantability at a time when some believed that sex with a virgin could cure venereal disease.

Stead had sent a former prostitute, Rebecca Jarrett into Marylebone to buy a child in order to show how easily girls could be found for this trade. The article recounted how the young Eliza Armstrong, referred to in the article as 'Lily', had been sold to Jarrett by her own mother for £5. Though never physically harmed, Eliza/Lily was put through what a real child victim would have experienced, including being 'certified' as a virgin, taken to a brothel and chloroformed. Afterwards, she was sent to France in the care of the Salvation Army. Unfortunately for Stead, Eliza's mother read the article, recognized her daughter and went to the police.

At his trial Stead told the jury, quite truthfully, that he had done what he did, 'not in order to abduct a girl, but to rescue her from what we believed to be her inevitable doom.' He was nevertheless convicted of abduction and indecent assault on the ground that he had acted without the permission of Eliza's father (who in those days had sole legal custody of the children).

Passing sentence of three months hard labour on Stead, Mr Justice Lopes said,

> 'Believing in the existence of most horrible depravity, it appears to me that you made statements about it which, when

challenged, you were unable to verify. You then determined to verify the truth of your assertions by an experiment with a child who was to be bought and subjected to all that a real victim would have been, but was to be rescued before any harm was done. For that purpose you selected a person of alleged reformed character, but who to your knowledge had passed a life–an infamous life, as I may say–pandering to and encouraging the very sins which you say–and I believe you–you were so anxious to repress. You chose your own agent, and, as might have been anticipated, having regard to her antecedents, which you fully knew, that agent deceived you... Your experiment, instead of proving what it was intended to prove, has absolutely and entirely failed, for the jury have found that Eliza Armstrong, the subject of that experiment, was never bought for immoral purposes at all.'

The conviction was technically correct, but the sentence was an appalling miscarriage of justice.

Stead served his time and every year thereafter celebrated the anniversary by wearing prison clothes.

Stead went down with the *Titanic* on 15 April 1912. He was last seen leading women and children to the lifeboats.

Rudyard Kipling once brought a private prosecution against his brother-in-law. It was an action wholly out of character with the author of the poem, 'If', and it was one he was to bitterly regret.

Kipling's humiliation

Joseph Rudyard Kipling married the American, Caroline ('Carrie') Balestier in 1892. During their honeymoon they visited her home State of Vermont where they bought some 11 acres of land in an idyllic site from Carrie's younger brother, Beatty. In the following year Kipling built a house on the site using Beatty as supervisor of construction and named it *Naulakha* after a novel which he had written in collaboration with Beatty's older brother, Wolcott.

At first, life was sweet in *Naulakha*. Here, Kipling wrote *'The Jungle Book'* and other stories, and Carrie gave birth to her second daughter. But Beatty, who acted as their caretaker, was a heavy drinker and a spendthrift with 'a tongue like a skinning knife'. Carrie soon fell out with her brother and Kipling followed suit. The result was disastrous.

It all began with a disagreement over the use of the pasture in front of the house which Carrie wanted to convert to a formal garden. Beatty was heard to abuse Kipling in public. Things got worse when Beatty, who was always short of money, came to believe that his sister was trying to buy him out of his house. On 6 May 1896 he drove over to *Naulakha* in a foul mood intending to speak to Kipling, but met the author on the road – quite literally since the poet had just fallen off his bicycle. Beatty, the worse for drink, shouted that he wanted to speak to his brother-in-law. Alarmed at his attitude, Kipling replied that if he had anything to say he should speak to his lawyers. Blue with passion, Beatty responded, 'By Jesus, this is no case for lawyers. You've got to retract the Goddamned lies you've been telling about me.' 'Do you mean personal violence?', asked Kipling. 'Yes', said Beatty, 'I'll give you a week, and if you don't do it I'll blow out your God-damned brains'. He then drove off shouting, 'Liar, cheat, coward.'

Fearful for his life, Kipling had Beatty arrested for assault and threats, but quickly realized his blunder. Going to law to settle a personal dispute was not consistent with his code of honour. Furthermore, as an incomer to Vermont he had little prospect of success against a local man who had already given his version of events to the newspapers. The ensuing trial in the Brattleboro opera house turned into a farce with Kipling wilting under a powerful cross-examination and sentiment in court strongly favouring the local man. When during an adjournment the judge gave the prisoner bail Kipling offered to put up the money. Beatty refused and his lawyer obliged instead.

It was all too much for the poet who fled Vermont for England along with his family before the date fixed for resumption of the trial. It was Kipling's greatest humiliation.

> Sir William Gordon-Cumming was caught cheating at cards. This would have been of little note had it not been for the fact that one of his fellow players was the Prince of Wales.

The Prince and the cardsharp

The forty nine year old Albert Edward, Prince of Wales was a guest of the shipping magnate, Sir Arthur Wilson at his Yorkshire mansion conveniently situated near the Doncaster races. Horses were one of the Prince's two passions. Another guest was the forty two year old Sir William Alexander Gordon Gordon-Cumming, who indulged the Prince's other passion by allowing him the use of his Belgravia home for his sexual encounters.

Gordon-Cumming was a Colonel in the Scots Guards and the epitome of a nineteenth century rake, gambler and adventurer. He was contemptuous of his social inferiors and had the reputation of being the most arrogant man in London.

On the evening of 8th September 1890 Wilson's guests were playing the then illegal game of baccarat. During the evening, Wilson's son noticed that Gordon-Cumming seemed to be cheating by altering the amount of his stake after the hand had been declared. The following night the Colonel was watched closely and his deceit was confirmed.

When the allegation was put to him next morning Gordon-Cumming flatly denied any wrong-doing, but agreed to sign a pledge that he would never play cards again in exchange for an undertaking that the affair would be kept secret. But the story soon got out through the indiscretion of the Prince's mistress, Daisy Brooke (known, not without reason, as 'Babbling' Brooke). Gordon-Cumming left the house the following morning, threatening to commit suicide. On reflection, he changed his mind and issued a writ against his accusers for defamation instead.

The trial of the action began on 1 June 1891 before the Lord Chief Justice, Lord Coleridge. Sir Edward Clarke QC was for the plaintiff and Sir Charles Russell QC for the defendants.

The Prince was summoned to give evidence for the plaintiff. Reluctant to testify, he was compelled to do so by virtue of his capacity as an army officer. In the witness box Edward had to admit that he had not reported the plaintiff's misconduct and to acknowledge his own part in the evening's entertainment. It was the first time that an heir to the throne had appeared before a court for at least five centuries. (See below.)

Despite Gordon-Cumming's protestation that he had signed the confession only in order to spare the Prince embarrassment, the jury found against him in a matter of minutes, to the sound of hissing in the public gallery. Dismissed from the army the next day, he resigned from his clubs and retired to his Scottish estate, his golf and his pet monkey.

Queen Victoria was not amused.

Prince Edward took up whist.

> The last time that a Prince of the royal blood had appeared in court was half a millennium before the baccarat scandal, at least if an old tale is to be believed.

The contemptuous Prince

In his youth Henry V was a bit of a lad, as famously portrayed in Shakespeare's two part play, Henry IV.

Shakespeare's picture of the young king is generally correct, but the story that he was committed to prison for contempt of court is unlikely to be true. It nevertheless deserves re-telling because of its authentic portrayal of the characters of those involved. This is how Sir Thomas Elyot told the tale in 1531:

'The most renowned Prince, King Henry the Fifth, late King of England, during the life of his father was noted to be fierce and of wanton courage. It happened that one of his servants whom he favoured well, was for felony by him committed, arraigned at the King's Bench; whereof the Prince being advertised, and incensed by light persons about him, in furious rage came hastily to the bar, where his servant stood as a prisoner, and commanded him to be ungyved and set at liberty.'[16]

Despite a warning from chief justice Sir William Gascoigne the Prince 'came up to the place of judgment [that is appeared before the court], men thinking that he would have slain the Judge, or have done to him some damage.' Gascoigne admonished him to remember the twofold duty he owed to the king his father. 'And now, for your contempt and disobedience, go you to the prison of the King's Bench, whereunto I commit you, and remain ye there prisoner until the pleasure of the King your father be further known'; whereupon the Prince laid down his weapon and tamely surrendered to custody.

On learning of the incident, the king his father was said to have praised God for giving him 'a judge who feareth not to minister justice, and also a son who can suffer and obey justice.'

---

[16] *The Boke named the Governour.*

Political parties are always in need of money; vain and self-important men long to see themselves 'honoured'. It does not take a genius to realize that there is profit to be made by anyone prepared to bring the two together. Arthur Maundy Gregory had a colourful career as a blackmailer, pimp and a spy. It is even likely that he was a multi-murderer. But it is for his role as an honours broker that Gregory is best remembered today.

Honours for sale

Maundy Gregory was the son of a clergyman who studied for the clergy at Oxford, but left university for the stage. In 1906 while manager of a theatrical company he was dismissed for fraud. He then tried to blackmail his boyhood friend, Harold Davidson, afterwards notorious as the vicar of Stiffkey (see below). After an unsuccessful venture into commerce Gregory started a detective agency, which led to contacts with British intelligence, for whom he acted on and off for years. This in turn brought him in touch with the highest levels of society, including the Duke of York, later king George V, and the Prime Minister, David Lloyd George.

Lloyd George quickly realised Gregory's value to him as a 'fixer' who could raise funds for the Liberal Party. In those days the sale of honours was an accepted way of raising money for political parties. There was nothing new in this. Baronetcies in their modern form had been conjured up by King James I for this purpose; Lloyd George and Gregory simply made it into a business. Soon, a knighthood was on offer for £10-12,000, a baronetcy for £35-40,000, while a peerage began at £50,000. During a six year period after Gregory set up his stall some 1,500 knighthoods and 91 peerages were awarded, twice as many as had been created in the previous twenty years. So widespread was the practice during the premiership of the Welsh solicitor, Lloyd George that Cardiff became known as the 'city of dreadful knights'.

The sale of honours enabled Gregory to buy *Burke's Landed Gentry* and to lease a hotel near Dorking where his friends could entertain young women for a small fee. He went too far, however, with the 1922 honours list, which included a number of thoroughly disreputable men, such as the South African magnate, Sir Joseph Robinson. Learning that Robinson had recently been ordered by a court to pay £420,000 in damages for his dodgy business dealings, King George described his inclusion in the list as 'little less than an insult to the Crown and to the House of Lords.' When it all came out Robinson at least had the grace to decline the offer.

There are strong reasons to believe Gregory of having been guilty of much worse than the sale of honours. In 1920 at the request of the police Special Branch he had spied on a former ILP Member of Parliament, Albert Grayson who was suspected of being a communist agent. Grayson tried to turn the tables by attacking Gregory: 'This sale of honours is a national scandal', he said, 'It can be traced right down to 10 Downing Street and to a monocled dandy with offices in Whitehall. I know this man and one day I will name him.' (Gregory had an office at 38 Parliament Street with a rear office in Cannon Row from which he sold honours on an industrial scale.) Soon after this attack on Gregory Grayson was beaten up in the street. A year later he disappeared altogether in suspicious circumstances. He was last seen entering a house belonging to Gregory.

Gregory now entered the Roman Catholic church in a successful bid to extend his customer base by starting a trade in Papal honours. For this he was rewarded by being made a Knight Grand Cross of the Holy Sepulchre.

Despite being a homosexual the 'short, paunchy, bald, rubicund, monocled, and epicene' Gregory lived for some years with an actress, Edith Rosse. By 1932 his funds were running short, but Edith refused him a loan. A few days after changing her will to make Gregory her only beneficiary she was found dead. At Gregory's instructions Edith was buried in a shallow grave beside the Thames with the coffin lid unsealed. When it was exhumed her body was too far decayed to offer any forensic assistance as to the manner of her death.

After the collapse of Lloyd George's coalition in 1922 the next government brought in legislation which for the first time made the buying or selling of honours a crime. It was not enough to stop Gregory, however, who continued in the profitable trade. But it all came to an end in 1933 when he tried to sell a knighthood to a Naval officer. The officer played along with the proposal, but turned the story over to the police. Gregory pleaded Guilty and was given a two month prison sentence. It is said that he also received a pension of £2,000 a year from the Conservative party, one of the beneficiaries of his activities.

Gregory died of natural causes in 1941 while a German internee in France.

'No direct evidence' of crime

Decades after Gregory's death suspicions arose that the old practice of raising money for political parties by the sale of honours had been resurrected in a different guise, namely loans at low rates of interest instead of 'gifts'.

In 2006, several men who had lent large sums of money to the Labour Party were nominated for life peerages by the then Labour Prime Minister, Tony Blair. The nominations were rejected by the House of Lords Appointments Commission and a police investigation followed. Lord Levy, the Labour fund raiser, was arrested and Tony Blair and other politicians were questioned, but no charges were ever brought. The Crown Prosecution Service explained: 'For a case to proceed, the prosecution must have a realistic prospect of being able to prove that the two people agreed that the gift, etc., was in exchange for an honour', and that, 'There is no direct evidence of any such agreement between any two people the subject of this investigation.'

Clearly, no offences had been committed, but the Labour Party repaid the loans and the Conservative Party followed suit. The temptations in this area of public life must be great and it is unlikely that this will be the last we shall hear of such practices.

Politics, violence and homosexuality combined to form a heady brew in a case involving a prominent twentieth century politician.

The assassination of Rinka

In 1979 the former leader of the Liberal Party, the Rt. Hon. Jeremy Thorpe PC, MP found himself in the dock at the Old Bailey charged with conspiracy to murder. He stood alongside four other men, including a nightclub owner and the Party's deputy treasurer. The ensuing proceedings were to reveal a bizarre and scandalous story.

Thorpe was a witty and talented man with a flamboyant taste in clothes. Called to the Bar in 1954, he combined a practice on the Western Circuit with a seat in Parliament where he led and reinvigorated the Liberal Party. In the early sixties he had met Norman Scott, a stable lad and former male model. A year or so later Scott went to the police alleging that he had had sexual relations with Thorpe, which was then a criminal act, even in private. He handed over letters which he had received from the MP; one of which included the immortal line, 'Bunnies [allegedly Thorpe's pet name for Scott] can and will go to France'. Peter Bessell, a former Liberal MP and failed businessman, used Liberal Party funds to pay Scott to return some of the letters and the police considered that the evidence was insufficient to take the matter further. In 1967 Thorpe became leader of his Party. Rumours concerning his sexuality persisted and the Party set up an inquiry into what was then a crime. It completely exonerated their leader.

Scott continued to talk about his supposed relationship with Thorpe. In October 1975 after attempts to silence him had proved fruitless he accepted a lift from a man claiming to have been secretly assigned to protect him. Andrew 'Gino' Newton, a former pilot, drove Scott and his Great Dane, 'Rinka' to Exmoor. While walking on the moor Newton drew a gun and shot and killed the dog. He then pointed the gun at Scott who was trying to resuscitate the poor creature, but, for whatever reason, it failed to fire and Scott ran off. In January 1976 Scott appeared in court on charges of defrauding the Social Security. During the course of the proceedings he repeated his claims against Thorpe, following which the Party leader resigned his position.

Later that year Newton was convicted of the illegal possession of a firearm with intent to endanger life and sentenced to two years imprisonment. During the proceedings Scott claimed that Thorpe had threatened to kill him if he spoke about their affair. Later, he sold to the press what he claimed were love letters written to him by the MP.

Upon Newton's release from prison in 1977 he revived the scandal by selling a story that he had been hired as a hit-man to kill Scott. The accusation led to Thorpe being charged with attempted murder and conspiracy to murder. He made a written statement to the police vehemently denying any homosexual relationship or any involvement in a murder plot. He had paid no money to Newton or Scott, with whom his relationship was purely philanthropic.

Thorpe and three others went on trial at the Old Bailey on 8 May 1979. Bessell had agreed in exchange for immunity to appear as the main witness for the prosecution. He gave evidence of a conspiracy within the Party to get rid of Scott by shooting him and disposing of his body down a disused tin mine. But his credibility was destroyed in the witness box by George Carman QC and devalued further when it was learnt that he had been paid a fee by *The Daily Telegraph* which would have doubled in the event of a conviction. Thorpe's defence was that he knew Scott, but that there had been no sexual relationship between them; he elected not to give evidence. Scott withdrew his claim to have had a sexual relationship with Thorpe, saying that it was a delusion. In his summing up to the jury Mr Justice Cantley described the mentally fragile Scott as 'a crook, a fraud, a sponger and a parasite. But, of course, he could still be telling the truth. It is a question of belief.' (The words were to be immortalised in a sketch by Peter Cook.) It took the jury 15 hours to arrive at a verdict of Not Guilty on all charges.

A service of thanksgiving was held in a church near Thorpe's home.

Shortly after the trial Thorpe was diagnosed as suffering from Parkinson's disease and never re-emerged into public life.

One of the most scandalous sex stories[17] ever to hit the White House involved the 42nd President of the United States of America.

'I did not have sexual relations with that woman'

On 19 December 1998 President William Jefferson ('Bill') Clinton was impeached by the United States House of Representatives. He was accused of having committed perjury before a Federal grand jury investigating his relationship with a White House intern, Monica Lewinsky, and of having obstructed justice by suborning a witness in a sexual harassment suit brought by a former Arkansas state employee, Paula Jones. The principal issue in both these sordid episodes was the veracity of the President.

When the Lewinsky scandal first broke Clinton, standing alongside his wife, Hillary, told a press conference that he wanted, 'to say one thing to the American people. I want you to listen to me. I'm not going to say this again: I did not have sexual relations with that woman, Miss Lewinsky. I never told anybody to lie, not a single time - never. These allegations are false. And I need to go back to work for the American people.' He also assured his aides, 'there's nothing going on between us.'

---

[17] One cannot say, 'the most' in view of the revelations of a former intern of JF Kennedy entitled *Once upon a Secret: my affair with President John F. Kennedys*, 2012.

Paula Jones' claim was dismissed before trial on the ground that she had failed to demonstrate any damages. When she appealed against this ruling the now former President settled out of court for $850,000.

So far as Monica was concerned, Clinton's position was that he had not had 'sexual intercourse' with her, but only 'sexual relations' as defined by the special investigator. It was a nice point from a former law professor, but for the rest of the world it was a distinctly unconvincing position. The President only made matters worse by telling the Grand Jury,

> 'It depends on what the meaning of the word 'is' is. If the - if he - if 'is' means is and never has been, that is not - that is one thing. If it means there is none, that was a completely true statement... Now, if someone had asked me on that day, are you having any kind of sexual relations with Ms. Lewinsky, that is, asked me a question in the present tense, I would have said no. And it would have been completely true.'

When it became clear that he had in fact participated in various imaginative sexual acts 'with that woman' in the Oval Office and elswehere, Clinton was forced, not once but repeatedly, to admit to having 'misled' the American people, including, of course, his wife, Hillary.

Voting in the Senate at the impeachment hearing divided almost entirely on party lines with a clear acquittal on the first charge. On the second the voting was equal but, since the American constitution requires a two thirds majority for the conviction of a President, Clinton was acquitted on that charge also. The whole episode was yet another demonstration of the weakness of trial by legislature.

Clinton's career, both before and during his presidency, was embroiled in scandals, sexual and financial (though the latter were never proved), but he left office with one of the highest approval ratings ever enjoyed by a President and continues to this day to enjoy the role of an international statesman.

3.5 GOD'S AWKWARD SQUAD

Higher standards are expected of the clergy than the rest of us and they can find themselves prosecuted in an ecclesiastical court for misconduct which falls short of the criminal. Here are three controversial examples of the genre.

> *The Beecher/Tilton adultery trial of 1875 came like a thunderclap to nineteenth century America. It revealed that, concealed beneath the trousers and crinolines of the men and women of God, were much the same sexual apparatus as those of their congregations. It also demonstrated that a man of genuinely liberal attitudes could at the same time be a hypocrite in his private life.*

The Great Seducer

Henry Ward Beecher was the nationally renowned pastor of a Congregational church in Brooklyn, New York. As befitted the brother of the author of *Uncle Tom's Cabin*, Beecher was a fierce opponent of slavery and a social reformer. He was also a man. In 1870 one of his congregation, a Mrs Elizabeth ('Lib') Tilton, confessed to her husband that she had been having a long term affair with his close friend, Beecher. The husband passed the story to a feminist writer whose advocacy of 'free love' had been denounced by Beecher. She had no qualms about publishing the story.

Beecher persuaded Lib to withdraw her confession and after an investigation the church declared their 'perfect satisfaction' of Beecher's 'entire innocence and absolute personal integrity' and expressed their disapproval of Mr Tilton by withdrawing his membership. Tilton, who had already lost his job as a newspaper editor over the affair, thereupon sued Beecher for 'criminal conversation' with his wife, seeking $100,000 in damages. The trial was a cause célèbre of its day with opera glasses being sold in the courtroom and the two contenders being showered with floral tributes as they entered court.

Typical of the lawyers' grandiloquent speeches was the opening address of Samuel D. Morris for the plaintiff which concluded:

> 'I call upon you to brand the seducer as his crime deserves to be branded. Let it be written on every door throughout the land: "Death, destruction to the seducer", and when you have rendered that verdict you will receive the prayers and blessings of every virtuous mother and of every virtuous daughter in the land, and a peaceful conscience will follow you through life, will be with you in the last solemn scenes on earth, and console you when at last you stand with your life-record before the ever-living God.'

Despite this awesome warning and six months of argument and evidence the jurors were unable to reach a verdict and the case was dismissed. The church chose to treat the hung jury as an acquittal and held another board of enquiry which exonerated Beecher for the second time. The triumphant pastor promptly undertook a purge of the 'non-believers' in his church and continued to retain his post and his credibility until his death in 1886.

Two years later Lib made a public confession of her adultery. Her membership of the church was withdrawn.

To this day no one knows the full story of a 63 year old Archdeacon's stay in a Peterborough hotel.

The girl in the cathedral

In 1921 The Venerable John Wakeford, Precentor[18] of Lincoln Cathedral and Archdeacon of Stow appeared before the Lincoln Consistory (or church) Court charged with adultery with an unknown woman at a commercial hotel.

At the trial it was common ground that Wakeford had stayed at the Bull hotel, Peterborough on the nights of 14–16

---

[18] A precentor is a director of music.

March and 2 April 1920. He refused to accept the entry in the hotel register that referred to himself and a woman described as his wife. He rejected evidence that he had been seen eating meals with a woman and that a woman's nightdress had been seen in his room, along with his pyjamas. A prosecution witness spoke of having seen the Archdeacon show a young woman round Peterborough Cathedral on his first stay at the hotel. Wakeford accepted that he had done this, but insisted that it was an innocent act of kindness towards a stranger. He had met the girl that day, offered his services to her as a guide and had not seen her before or since. A maid at the hotel gave evidence of an apparently incriminating remark which turned out to have been made by another guest. Wakeford claimed to have gone to Peterborough the first time because it was a quiet place to prepare himself for a series of sermons he had to give. He had gone there again a fortnight later because of difficulties in getting a direct train home from London. The charges, he claimed, were the result of a conspiracy between two clergymen, his brother in law, who held a grudge against him, and the informant who had himself been disciplined for immorality.

After a seven day hearing Wakeford was found guilty and ordered to be deprived of his offices, although he was allowed to remain in holy orders. With his wife's support he appealed to the Privy Council where a hearing took place before the judicial committee under the chairmanship of the Lord Chancellor, Lord Birkenhead. The appeal, which was conducted as a re-trial, was unanimously dismissed and Wakeford was ordered to pay the costs of the bishop who had defended the appeal.

The Privy Council's reasons for rejecting the appeal seem unconvincing. The court agreed that the facts were difficult to disentangle. They accepted that the prosecution witnesses had been inconsistent on many points. Among the prosecution witnesses were two police officers who said that they had been looking out for a man posing as a clergyman who had been passing dud cheques. Their evidence, the court went so far as to say, lacked candour, 'even positive mis-statement'. Nevertheless, while accepting that the informant had considerable animus against the Archdeacon the court rejected Wakeford's suggestion that the prosecution was a conspiracy against him.

The Privy Council dismissed the evidence of defence witnesses who had seen Wakeford eating alone on the ground that it showed 'nothing more than that his companion was late for that meal'. They simply dismissed as 'a mystery' Wakeford's evidence, which was confirmed by his wife and others, that he never wore pyjamas. They were impressed by the fact that the hotel restaurant recorded sums paid by Wakeford suggesting bills for two, not one, though the evidence on the point was far from clear. (Champagne was included in the bill, though Wakeford never drank the stuff.) The court also placed significance on the failure of the 'girl in the cathedral' to turn up to give evidence for the Archdeacon.

'[P]erhaps the crucial point in the case', said the court, was the entry in the hotel register which recorded the room as having been taken by 'J Wakeford and wife', despite the fact that the former hotel manager admitted having added the words 'and wife' himself in handwriting that bore a strong similarity to the Archdeacon's. The court heard expert evidence on the authorship of the writing, to which it saw fit to add its own untutored opinion.

At the very least the court's reasons are unconvincing, particularly taking into account the appellant's good character and the improbability of a clergyman twice undertaking an illicit rendezvous with a woman in a public place while dressed in gaiters and full clerical outfit.

But there was more. Shortly after the Privy Council hearing the 'girl in the cathedral' was traced with the help of Horatio Bottomley's paper, *John Bull*. She confirmed Wakeford's account of their innocent meeting. As a recently married young woman she had not come forward earlier out of fear of the consequences of publicity.

After the trial the bishop's solicitor claimed that the former Archdeacon was a frequent adulterer. Wakeford sued for defamation, but lost on a technicality: it bankrupted him and he was only rescued by a fund set up by three bishops. Wakeford had borne the legal proceedings with a brave dignity. Unable to get the case re-opened, his health deteriorated and he spent the last two years of his life in an asylum.

Whether Wakeford was an adulterer and a hypocrite is a fact known only to his God, but there can be no doubt that he should never have been convicted on the basis of the facts.[19]

The Vicar of Stiffkey was de-frocked in 1932 by the Consistory Court for numerous offences against young girls. It was a charge he was to deny until the day of his extraordinary death.

'It wasn't the lion that killed him'

Harold Francis Davidson had always been fascinated with the stage. As a young man he had joined a group of entertainers, but after a few years gave it up in order to enter theological college. From there he went to Exeter College, Oxford, where he was able to return to his first love by joining the university's dramatic society, OUDS.

Davidson was ordained in 1903. After a curacy in St Martin in the Fields he was appointed rector of Stiffkey (pronounced 'Stukey') in Norfolk. During the Great War he served as a Royal Navy chaplain and afterwards had a brief spell as tutor to a Maharajah's son before returning to Stiffkey. Davidson was interested in social reform and was party to the setting up of the Dockland Settlement. In 1925 he was swindled out of a large sum of money and forced to go bankrupt. When he became solvent again he was authorized by his bishop to maintain a ministry around Covent Garden. He threw himself into the task with gusto, taking particular concern for the impoverished young women who worked in the area as prostitutes. He found jobs for them and even paid for

---

[19] I am grateful to the Ministry of Justice for unearthing the reasoning of the Privy Council which was redacted from the published version of the report.

their medical treatment. For this, he became known as 'The Prostitute's Padre'.

But not everyone loved Davidson. A Norfolk landowner with a grudge against him hired private investigators to look into his private life, but they turned up nothing. However, when an anonymous complaint was made to the Bishop of Norwich he ordered his own investigation, which resulted in Davidson being put on trial before the Chancellor of the diocese of Norwich on charges of immorality with the young girls of Covent Garden.

Davidson hotly denied the accusations. The help he had given the young women was of a selfless nature. The Bishop's investigators had interviewed forty girls but chose to call only one to give evidence against the Rector. Sixteen year old Barbara Harris accused him of pretending to be her uncle and paying her rent. Photographs were produced, including one of Davidson talking to another young girl who was dressed in a shawl but little else. Despite strong support from his parishioners the court rejected Davidson's evidence as a tissue of lies and he was convicted on all counts. In accordance with the order of the court he was defrocked at Norwich cathedral on 21 October 1932.

The disgraced Rector's end was a sorry one: he was forced to become a street entertainer on Blackpool promenade, standing in a barrel or appearing to be roasted in an oven by the Devil. In 1936 he was fined for trespass in Victoria station, possibly as a public entertainer. His last job was in the amusement park in Skegness where he would enter a lion's cage and stay there for ten minutes. The act ended for good when he tripped on the lion's tail and was mauled badly.

Strangely, it wasn't the lion that did for Davidson. When he was taken to hospital, he was found to be suffering from diabetes and died in a diabetic coma. The last words of this enigmatic man were said to be, 'Don't miss ... the evening edition.'

Three thousand mourners attended the funeral, the late minister's wife among them.

Doubts still surround the decision of the Consistory Court. A letter from Davidson subsequently came to light which proved the sixteen year old girl (who had been paid for her evidence) to have been a liar; and the incriminating photographs showed signs of having been tampered with.

> The law is a good way to settle many disputes, but not all. A good example was the famous occasion when the legal and the artistic worlds came dramatically into conflict over the merits of a painting.

'Two hundred guineas for flinging a pot of paint in the public's face.'

James Abbott McNeill Whistler was an American painter of Scottish/Irish descent who had made his home in London. His impressionistic use of colour was revolutionary for its time, and not everyone appreciated it.

In 1877 Whistler was invited to display his paintings at a Bond Street Gallery alongside works of the Pre-Raphaelite and aesthetic movements. John Ruskin, the most distinguished art critic of the day, wrote a review of the exhibition in his journal, *Fors Clavigera*. He began by praising the talent of the Pre-Raphaelite, Edward Burne-Jones ('the best that has been, or could be'), and went on to compare Whistler's work unfavourably with his. Ruskin's ire was directed particularly at Whistler's painting, '*Nocturne in Black and Gold: The Falling Rocket*,' which depicted fireworks as gold and red flecks exploding in the smoke filled night sky over the Cremorne Pleasure Gardens beside the Thames at Chelsea. Ruskin wrote:

> 'For Mr. Whistler's own sake, no less than for the protection of the purchaser, Sir Coutts Lindsay ought not to have admitted works into the gallery in which the ill-educated conceit of the artist so nearly approached the aspect of wilful imposture. I have seen, and heard, much of Cockney impudence

before now; but never expected to hear a coxcomb ask two hundred guineas for flinging a pot of paint in the public's face.'

The furious artist issued a writ for libel, claiming £1,000 in damages for loss of reputation. The case came for trial before Baron Huddleston and a special jury in the newly created Exchequer Division of the High Court. Ruskin, who was absent from court through illness, was represented by the Attorney General, Sir John Holker, Whistler by Serjeant John Humffreys Parry.[20]

Parry's case was that only the artist, not the writer, was qualified to pass judgement on paintings. Holker responded robustly, 'In the present mania for art it had become a kind of fashion among some people to admire the incomprehensible, to look upon the fantastic conceits of an artist like Mr. Whistler...; but the fact was that such productions were not worthy the name of great works of art.' Ruskin's article, he argued, enjoyed a privilege against legal action as a fair and bona fide criticism of a painting.

There followed a spirited exchange between the lawyer and the painter. Whistler agreed with Holker that two hundred guineas was a 'stiffish price' for the painting.

When asked, 'Can you tell me how long it took you to knock off that nocturne?' Whistler replied, 'I beg your pardon?'

Holker, 'Oh! I am afraid that I am using a term that applies rather perhaps to my own work. I should have said, How long did you take to paint that picture?'

'Oh,' said Whistler, 'I "knock one off" possibly in a couple of days – one day to do the work and another to finish it...'

Holker: 'The labour of two days is that for which you ask two hundred guineas?'

Whistler: 'No, I ask it for the knowledge I have gained in the work of a lifetime.'

---

[20] A Serjeant was a rank of barrister from which judges were chosen.

Burne-Jones then went into the witness box to confirm that 200 guineas was a large price for Whistler's painting, but conceded under cross-examination that the artist 'had an almost unrivalled appreciation of atmosphere, and his colour was beautiful, especially in moonlight scenes.'

At the end of the two day hearing the jury found for Whistler but awarded him only one farthing in damages. The judge, who had indicated that such an award would amount to saying that the case should not have been brought, confirmed this by letting the costs lie where they fell.

Ruskin's costs were paid by public subscription, but he felt it necessary to resign from the position of Slade Professor of Fine Art. Whistler, wore the farthing on his watch chain, but was bankrupted by the action. Years later he was able to sell the *Nocturne in black and gold* for £800.

Chapter 4

DISCONTENT

4.1 'UNEASY LIES THE HEAD'

> 'For God's sake let us sit upon the ground
> And tell sad stories of the death of kings:
> How some have been deposed, some slain in war,
> Some haunted by the ghosts they have deposed,
> Some poisoned by their wives, some sleeping killed;
> All murdered ...'
>
> (Shakespeare, *Richard II.*)

Three years after Henry VIII married Anne Boleyn she was dead, the victim of a cynical conspiracy and a rigged trial.

'I have a little neck'

Henry's twenty one year marriage to Catherine of Aragon had not been one of undiluted happiness. The king had had numerous affairs, including one with Mary Boleyn, the married daughter of one of his courtiers. Eventually tiring of Mary, he turned his attention to her younger sister, Anne, then one of his wife's maids of honour and some fifteen years her junior.

Anne was no beauty, but her lively character, coupled with the attainments she had acquired at the French court made her a desirable catch. She played her cards cleverly in the marriage stakes, refusing any intimacies until Henry agreed to regularize her position. Finding an excuse to divorce his wife was no great challenge for a man with a remarkable facility for accommodating his beliefs to whatever best suited his interests. In the end, and with Anne's active support, he got the divorce he wanted, and in 1533 married his new love, at first in secret then, after she became pregnant, publicly.

A major reason for Henry's marriage was the hope that Anne could, unlike Catherine, produce a male heir. Her first child proved to be a girl (and a future Queen of England, as it turned out). Anne went on to suffer two miscarriages, but never bore Henry a son. This 'fault' in her husband's eyes was compounded when she made the mistake of offending his chief minister, Thomas Cromwell, by criticizing the way he went about dissolving the monasteries. No one can be sure whether it was Cromwell who prompted the king to rid himself of Anne or Henry who instructed Cromwell. In any event both were involved in the setting up of a commission, chaired jointly by Cromwell and Anne's uncle, the Duke of Norfolk, to investigate her conduct. The commission's first act was to arrest Mark Smeaton, an insignificant court entertainer, who broke down under questioning and possibly torture, and confessed, almost certainly untruthfully, to having committed adultery with Anne. When this was whispered in the king's ear at the May Day joust he left without a word to his Queen, never to see her again. Thereafter, events moved swiftly.

Anne and her brother, George, Viscount Rochford, were arrested, questioned by the commission and committed to the Tower of London, where the Queen broke down in distress. Sir Henry Norris, a close friend of the King, was the next to be arrested, then the courtiers, Sir Francis Weston, the elderly Sir William Brereton, Sir Thomas Wyatt, the poet, and Sir

Richard Page. Wyatt and Page were released without charge, possibly because of their friendship with Cromwell. Norris was offered a pardon if only he would confess: he chose not to accept it rather than admit a non-existent relationship with the Queen. Tried in Westminster Hall, all but Smeaton pleaded Not Guilty of treason by reason of their adultery with the Queen. The evidence against them amounted to no more than their proximity to Anne and the flirtatious banter that was commonplace at court, but the jurymen had been hand picked by Cromwell and knew exactly what was wanted of them. All the accused were convicted and executed five days later. As was customary in such circumstances, courtiers had written in begging to be given the properties of the accused, even before they had been convicted.

Three days later Anne and her brother were brought to stand their separate trials in the Great Hall of the Tower on charges of adultery and incest with each other. Henry, who was already courting his next wife to be, needed the validation of the mob and some 2,000 of them were packed in to witness the show. Brother and sister both pleaded Not Guilty and put up a brave defence, but they too were convicted and condemned to be burned or executed at the king's pleasure. When passing sentence Anne's uncle Norfolk is said to have had tears in his eyes. (Ah!)

As with the others the trial was a fix: the charge of incest was a nonsense and there was no real evidence of adultery. But that did not matter: the prosecution were so sure of themselves that they had not always bothered to check that the allegedly adulterous parties were in the same places at the same times. Otherwise, the proceedings were cunningly planned. The Queen was not brought to trial until the courtiers had been convicted of adultery with her. According to the practice of the day this left the court with little option but to find her guilty too. George was similarly convicted of incest before Anne ever entered the court – with the same result.

George went to the block on 17 May before a large crowd. His sister followed him two days later. Henry 'mercifully' allowed her a private execution with a sword instead of the axe, and brought an expert over from Calais to wield it. On the night before her death the poor woman remarked, 'I heard say the executioner was very good, and I have a little neck,' putting her hands about it and laughing. No arrangements had been made for her funeral and after her execution her body parts were thrown into an arrow box and buried in an unmarked grave, not to be seen again until they were discovered in the reign of Queen Victoria.

A fortnight later the bells rang out to celebrate the marriage of Henry to his new mistress, Jane Seymour.

At the end of the English civil war Parliament and the army fell out over what to do with the captured King. When it came to light that Charles had been plotting with foreign powers while pretending to negotiate with his Parliament the army determined to put him on trial. The House of Commons refused to consent to the trial and the army's reaction was swift.

Pride's Purge

As the Honourable Members arrived at the Palace of Westminster on the morning of 6 December 1648 they found the entrance to St Stephen's Chapel, where the Commons then sat, barred by an army Colonel, Thomas Pride, and a troop of soldiers from his regiment of Foot. A regiment of Horse was standing nearby ready to support them, if needed. Using a list which had been provided to him, the Colonel arrested 45 Members who were not in favour of putting the king on trial and kept them imprisoned in a public house until six days later, during which time 186 more Members were turned away from the Commons. Some fifty Members were allowed to enter to comprise what became known, inevitably, as the Rump Parliament. On 4th January 1649 the compliant Rump committed the King for trial on charges of treason and other high crimes.

When the King's trial began on 20 January he refused to enter a plea and boldly demanded to be told,

> 'by what power I am called hither ... by what Authority, I mean, lawful; there are many unlawful Authorities in the world - Thieves and Robbers by the highways - but I would know by what Authority I was brought from thence, and carried from place to place, (and I know not what), and when I know what lawful Authority, I shall answer.'

Charles had a good point. Some speculate that it was suggested to him by the rising young barrister, Sir Matthew Hall, subsequently Lord Chief Justice. But Charles' question received no answer, for the simple reason that there was none. The Lords and Commons together have always formed a court, known as The High Court of Parliament, with power to try people for crimes, but this power is available only if both Houses agree. In Charles' case the Lords refused their consent and the truncated Commons unilaterally declared themselves the supreme authority in the land.

Their action was illegal, but who was in a position to challenge it successfully?

Nearly a century and a half after the death of king Charles French revolutionaries condemned their king to death in a show trial. Nine months later his former Queen, Marie-Antoinette de Lorraine of Austria suffered the same fate. The proceedings were a travesty of justice, the outcome pre-determined.

Revolutionary 'justice'

On 14 October 1793 the thirty nine year old Marie-Antoinette was brought, pale and exhausted, before the revolutionary tribunal in the great hall of the former *Parlement* building in Paris. She was prematurely aged from her lengthy imprisonment and suffering from vaginal bleeding.

The charges against her included sending state money to France's enemy, Austria, of plotting to kill the Duke of

Orléans, and of responsibility for the massacre of the Swiss Guards. She was also charged with arranging orgies at the Palace of Versailles, and, most outrageously of all, with sexually abusing her eight year old son, known as the Dauphin. The poor woman's plea for time to prepare her defence was refused.

The state prosecutor, Antoine Quentin Fouquier-Tinville began by calling the deputy *procureur* of the commune, René Hébert to give evidence concerning the Queen's alleged abuse of her child. In fact, there was no evidence, merely Hébert's account of someone else's reported conversation with the Dauphin. Marie-Antoinette replied curtly to all questions put to her, but when asked about the scandalous allegations concerning her son she remained silent. When a juror demanded that she answer the Queen hit back passionately: 'If I have not replied it is because Nature itself refuses to answer such a charge laid against a mother. I appeal to all mothers here present – is such a crime possible?' The women in the public gallery were visibly moved and the President of the Tribunal, Armand-Martial-Joseph Herman, threatened to clear the room. The charge was of course groundless. Even Robespierre, when told of this clumsy attempt to blacken the Queen's name, is said to have thrown his dinner plate to the floor in disgust.

Asked whether she had anything to say in her defence, Marie-Antoinette was able to demonstrate that many of the 'facts' produced by the prosecution were misconceived. For example, a 'packet marked with ciphers' turned out to be a table on which she taught her children to read. Hébert sought to implicate her in the 'affair of the necklace' (a notorious court fraud), but she had never even met the people involved. She was accused of signing large cheques, but none was produced. And so it went on. As to the other charges she replied, 'I have no knowledge of the facts of which Hébert speaks.'

The two day 'trial' came to an end in the early hours of 16 October. After a two hour's retirement the former Queen was convicted of all charges except those relating to the Dauphin, which were quietly dropped.

Later that morning Marie-Antoinette was taken to the tumbrel dressed in a white piqué dress and with her hands tied behind her back. (They had to be untied to allow her to relieve herself by the wall.) Mounting the scaffold in the Place de la Révolution, now the Place de la Concorde, she trod on the executioner's foot and pathetically exclaimed, 'Monsieur. I beg your pardon. I did not do it on purpose.' The blade of the guillotine fell at 12.15 pm that day.

Hébert suffered the same fate some six months later, Herman and Fouquier-Tinville a year after.

It is ironic that enthusiasts for the rights of man have sometimes been the worst abusers of those rights. This fact was born home with particular poignancy to one of the architects of the French revolution.

The Committee of Public Safety

After the successful overthrow of King Louis XVI rivalry between the leaders of the French revolution led to them turning on each other. The violence culminated in the ten month period of bloodletting known to history as The Terror. One of the revolution's founding fathers, the attorney Georges Jacques Danton, was caught up in The Terror and thrown into the Luxembourg prison by the Committee of Public Safety on 30 March 1794. He was heard to exclaim, 'This time twelvemonth, I was moving the creation of that same Revolutionary Tribunal. I crave pardon for it of God and man.'

Danton's 'trial' began two days later when he appeared in the great hall of the Paris *Parlement*. In the dock along with him were fourteen others, some of them simple criminals who had been added for no other reason than to blacken his name. He was accused of organising a massacre on the Champ de Mars, of enriching himself at public expense and of conspiring to overthrow the Republic. Asked for his particulars, Danton replied, 'My address will soon be in oblivion;

as for my name, you will find it in the Panthéon of history.' The prosecutor, Antoine Quentin Fouquier-Tinville called his only witness, the financier, Cambon, once a fellow member with Danton of the Committee of Public Safety; it was not a wise move. Observing that the witness could not conceal his emotions, Danton remarked, 'Come, Cambon, do *you* think we are conspirators? Look, he is laughing, he believes no such thing.'

Danton answered his accusers: 'I put against your accusation – of which you cannot furnish a proof nor the hint of a proof, nor the shadow, nor the beginning of a witness – the whole of my revolutionary career.' When he went on to accuse his accusers the tribunal immediately adjourned the hearing. Overnight, the prosecutor gave a false account of the proceedings to the National Convention which responded by decreeing that any prisoner who should attempt to interrupt the course of justice by threats or revolt should be outlawed.

Next morning, the tribunal convened at 8.30 am instead of the usual 10 in order to get its sordid business over before the public arrived. No sooner had the decree had been read out than the jurors, prompted vigorously by the tribunal's president, Armand-Martial-Joseph Herman, asked leave to proceed at once to judgement. The prisoners were hurried out of court while sentences of death were passed in their absence.

Danton was far from a saint, but he was one of the first leaders of the revolution to realize that their ideals had turned to dust.

Sir Robert Peel narrowly escaped assassination in 1843. The resulting trial and sentence of his assassin led to a re-examination of the defence of insanity in a criminal trial.

Death by mistaken identity

While walking in Whitehall on the afternoon of 20 January 1843 Edward Drummond was shot in the back at point blank range by a man who wrongly assumed his victim to be the Prime Minister, Sir Robert Peel. In fact, he was Peel's private secretary making his way home from work. Though Drummond managed to walk away from the scene, he died of complications five days later.

The assassin was Daniel M'Naghten (the name is variously spelled) the owner of a successful woodturning business in Glasgow. M'Naghten was a man of radical views who believed that he was being persecuted by the Tories. When asked to plead to the charge of murder he answered, 'I was driven to desperation by persecution', and 'I am guilty of firing'. His counsel, Alexander Cockburn, later to become Lord Chief Justice, ran a defence of insanity, claiming that his client was 'the victim of a fierce and fearful delusion'. Medical evidence suggested that the prisoner was deprived of 'all restraint over his actions'. The result was a verdict of not guilty by reason of insanity and M'Naghten was committed to Bethlem asylum.

Queen Victoria, who had been the target of more than one assassination attempt herself (see below), let it be known that she was outraged. The House of Lords decided to investigate whether the law of insanity should be improved and put a number of questions to the judges of the Court of Common Pleas. The judges answered in words which were to become the test for legal insanity for many years:

> 'To establish a defence on the ground of insanity it must be clearly proved, that, at the time of committing the act, the party accused was labouring under such a defect of reason from disease of the mind, as not to know the nature and quality of the act he was doing, or if he did know it, that he did not know that what he was doing was wrong'.

Such a definition of insanity, had it been in force at the time of M'Naghten's trial, would probably have resulted in his conviction and execution.

While M'Naghten is remembered today only as a name in the law books, some still wonder if his famous claim to insanity was merely a smokescreen. M'Naghten was heavily involved in radical politics, a Chartist leader and a spokesman for the Glasgow trade unions. His library ticket reveals that he had investigated the symptoms of insanity which, in the words of the Dictionary of National Biography, he may have been feigning.

M'Naghten died in Broadmoor asylum of natural causes in 1863, but the 'M'Naghten test' proved to be remarkably robust, lasting until 1957 when it was replaced by the defence of diminished responsibility. It is, however, still in use in the United States of America.

Although she ended her days as the most beloved of England's monarchs, during her forty year reign Queen Victoria was not always popular and was the subject of at least eight attempts on her life.

Victoria under threat

The first attempt on the life of Queen Victoria occurred on 10 June 1840, though just how serious it was is still in doubt. The pregnant Queen was riding in a carriage with Prince Albert on Constitution Hill on the way to visit her mother when eighteen year old Edward Oxford stepped out of the crowd and fired first one pistol and then another directly at her. Albert pulled the Queen down (but did not take a bullet on her behalf as a recent film suggested[1]) and she was not hit. Oxford offered no resistance to arrest, shouting with somewhat confused grammar, 'It was I, it was me that did it.' Documents found at his house revealed that he was a member of a fictitious society devoted to violence. Charged with high treason, the jury found that 'the prisoner Edward Oxford discharged the contents of two pistols at her Majesty, but whether they were loaded with bullets or not has never been satisfactorily proved, he being at the time insane'. He was detained indefinitely in an asylum where he proved to

---

[1] *The Young Victoria*, 2009.

be a model patient. In 1867 he accepted a discharge on the condition that he would leave the country. He is thought to have died in Melbourne around the year 1900.

On 29 May 1842 at a time when the Queen was not in good odour with her people she was riding in the Mall when a man by the name of John Francis fired a pistol at her. Victoria was not injured but her assailant escaped. In an attempt to flush out the assassin the Queen agreed to travel the same route the following day. (Monarchs were made of sterner stuff in those days.)[2] The plan worked: as the Queen's carriage passed by Francis stepped forward and was immediately arrested by a plain clothed policeman. 'Damn the Queen,' he said, 'why should she be such an expense to the nation'. Convicted of high treason, Francis was sentenced to death, a sentence which was later commuted to transportation for life.

After that, the palace gates were surrounded daily by spectators anxious to see the action; and they were not disappointed. Two days later a man named John William Bean fired a pistol at Victoria, but, being loaded only with gravel, paper, tobacco and broken clay pipes, it had no effect. Described as a 'deformed boy age 16, a wretched and diminutive looking being', Bean received a sentence of eighteen months imprisonment for his pains.

It was all too much for Prince Albert. At his suggestion Parliament passed an Act making it an offence punishable by seven years imprisonment and flogging to aim a firearm at the Queen, or otherwise hurt or threaten her.

All was quiet for the next seven years, but on 19 May 1849, shortly after the birth of the Queen's seventh child, an unemployed Irishman, William Hamilton fired at the royal carriage in Constitution Hill. Despite the fact that his pistol was loaded only with powder he was sentenced to seven years in a penal colony.

The next attack on the Queen took place on 27 June 1850 and was the only one which left its mark. It happened when

---

[2] I do the present royal family an injustice. When in 1974 Princess Anne was faced in the Mall with an armed kidnapper who ordered her out of her car she is said to have refused with the words, 'Not bloody likely.'

Victoria's carriage was leaving the courtyard of her uncle's house in Piccadilly. A former army officer named Robert Pate ran up behind and managed to strike the Queen quite violently on the head with a walking cane. English newspapers played down the injury, but at the end of the century the *New York Times* carried a story that Victoria still bore the scar. Pate's plea of insanity was rejected and he was found guilty and sentenced, like Hamilton, to seven years transportation. After returning to England in 1860 he inherited his father's estate and died a wealthy man.

In 1872, while returning in her landau to Buckingham Palace a young Fenian named Arthur O'Connor climbed into the grounds of Buckingham Palace and flourished a broken pistol at the Queen before being disarmed by her faithful servant, John Brown. O'Connor's gesture had been designed to secure the release of some Irish nationalists, but it cost him a year in prison and twenty strokes of the birch. Brown got a medal and the Queen intervened to spare her assailant the birching. Brown was rewarded with a medal.

The last assassination attempt came on 2 March 1882, and was the most bizarre of all. Victoria was leaving Windsor railway station in her carriage for the castle, along with her daughter, Princess Beatrice when a young unemployed clerk by the name of Roderick Maclean stepped out of the crowd, lifted a pistol and 'fired' it at her. Fortunately, the weapon was unloaded. He was overpowered by two boys from Eton College who beat him with their umbrellas. Maclean turned out to be a budding poet who had sent a loyal address to Her Majesty and had been offended by its reception. Found 'not guilty, but insane', he was committed to Broadmoor, where he ended his days in 1921.

The event was celebrated, appropriately, by another poet, the eccentric Scot, William McGonegall, in his own inimitable style:

> Maclean must be a madman,
> Which is obvious to be seen,
> Or else he wouldn't have tried to shoot

Our most beloved Queen.

Horrified at the fact that Maclean had escaped a prison sentence, Victoria declared that the law must be changed. A year later a Bill was introduced to permit the courts to enter the verdict of *'guilty* but insane'.

No further attacks were made on the Queen, who died peacefully in her bed in 1901.

The punishment of a once powerful tyrant is usually greeted with joy, at least so long as his fate has been determined fairly by an independent tribunal. The tribunal which sentenced the former President of Iraq, Saddam Hussein to death could lay claim to no such safeguards.

Saddam in court

Months after the overthrow of Saddam Hussein's government in 2003 by the US led coalition Saddam himself was caught hiding in a hole in the ground outside his home town of Tikrit. Eight months later he was brought, weak and pale but full of defiance, before an investigating Iraqi judge. When asked to identify himself he answered, 'You are an Iraqi, you know who I am ... I am still the president of the republic and the occupation cannot take that away'.

The following year Saddam and other members of his party appeared before the Supreme Iraqi Criminal Tribunal to answer charges concerning the killing in 1982 of 148 Shiite civilians in the town of Dujail in retaliation for an attempt to assassinate Saddam. The former dictator pleaded Not Guilty, but refused to acknowledge the legitimacy of the court. At one stage he even refused to enter court, claiming that he had been beaten by his guards and denied showers and access to writing materials.

Saddam's defence team claimed that the Dujail men had been sentenced to death after a fair trial and that the action was a legitimate response to an attempted assassination of the head of state.

Further charges were made against the ex-dictator in August 2006. He and six co-defendants were accused of the massacre in 1988 by mustard gas and nerve agents of some 5,000 civilians in the Kurdish town of Halabja.

On 5 November 2006 Saddam was convicted of the murder of the Shiites. The charge of killing the Kurds was dropped without explanation. When sentenced to death by hanging the prisoner shouted bitterly at his judges, 'You don't decide anything. You are servants of the occupiers and their lackeys. You are puppets'. His appeal was rejected and he went to his death. Some say the execution was bungled. The trial itself has also been the subject of disturbing criticism.

The right of an accused to a 'competent, independent and impartial tribunal' is guaranteed by various international treaties, but the trial of Saddam fell far below these standards.

The first chief judge was assassinated and replaced by another who had to suspend the session because he was unable to control the prisoner's contemptuous outbursts. He in turn left the bench, claiming ill-health. His replacement never took up post after it was discovered that he had been a member of Saddam's Ba'athist party. The next nominee was a Kurd who resigned on grounds of political pressure even before he took up post. During the course of the proceedings three of the defence lawyers were kidnapped; two of them were murdered and a third ran off in fear of his life.

The proceedings of the 'High Tribunal' were chaotic at best, with the judges intervening frequently with remarks prejudicial to the defendants. According to *The Daily Telegraph* newspaper, the deliberations were often so embarrassing that the microphones had to be turned off. The UN Secretary-General declined to support the trial, which was also condemned by groups such as Amnesty International and Human Rights Watch. Their criticisms were supported by the defence team. By itself, this would not have been surprising, save for the fact that one of the team's lawyers was a former US Attorney-General.

The American and British governments expressed no criticisms of the trial, though Tony Blair deplored the imposition of the death penalty.

4.2 WAR'S ALARMS

Law struggles to exist in times of war. The writ of habeas corpus, for example, regarded throughout the common law countries as a pillar of our freedoms, has been suspended during hostilities by both Britain and the United States of America.[3] And when the war is over the victor often uses the device of a show trial to justify the persecution of its enemies. It is a stratagem that sometimes backfires.

> *Everyone knows the story of how Joan of Arc beat the British and claimed the crown for the Dauphin of France before being betrayed and handed over to the Inquisition. Arguably her greatest accomplishment, however, was her bravery in the face of her inquisitors.*

A Maid undaunted

The British had been fighting the French on and off for over a century before they were pushed into retreat by the army of the Dauphin inspired (though not led) by a nineteen year old girl from Orléans called Joan, but widely known as The Maid. When Joan was captured by a dissident French baron she was sold to the British who handed her over to the Inquisition for trial - after first making it clear what outcome they expected.

Following a long incarceration and weak from fasting for Lent, Joan was finally brought before her inquisitors. No one reading the transcript of the proceedings can fail to be

---

[3] Habeas corpus is an order of the court to produce someone to court in order to challenge the legitimisation of his incarceration.

impressed at the way this unlettered, sickly and unrepresented young woman stood up for herself over long hours of questioning by skilled interrogators.

When asked a question she had already answered Joan would reply brusquely, 'That does not concern your trial' or 'Move on to the next question.' If the inquisitor referred to matters she was reluctant to discuss she would undertake to respond the following day (but never did). At one point she tartly told her questioner that he would find the answer to his question in the minutes of the previous session.

Joan's skill in answering difficult questions was formidable. Once, when she said that her voices had assured her that in the end she would come to the kingdom of heaven the inquisitor jumped in to ask whether this meant she believed that she could not commit mortal sin. Joan confounded him by replying, 'As to this I know nothing; but commit myself in all things to Our Lord.' Asked whether she knew she was in a state of grace, Joan deftly replied, 'If I am not, may God bring me into it; if I am, may God keep me in it.' Asked whether she approved of the murder of the former Duke of Burgundy (who had been assassinated by the Dauphin), she said that it was a great tragedy for the kingdom but that, whatever occurred between them, she had been sent to help the King. Another 'trap' question was whether God hated the English. Joan answered that she did not know but she did know that God would drive all the English out of France except those who died there.

But nothing Joan said could deflect the court's determination to condemn her to a frightful death at the hands of her enemies. She was tricked into a 'confession' which she immediately withdrew and was then tricked into appearing to defy the court by resuming the wearing of men's clothing. After she had been convicted the Inquisition handed her over to secular 'justice' (a fine name for the British executioner, to whom the inquisitors knew she would be committed) hypocritically 'praying the same to treat you with kindness and humanity in respect of your life and your limbs'. Whether intentionally or not, the stake was built in such a way that the usual steps could not be taken to hasten the prisoner's end and Joan died in agony.

It was 30 May 1341. It took the church over a century to acknowledge the great injustice they had done to this exceptional young woman, and another five centuries before she was canonized and made a patron saint of France.

The deaths of four Bostonians and a slave at the hands of British soldiers provoked outrage among the colonists, already aggrieved by supposedly unjust taxes and by the practice of billeting soldiers upon ordinary citizens. The ensuing trials illustrate the best features of the common legal tradition of the two nations (as they now are). And it all began with a row over the payment of a bill.

The snowball 'massacre'

It was a cold, snowy night in Boston on 5 March 1770 when a British officer, Captain Goldfinch was accosted in the street by Edward Garrick, a wig-maker's apprentice. Garrick called out, 'There goes the fellow who hath not paid my master for dressing his hair'. Goldfinch ignored him and walked off. Garrick followed, repeating his accusation assertively. A British sentry, Hugh White intervened to say, 'He is a gentleman, and if he owes you anything he will pay for it.' Garrick unwisely replied that there were no gentlemen left in the regiment, upon which White promptly knocked him to the ground. Very soon a crowd of Bostonians, many of them armed with cudgels, swords and bats, surrounded the two soldiers, calling for the sentry's death.

When the mob began pelting White with stone packed snowballs, ice and sticks he called for the guard to turn out. Not to be outdone, the Bostonians rang the church bells to summon help. Another much larger mob who had been taunting soldiers elsewhere in town hurried to the scene, making over three hundred in all.

The officer of the day was Captain Thomas Preston of the 29th Regiment of Foot (later to be known as the Worcester Regiment). He doubled into the street accompanied by a corporal and six men. After forcing their way through the crowd the soldiers stood in a semi-circle protecting White from the townsmen.

The crowd responded by striking the soldiers' muskets and bayonets with their clubs. When they pulled one of them, Hugh Montgomery to the ground he called on his fellows to fire. The crowd's reaction was to taunt the soldiers with cries of 'Fire, Fire'. Eventually a single shot rang out. (After the court proceedings were over Montgomery admitted that it was he who had fired after being knocked down by the crowd.) It was followed by a ragged volley from the soldiers. When the firing died out three of their tormentors were found to be dead and others injured, two of them dying later of their wounds. Because soldiers were prohibited from using their weapons except by authority of a magistrate Captain Preston and eight of his men were arrested and charged with murder.

After eight months in custody Preston was put on trial for murder. The noted Bostonian lawyer and 'patriot', John Adams was the only attorney willing to act for him and his soldiers, well knowing that to do so might prejudice his political ambitions. After a six day trial the judges ruled that Preston had not ordered his men to fire, but that if he had, the assault on the soldiers had been so violent that it could not even amount to manslaughter, but was excusable homicide. The jury duly returned a verdict of Not Guilty.

The private soldiers were tried separately a few weeks later. Adams argued that they had been entitled to defend themselves against 'a motley rabble of saucy boys, negroes and molattoes, Irish teagues and outlandish jack tarrs'. All were acquitted of murder, but Montgomery and another Private were convicted of manslaughter (a finding seemingly in conflict with that of Preston's court).

Adams reacted by pleading benefit of clergy on their behalf and they were branded on the thumb instead of being executed.

Four civilians were also prosecuted on the basis that they had fired at the crowd from the Customs House, but the evidence against them was thin and they were discharged.

Adams justly described his role in the affair as, 'one of the most gallant, generous, manly and disinterested Actions of my whole Life, and one of the best Pieces of Service I ever rendered my Country. Judgment of Death against those Soldiers would have been as foul a Stain upon this Country as the Executions of the Quakers or Witches, anciently. As the Evidence was, the Verdict of the Jury was exactly right'. Ironically, John Adams' cousin, Sam, may have been responsible for arranging the deliberate harassment of the British soldiers.

Adams went on to become one of the Founding Fathers of the United States of America and, subsequently, its second President.

And the apprentice Garrick was mistaken: Captain Goldfinch had paid the wigmaker's bill the day before.

All servicemen are bound to obey the orders of their superiors, but the exigencies of seafaring demand the strictest compliance with the orders of a ship's captain. The most famous mutiny in British naval history occurred on 28 April 1789.

Mutiny on the South Seas

His Majesty's Ship *Bounty* had been bought by the Admiralty for the purpose of bringing breadfruit plants from Tahiti in the Windward islands to the West Indies, where it was hoped to use them as a cheap source of food for the slaves. The ship's Captain was 35 year old Lieutenant William Bligh RN. After an idle six months in Tahiti the *Bounty* left for home with over 1,000 breadfruit plants on board. The crew were reluctant to leave the island paradise where many of them had acquired dark skinned 'wives'.

The first that Bligh knew of the mutiny was being awoken at pistol point and dragged onto the deck of his ship, dressed in his nightshirt with his hands tied behind his back. Along with five other members of the crew he was forced into the ship's 23 foot launch, where thirteen more opted to join him before they were cast adrift on the High Seas.

Equipped with only a sextant and a pocket watch and with no more than a few inches of freeboard, Bligh sailed the open boat safely from just West of Tahiti to Timor in the Dutch East Indies, an epic voyage of some 3,600 nautical miles which has never been equalled.

The leader of the mutiny was the master's mate, Fletcher Christian, formerly a close friend of Bligh's. The two men seem to have fallen out following Bligh's criticism of Christian, though exactly what gave rise to the quarrel is not known. After the mutiny Christian took the *Bounty* and the rest of its crew back to Tahiti, where they picked up the 'wives' they had accumulated during their stay on the island. They then set sail for the isolated island of Pitcairn, where they burned the Bounty. A year later fourteen of the mutineers were captured in Tahiti by a naval ship sent out for that purpose. On the way home it foundered with the loss of 31 crew and four of the prisoners.

The court-martial of the surviving mutineers began on 4 April 1792 in the Captain's cabin of Lord Hood's ship, *The Duke* in Portsmouth harbour. The prosecution claimed that the accused had not resisted the mutiny, that they failed to get into the launch with Bligh and that they made no effort to return to England afterwards, each of which constituted mutiny. Bligh wrote to the court exonerating two of the accused, who were duly acquitted. Six others were convicted and received the mandatory sentence of death. Of these, two were later pardoned on the court's recommendation and a third on the ground that he had been denied the opportunity to call witnesses. One of those who escaped the rope was Midshipman Peter Heywood, who went on to justify the leniency he had received by rising to the rank of Captain.

At 11.26 in the morning of 29 October the three remaining men were hanged at the yardarm of *HMS Brunswick* in Portsmouth Harbour. It was not a speedy death and their dead bodies were left swinging for two hours in the rain.

Bligh was subject to the usual mandatory court-martial for losing his ship, and was acquitted. It did not affect his career. He served with distinction under Nelson at Copenhagen and was later appointed Governor of New South Wales, where, ironically, he was to be arrested by mutinous troops in what is known as the rum rebellion. After his release Bligh was appointed Vice Admiral of the Blue[4].

Fletcher Christian was never found. There were reports that he was killed by Tahitians he had brought with him to Pitcairn, though there were also persistent rumours that he had found his way back to England. The last mutineer died on Pitcairn island in 1829, where descendants of the mutineers still live to this day.

When a few breadfruit plants finally got to Jamaica the slaves refused to eat the unpalatable fruit.

It might be thought that especial care would be taken to ensure that the trial of someone accused of assassinating the head of state of a modern democratic country would be conducted in accordance with all due process, but that was not the case with the alleged assassins of America's greatest President.

The flawed trials of the Lincoln assassins

Abraham Lincoln was shot dead in a box at the theatre in 1865. His assassin, the actor, John Wilkes Booth escaped, only to be shot a week or two later by one of the pursuing soldiers.

By then, Booth's accomplices had been rounded up. After being kept shackled and hooded for weeks in inhumane conditions they were tried and convicted by a military commission without being given any prior warning of the charges.

---

[4] That was the junior of the three vice Admirals.

Four of them, three men and a woman, went to the scaffold the following morning despite a recommendation for mercy in the case of the woman.

Strangely for such a litigious minded country, the proceedings were probably illegal. As the US Supreme Court was to rule shortly after in another case, military courts had no authority to act in civil cases while the ordinary courts were open.[5] And at the time of the Lincoln commission the ordinary courts were open in the District of Columbia where the commission sat.

The commission could also have been objected to on the ground that many of its members were personal friends or acquaintances of the victim. Furthermore, throughout the trial one of their number, a noted phrenologist, was observed to be studying the shape of the defendants' heads. Modern sensitivities might feel disquiet at the fact, and it was probably insufficient to disqualify him for bias – though not, perhaps, for inattention.

Though it has no bearing on the court-martial's legitimacy, it is interesting to note that another of its members was General Lewis (Lew) Wallace who went on to write the famous novel, *Ben Hur: a Tale of the Christ*.

Should the ordinary laws be tempered in times of war? A senior judge got into hot water when he delivered his frank opinion on the subject.

'Amidst the clash of arms'

At the height of the Second World War the Appeal Committee of the House of Lords were faced with a case involving the power of the executive to detain 'persons of hostile origins or associations' under the notorious wartime regulation 18B. In the course of his speech Lord Atkin said:

---

[5] *Ex parte Milligan*, 1866.

'I view with apprehension the attitude of judges who on a mere question of construction, when face to face with claims involving the liberty of the subject, show themselves more executive-minded than the executive. Their function is to give words their natural meaning, not perhaps in war time leaning towards liberty ... In this country amidst the clash of arms the laws are not silent. They may be changed, but they speak the same language in war as in peace. It has always been one of the pillars of freedom, one of the principles of liberty for which on recent authority we are now fighting, that the judges are no respecters of persons and stand between the subject and any attempted encroachments on his liberty by the executive, alert to see that any coercive action is justified in law. In this case I have listened to arguments which might have been addressed acceptably to the Court of Kings Bench in the time of Charles I...

'I know of only one authority which might justify the suggested method of construction. "When I use a word," Humpty Dumpty said in rather a scornful tone, "it means just what I choose it to mean, neither more nor less." "The question is," said Alice, "whether you can make words mean different things." "The question is," said Humpty Dumpty, "which is to be master– that's all." After all this long discussion the question is whether the words "If a man has" can mean "If a man thinks he has." I am of opinion that they cannot, and that the case should be decided accordingly.'[6]

The Lord Chancellor, Viscount Simon wrote to Atkin asking him to moderate his language, but he refused and his words were printed as written. Later opinion has been more favourable to Atkin.

---

[6] *Liversidge v Anderson*, 1941. The reference to the laws not being silent in times of war was lifted from Cicero.

A man at the centre of the Nazis' 'Final Solution of the Jewish Question' sought to excuse himself to an Israeli court by arguing that he was only obeying orders. His defence exposed an inconsistency in the attitude of the victorious Allied powers.

'I was only obeying orders'

Adolf Eichmann was a 26 year old sales clerk when he joined the SS in 1932. Ten years later he had risen to the rank of SS-Obersturmbannführer (or Lieutenant Colonel) in which capacity he was called upon to act as secretary to the Wannsee conference[7] at which the 'final solution of the Jewish question' was planned. Eichmann was later given responsibility for transportation of the victims to the gas chambers, a task which, as a good Nazi, he performed with efficiency and enthusiasm. At the end of the war he escaped with his family to Argentina where he engaged in a variety of jobs, including that of rabbit farmer. In 1960 he was seized, illegally, by agents of the Israeli secret service, Mossad, and smuggled out of the country to Israel.

At his trial the following year Eichmann did not dispute his role in the arrest, torture and murder of millions of Jews, relying on the defence that he did so on the orders of those above him in the Nazi hierarchy. Eichmann argued that 'one must be loyal to the head of state' and that Germany had the misfortune of a having a bad head of state. He went on, 'Ethically I condemn myself and try to argue with myself ... I have regret and condemnation for the extermination of the Jewish people which was ordered by the German rulers, but I myself could not have done anything to prevent it. I was a tool in the hands of the strong and the powerful and in the hands of fate itself'. The defence was rejected and he was convicted and sentenced to death by hanging. The Israeli Supreme Court rejected his appeal, commenting, 'Eichmann

---

[7] The conference was held in a mansion by the side of the Wanseee, a lake near Berlin.

received no superior orders at all... He was his own superior and he gave orders in matters that concerned Jewish affairs.'

If the court was correct and Eichmann was, indeed, an enthusiastic participant in the holocaust there is little more to say about this evil man. But his defence poses the question: what should be the responsibility of those who commit grave crimes on the orders of their superiors?

The British army's *Manual of Military Law*, edited by Professor Lauterpacht, was clear on the point. It provided that: '[T]he fact that a rule of warfare has been violated in pursuance of an order of the belligerent Government or of any individual belligerent commander does not deprive the act in question of its character of a war crime; neither does it, in principle, confer upon the perpetrator immunity from punishment by the injured belligerent.'

But this had not always been the official British view. The previous (1914) edition of the *Manual*, edited by Professor Oppenheim, which was in force throughout most of the second world war, actually accepted Eichmann's view of the defence of 'superior orders' by advising that: '[m]embers of armed forces who commit ... violations of the recognized rules of warfare as are ordered by their Government or their commander are not war criminals, and cannot, therefore, be punished by the enemy.' It was only in 1944 that this guidance was replaced by the new. Most of the acts on which the Nuremberg charges were based were committed at a time when the old, more forgiving, guidance was in operation.

It was not only the British who changed their view on this point: the Americans had undergone a similar change of heart also and it was the later view of the two countries that was incorporated in the Nuremberg charter, which stipulated that, 'The fact that a person acted pursuant to order of his Government or of a superior does not relieve him from responsibility under international law, provided a moral choice was in fact possible to him.' The Allied volte face was embarrassing, but the Eichmann tribunal opted to follow the charter in this regard. Whether it acted justly in so restricting the defence of 'superior orders' is another matter.[8]

It is not generally known that throughout the Second World War there was a unit of the German army dedicated to the exposure of war crimes, both Allied and Axis.

War crimes investigations by the German army

Following in the steps of a similar body set up during the First World War the Wehrmacht-Untersuchungstelle, or army war crimes investigation bureau, was set up by General (later Field Marshall) Keitel in 1939 within the legal department of the German army. Its role was to examine violations of the laws of war by enemy civil and military personnel, as well as by the German armed forces.

The bureau was solely an investigative body; it had no power to prosecute or try. It was staffed by German military judges of the old school and, although there were occasional examples of National Socialist influence, in general their investigations were thorough and fair. This little known department continued its work until almost the last days of the war. An exhaustive review of the bureau confirmed that it:

'did function in a trustworthy manner, that its investigations were authentic and its documents reliable ... The Bureau was not a propaganda arm of the Nazi regime ...'[9]

---

[8] Half a century after Nuremberg a statute of 1998 set up the International Criminal Court. It offered a much more nuanced approach towards the defence of superior orders. Such orders, the statute provides, do not relieve an accused of criminal responsibility unless three conditions apply, namely he was under a legal obligation to obey the order, he did not know that the order was unlawful; and the order was not manifestly unlawful. The statute declared genocide and crimes against humanity to be manifestly unlawful. The British armed forces have since adopted a similar view (Manual of the Law of Armed Conflict, 2005) and it is one which seems likely to prevail in future.

[9] *The Wehrmacht War Crimes Bureau, 1939-1945*, by the American lawyer, Alfred M. de Zayas. Nebraska University Press, 1989.

Hardly any Allied soldiers were prosecuted for war crimes, although many such crimes were committed by the Allies, notably the Soviets.

Keitel, Hitler's lickspittle warlord, was hanged as a war criminal in 1946.

No one who lived through the war years can forget the nasal monotone of William Joyce pouring contempt on Britain's war effort. The whole nation wanted to see him silenced, but when he was finally brought to book there were grave misgivings about the outcome.

'Lord Haw Haw'

Throughout the Second World War the extreme right wing politician, William Joyce made propaganda broadcasts in Germany for the Nazis. He was caught at the end of the war, put on trial for high treason, convicted and hanged.

This gave rise to considerable unease from many who felt that Joyce's offence amounted to little more than making a false declaration on a passport application. Treason is normally a crime committed by a citizen of the state in question, but, despite a wide impression to the contrary, Joyce was not British, but an American citizen[10]. The English courts nevertheless found him guilty of treason because he had applied for and been granted a British passport which entitled him to the protection of this country. To get the passport he had told lies about his nationality and place of birth.

The distinguished jurist, Dr Glanville Williams expressed a common view among lawyers when he wrote:

'Despite the unanimity of the Bench in Joyce's case, the great body of contemporaneous opinion at the Bar, so far as one could gather it from private conversations, was against the decision. As soon as it became generally known that Joyce was not a British subject, and that the continuation of the

---

[10] His father was born in Ireland, but became a naturalized American citizen.

charge against him was made possible only by the fact that he possessed a British passport, there was a remarkable revulsion of feeling even in lay circles against a conviction. To many men in the street, notwithstanding the odious character of Joyce's activities in Germany, a conviction seemed undesirable when it could be gained only by what was regarded as a legal device.'[11]

But laws are not decided by academics and Joyce went to his death in Wandsworth prison. Thirty years later his remains were disinterred and sent to Ireland for burial.

Wartime events can sometimes give rise to litigation many years later.

Echoes of war

Over forty years after the second world war Count Nikolai Dmitrievich Tolstoy-Miloslavsky (a distant cousin of the writer, Leo Tolstoy) published a book, *The Minister And The Massacres* claiming that Lord Aldington, while plain Brigadier William ('Toby') Low DSO, had in May 1945 been an accomplice to the murder by Soviet Russia of some 70,000 men, women and children. Aldington ignored the book, as he had previous allegations of a like nature, until a property developer, Nigel Watts intervened. Watts was in dispute with the Sun Alliance insurance company over his brother-in-law's insurance claim and Aldington was chairman of the Sun Alliance. Watts stirred up the old calumny by distributing 10,000 copies of a pamphlet he had written with Tolstoy's help. It asserted that:

> 'The evidence is overwhelming that [Low] arranged the perpetration of a major war crime in the full knowledge that the most barbarous and dishonourable aspects of his operations were throughout disapproved and unauthorised by the

---
[11] *Cambridge Law Journal*, 1948.

higher command, and in the full knowledge that a savage fate awaited those he was repatriating.'

An appalling war crime had indeed occurred, but the allegations against Aldington were quite unjustified. At the end of the Second World War Churchill, Roosevelt and Stalin had agreed at the Yalta conference that Soviet citizens and Yugoslavs who had fought for the Nazis would be turned over to the Russians and the Yugoslav partisans respectively. At the time Brigadier Low was chief-of-staff to Field Marshal Alexander and it had been his unsavoury duty to carry out this task, acting upon the orders of Harold Macmillan, then Churchill's minister resident in the Mediterranean. The people concerned were White Russian Cossacks who had fought in the Waffen SS, as well as Croation Ustachi and their families.[12] Some of them resisted repatriation violently. As soon as they were in the hands of the Soviets most were summarily executed.

In 1989 Aldington, now chairman of the Conservative Party, brought a libel action against Watts which was supported financially by the Sun Alliance. Tolstoy was joined as co-defendant at his own request. After a nine week trial the jury ordered the two defendants to pay Aldington £1.5 million in damages, approximately three times the largest amount previously awarded by an English libel jury. The size of the award may have been aggravated by the fact that Tolstoy and Watts had pleaded the defence of what is called in law 'justification', that is an assertion that the libels were in fact true. They had also rejected an offer of £300,000 in settlement.

An appeal to the European Court of Human Rights led to the size of the award being reduced substantially on the ground that it was disproportionate to the aim of the proceedings.

---

[12] It is easy to despise anyone who fought on Hitler's side during the war, and members of both the massacred groups committed atrocities, but the Cossacks saw themselves, not so much as supporting the Nazis, as seeking to defeat the Communist dictatorship of their own country. Much the same goes, mutatis mutandis, for the anti-Tito Ustachis.

In 1994 Tolstoy issued a writ against Aldington, applying for an order that the judgment of 1989 be set aside on the ground of fraud. The writ was struck out as being an abuse of the process of the court and in an unusual step Tolstoy's pro bono solicitors were ordered to pay 60% of Low's costs.

In 1995 Watts was gaoled for eighteen months for repeating the libel in another pamphlet.

Aldington died in the year 2000. Two days after his death Tolstoy paid his estate the sum of £57,000.

The invasion of Iraq in 2003 was one of the most fiercely controversial military actions of this century. Suspicions that the British Attorney General had trimmed his advice to the Prime Minister on the legality of the projected invasion led some to question his good faith and that of the Blair government, but were the suspicions justified?

Counsels of war

Saddam Hussein, the dictatorial President of Iraq (whose trial and execution is described above), was no stranger to weapons of mass destruction. There is no question that he had used poison gas against the Kurdish people and was attempting to obtain atomic missiles, for which he already possessed delivery systems. After he had failed to comply with a number of UN resolutions requiring him to desist in these efforts the United States and its allies began to examine the military options.

On 30 January 2003 the British Attorney General, Lord Goldsmith PC, QC gave his advice to Tony Blair, the Prime Minister concerning the legality of waging war on Iraq. It consisted of a memorandum which examined among other issues the key question of whether a further UN resolution was necessary to revive an earlier one authorising war. 'A narrow textual reading of the resolution,' the advice concluded, 'suggests that [another resolution was] not needed, because the Council [of the United Nations] has predetermined the issue.' But it conceded that a court might take a different view. Goldsmith added that: '... the safest legal course would be to secure the adoption of a further resolution to authorise the use of force,' adding: 'The legal analysis may, however, be affected by the course of events over the next week or so...'

On 17 March Goldsmith declared in a written answer to a Parliamentary Question that, 'having regard to the information on the negotiating history which I have been given and to the arguments of the US Administration which I heard in Washington, I accept that a reasonable case can be made that resolution 1441 [of the UN] is capable in principle of reviving the authorisation in [resolution] 678 without a further resolution.' The Attorney later explained that he had given this further advice because the military deserved an 'unequivocal' judgement on the legality of the action before troops went into battle.

Three days later, just after the war had begun, a deputy legal adviser at the Foreign and Commonwealth Office resigned, claiming that Goldsmith had 'changed his advice twice just before the war to bring it in line with 'what is now the official line'. The ensuing controversy divided largely along party lines.

So, did the Attorney trim his advice to the wishes of his political masters and their transatlantic allies? Goldsmith's first advice was a measured opinion, marginally in support of the legality of war, but conceding that the point was arguable. When the UN resolution he hoped for failed to materialize the Attorney took further advice and obtained further information which reinforced his original view, which he thereupon delivered to the government in order that the armed services could be given the clear assurance he believed they needed, and his second opinion was no way inconsistent with his first.

The job of the Attorney, like that of any lawyer, is to give honest and helpful advice to his client; it is not always an easy task.

4.3   THE VOICE OF PROTEST

Contrary to rosier views of our island history, unrest, even revolt, has seldom been far below the surface of society. At the time of writing, it is not long since mobs of young criminals devastated large swathes of London and other great English cities in an orgy of burglary, vandalism and violence. Sometimes the law has been on the side of the oppressed, sometimes it has been the object of their hate.

The feudal system which the Normans had brought with them to Britain required the labours of some 15 to 30 peasant families to maintain the living standards of a knight, more for a baron. The manorial lord enforced his privileged position through his own court, known as the manorial court. But that was when labour was cheap. Between 1348 and 1350 about 1.4 million English men and women died of the plague[13] out of a population of 4 million. Labourers were now in short supply, but their wages were held down artificially. At the same time food prices were rising and a new poll tax was imposed. Something had to give.

And it all began with a rumour.

'The Great Rumour'

In 1377 a bright, but sadly unidentified peasant realized that he could ignore his lord's demands for what was called seigniorial service if he could only show that his tenancy was one of 'ancient demesne', that is free of the lord's demands. This he did by getting hold of certified copies (called exemplifications) of extracts from the Domesday Book. The good news spread like wildfire in Berkshire and among some forty villages across the South in what came to be called the 'Great Rumour'. A surprising number of peasants were prepared to

---

[13] To this day there is no general agreement among experts as to the nature or origin of this disease, which did not fully die out in this country until the seventeenth century.

spend their modest savings on a lawyer in pursuit of their desire to acquire their freedom. Suddenly, the legal profession was popular. Don't worry: it didn't last long.

Under pressure from the gentry the ten year old King Richard II was persuaded to enact a law to suppress this menace to the established order. It declared:

> 'In many lordships and parts of the realm of England' the Act recited, 'the villeins[14] and holders of land in villeinage refuse their customs and service due to their lords, under colour of certain exemplifications made from Domesday Book concerning the manors in which they dwell; and by virtue of the said exemplifications, and their bad interpretation of them, they affirm that they are quit and utterly discharged of all manner of serfdom due whether of their bodies or of their tenures, and will not suffer distresses to be levied on them, or justice done on them, but menace the servants of their lords in life or members, and what is more, they draw together in great bands, and bind themselves by confederation that each shall aid the others to constrain their lords by the strong hand.'

Special commissions were issued to the justices of the peace to punish such bold peasants, as well as their lawyers, who were considered to be their 'maintainers and abettors'.

But the royal action did nothing to remove the underlying discontent and four years later the Peasants' Revolt broke out.

The largest insurrection in English history had no single objective. In so far as those involved could be said to have had a common purpose it was to destroy the laws which bound them to their feudal lords and the lawyers who administered them.

Lawyers under attack

The revolt began when a tax collector called Thomas Bampton visited the Essex village of Fobbing to assess the inhabitants

---

[14] A villein was the lowest class of farmer.

for the much resented poll tax and was beaten up and kicked out of town. Soldiers arrived to establish order and they too were thrown out. Discontent spread swiftly to other villages. Manors were burned down and legal records destroyed with the aim of destroying the landowners' proof of title. Discontent jumped across the Thames to Kent, where a mob found a popular hero, the radical preacher, John Ball locked up in Maidstone castle. (Ball was the originator of the bitter saying, 'When Adam delved and Eve span who was then the gentleman?'). The mob seized the castle, released Bell and went on to attack Canterbury.

An unknown veteran of the French wars by the name of Wat Tyler somehow emerged as the leader of the Kentish men, who by this time numbered about sixty thousand, and led them in a march under his banner to London. Here they were joined by a similar host from Essex. As soon as the multitude were seen approaching the gates of London bridge were opened by the fearful citizenry and the peasants swarmed across. Once inside the City walls, they broke down the gates of the Fleet prison and went on to ransack and burn the Savoy palace of John of Gaunt, whom they saw as responsible for the hated poll tax.

John Ball had exhorted the people "that they might destroy first the great lords of the realm, and after the judges and lawyers, questmongers [people who promoted litigation], and all other whom they took to be against the commons.' The peasants took his advice to heart. A chronicler recorded how they 'broke open the chests found in the [Temple] church or the chambers of the apprenticii [or junior barristers] and tore up whatever books they found, whether ecclesiastical or charters and muniments [or title deeds] in the safety chests of the apprenticii, and fed them to the fire.'

Revolt spread far beyond London to places such as Hertfordshire and Norfolk (where the castle was seized), even York. In Bury St Edmunds the Prior was put on trial and beheaded. When Cambridge was sacked and the university charters burned a townswoman was heard to shriek, 'Away with the learning of the clerks!'

Eventually, the fourteen-year-old king Richard II plucked up enough courage to meet the rebel leader face to face at Mile End. This is how the chronicler described the meeting:

> Wat Tyler of Maidstone, ... came to the King with great confidence, mounted on a little horse, that the commons might see him. And he dismounted, holding in his hand a dagger which he had taken from another man, and when he had dismounted he half bent his knee, and then took the King by the hand, and shook his arm forcibly and roughly, saying to him, "Brother, be of good comfort and joyful, for you shall have, in the fortnight that is to, praise from the commons even more than you have yet had, and we shall be good companions." And the King said to Walter, "Why will you not go back to your own country?" But the other answered, with a great oath, that neither he nor his fellows would depart until they had cut their charter such as they wished to have it, and had certain points rehearsed and added to their charter which they wished to demand.

In the hope of calming the mob Richard promised to do away with the poll tax and remove the servile status of villein[15]. What he did not know was that, while this meeting was going on, another part of the mob had taken over the Tower of London, where they beheaded the unpopular archbishop of Canterbury as a prelude to an orgy of robbery and murder.

King and commoner met again the following day at Smithfield. Tyler, whose success was causing him to lose his grip on reality, started to berate his king. It was too much for the Lord Mayor, Sir William Walworth who drew his dagger and slashed at Tyler's throat. The rebel leader was knocked off his horse and run through on the ground by an esquire.[16] The king seized the opportunity to call on the crowd to follow him, promising that they would be granted charters and pardons.

---

[15] A villein was a peasant legally subservient to the local lord, a status barely above that of slave.

[16] Walworth was knighted by the king for his efforts and his statue now stands at Holburn Viaduct.

It was a false promise that Richard had no intention of keeping. What remained of the revolt was ruthlessly put down at the king's command. 'Villeins ye are', Richard is said to have declared, 'and villeins ye shall remain.' The charters and pardons he had promised to grant were torn up or ignored and thousands perished in the aftermath of the rebellion.

The poll tax was not reintroduced until 1988, when it proved to be as unpopular as ever and had to be withdrawn. No lawyers are known to have been harmed in the process.

King and lords failed to learn their lesson from the Peasants' revolt and nearly seventy years later another rebellion broke out under the leadership of the mysterious 'Jack Cade'. It gave rise to the most oft-quoted fictional attack on the legal profession.

'Let's kill all the lawyers'

By 1450 the men of Kent were unhappy once again - at the forced labour laws, the corrupt courts, the land seizures and the general mismanagement of the economy under the deeply unpopular King Henry VI. Unlike the Peasant's revolt of their grandfather's day, the aggrieved comprised, not merely peasants, but small landowners and clergy too.

In other respects it was like a re-run of the Peasants' revolt when some 20,000 Kentish men assembled at Blackheath under the leadership of Jack Cade where support for their grievances was expressed even by some supporters of the king. Little is known about Cade, though rumour had it that he was an Irishman, possibly a veteran of the French wars, who had had to flee Sussex after killing a man.

After sending his grievances in writing to the King's Council Cade, now calling himself 'Captain of the Great Assembly of Kent', seems to have thought he had done enough and agreed to retire. But it was not enough to satisfy his followers, now reinforced by contingents from Surrey, Sussex and

Essex, and riot and disorder broke out. There was a skirmish near Sevenoaks at which the royal force was brushed aside by the mob, now once again led by Cade, who took their chance to march to Southwark, then on to London, where the gates were opened by a sympathetic populace. Once inside, the Captain of Kent, as Cade was called, declared himself Lord Mayor of London also by striking the London Stone with his sword in the traditional manner.[17]

Fearful of what might happen, the Council had committed two of the people most detested by the mob to the Tower of London. They were James Fiennes, first baron of Saye and Sele, the hated former sheriff of Kent, and his son-in-law, William Cromer, the current sheriff. Once the Kentish men had control of the Tower a commission was set up to put Fiennes on trial for treason and extortion. He was convicted and executed, along with Cromer. The two men's decapitated heads were arranged on London Bridge so that they appeared to be kissing each other.

After a day of plunder and mayhem the mob spent the night at Southwark, but by then they had lost the support of the Londoners who forcibly removed them from the City. The following day the rebels reached a settlement with a delegation of churchmen in return for some 30,000 pardons. (Do they never learn?) This gave the royal forces time to re-form, at which the rebels dispersed. Cade sought unsuccessfully to take refuge in Queenborough castle in Kent, later fleeing to his native Sussex, while the booty he had seized was sent by barge to Rochester. He was finally captured in Sussex after a fight and died of his wounds on the way back to London. His lifeless body was ritually decapitated at Newgate. But it took some years before the disorders finally ceased, many of Cade's followers dying in what was sinisterly known as 'the harvest of heads'.

The rebellion was immortalized by Shakespeare in his play, Henry VI, Part II, in which the fictional Jack Cade declared,

---

[17] The London stone is thought to have been used by the Romans as a measuring point. It played a part in the commercial arrangements of the mediaeval City and can still be seen displayed in a wall in Canon Street.

'There shall be in England seven halfpenny loaves sold for a penny; the three-hooped pot shall have ten hoops; and I will make it a felony to drink small beer. All the realm shall be in common, and in Cheapside shall my palfrey go to pass. And when I am king - as king I will be - there shall be no money; all shall eat and drink on my score; and I will apparel them all in one livery, that they may agree like brothers, and worship me their lord.'

His friend, Dick the butcher replied, 'The first thing we do, let's kill all the lawyers'.

Cade answered in the same vein,

'Nay, that I mean to do. Is not this a lamentable thing, that of the skin of an innocent lamb should be made parchment? that parchment, being scribbled o'er, should undo a man? Some say the bee stings: but I say, 'tis the bee's wax; for I did but seal once to a thing, and I was never mine own man since.'

As every schoolboy knows, the Gunpowder Plot was an attempt by a group of English Catholics to assassinate the King and his Parliament in order to usher in a return to the old religion. One of the less well known stories of the plot is that of the Jesuit priest who was caught up, almost unwittingly, in the affair.

Equivocation

Henry Garnet was a Derbyshire boy who had been educated at Winchester college and studied law in London. After converting to Catholicism he abandoned his studies in order to train for the Jesuit order in Rome. From there he was sent to England to advance the Catholic faith, eventually becoming head of the very successful Jesuit mission to this country. After King James I failed to deliver the tolerance he had promised to Catholics a small group of them determined on his overthrow.

In the course of a meeting with Robert Catesby, the leader of the plotters, in London on 9 June 1605 Catesby indicated to the priest that some great plot was under way and asked him about the morality of 'killing innocents'. Garnet answered that during war innocents were often killed alongside the enemy. He was later given a detailed account of what was proposed from a Father Oswald Tesimond. It was received under the seal of the confessional and on the understanding that if the plot were discovered Garnet would be able to go to the authorities. Later that month Garnet met Catesby again and told him that he 'wished him to look what he did if he intended anything. That he must first look to the lawfulness of the act itself, and then he must not have so little regard of Innocents that he spare not friends and necessary persons for the Commonwealth.' When Catesby offered to tell the priest more, Garnet refused to listen: 'I told him what charge we all had of quietness and to procure the like in others.'

After the plot was discovered Garnet wrote to the authorities protesting his innocence and went into hiding. During this time he wrote a letter to the Privy Council in which he declared his abhorrence for "the late most horrible attempt" to which he admitted being an accessory by administering "the Most Holy Sacrament to six of the confederates at their very undertaking so bloody an enterprise". He begged the Council to give him a hearing, and protested that the conspirators never made him privy to the plot.

The proclamation for his arrest gave a good description of the man:

> 'Henry Garnet, alias Walley, alias Darcy, alias Farmer, of a middling stature, full faced, fat of body, of complexion fair, his forehead high on each side, with a little thin hair coming down upon the middest of the fore part of this head; his hair and beard griseled. Of age between fifty and three score. His beard on his cheeks close cut, and his chin very thin and somewhat short. His gait upright, and comely for a feeble man.'

Garnet was discovered in a 'priest hole' in Hindlip Hall in Worcestershire. He was arrested and taken before Sir Robert

Cecil, the Lord Privy Seal, and questioned on twenty-three different occasions before being sent for trial at the Guildhall charged with compassing the death of the king, as the crime of treason was known.

At his trial the prosecution attempted to portray Garnet as having tried to avoid giving a straight answer to the questions put to him. There was some force in this. Since the thirteenth century Catholics had been permitted for grave reason to make mental reservations to anything they said to civil authorities, provided that no outright lie was involved. It was a tactic which was known as equivocation. Shakespeare's *Macbeth* (which was written about this time) refers to 'an equivocator that could swear in both the scales against either scale; who committed treason enough for God's sake, yet could not equivocate to heaven.' And Garnet himself had written about the doctrine.

Garnet's defence was that Catesby had told him that 'he had some great thing in hand for the good of Catholics. I much disliked it and dissuaded him'. He had to admit, however, to having done nothing to frustrate the plot. Coke met this explanation with a display of childishly alliterative sarcasm. The accused, he said, 'hath many gifts and endowments of nature, by art learned, a good linguist and, by profession, a Jesuit and a Superior as indeed he is Superior to all his predecessors in devilish treason, a Doctor of Dissimulation, Deposing of Princes, Disposing of Kingdoms, Daunting and deterring of subjects, and Destruction'.

The trial ended with Garnet being convicted and sentenced to the horrible death reserved for traitors.

On 3 May 1606 speaking from the scaffold erected in the Churchyard of old St Paul's Garnet once again admitted his failure to disclose his 'general knowledge' of the plot, but maintained that he neither sanctioned nor approved of violence against King or state. When he was turned off the ladder a sympathetic crowd pulled on his legs so that he was dead before the rest of the gruesome sentence could be carried out.

Garnet seems genuinely to have believed that he was innocent of any part in the gunpowder plot, but it is hard to believe that his was anything other than a case of wilful blindness towards a projected act of mass murder.

There can be few men who have been made a judge with their ears clipped, their nose slit and their cheeks burned.

'Ye who have ears to hear'

William Prynne was a farmer's son who went to grammar school and took a degree at Oxford before being called to the Bar at Lincoln's Inn. While there he fell under the influence of militant Puritanism and spent the rest of his life hectoring and vilifying almost every aspect of contemporary life, from religion and the monarchy to divorce, the stage, even the length of men's hair.

But he went too far in 1633 when he referred to women actors as 'notorious whores'. The Queen, Henrietta Maria, whose pleasure it was to act in court masques, took the words to be an insult aimed directly at herself. Accused of sedition, Prynne was brought before the Court of Star Chamber. It was an 'iffy' charge because he had not criticized the king in person, only his wife, but in the rough and ready jurisprudence of the day it did not stop him being convicted and sentenced to life imprisonment. He was also fined heavily and ordered to have his ears lightly clipped in the pillory. In consequence of this he was expelled from Lincoln's Inn and deprived of his Oxford degree.

Prynne was incarcerated in Mount Orgueil castle in Jersey. With the help of a friendly governor he continued to vent his displeasure from his cell, notably against Archbishop Laud, whom he believed to be his tormenter. Three years later Prynne wrote a pamphlet denouncing the bishop of Norwich. It led to him being prosecuted for an 'infamous libel against their majesties, state and government' and a second sentence of life imprisonment, as well as an order of exile. In addition, he was fined £5,000 and ordered to lose the rest of his ears and have his nose slit. Finally, he was to be branded on both cheeks with the letters S. L. for 'seditious libeller'. The 'surgery' was so badly done that Prynne nearly lost his life. But it did not deter him: with all the passion of a fanatic he declared, 'The more I am beat down the more I lift up.'

Released from prison by the Long Parliament in 1640, Prynne became an MP and pamphleteered in support of Parliament's case against the tyrannical king. He also had the satisfaction of hounding his tormentor, Laud to death. But when the army proposed to put king Charles on trial he thought that they had gone too far and did not refrain from saying so. Like other dissenting MPs, he was excluded from the Chamber in what is called Pride's Purge (see above) and imprisoned. Released from prison in 1653, Prynne was elected MP for the second time. The antiquary, John Aubrey, who, though not always reliable, usually got the best stories, tells how Prynne proudly re-entered the Commons flourishing his grandfather's basket handled sword. Unfortunately, '(his) long sword got between Sir W. Waller's short legs, and threw him down, which caused laughter'. As a good Presbyterian he refused to kneel with the rest of the House at prayers, but it did no harm to his career and he was appointed Recorder (or judge) of his native city, Bath, a post he held for two years.

Prynne enjoyed a successful Parliamentary career, becoming chairman of important committees and drafting and introducing Bills. Eventually, King Charles II rewarded his father's old supporter with the post of keeper of the Records in the Tower of London. It suited the old lawyer perfectly and his careful work in the organisation and preservation of state documents is still remembered.

Prynne died in his chambers in 1669. He is buried 'in the walk under the chapel' of Lincoln's Inn. Exactly how he kept his spectacles on is not known.

The case of John Bunyan shows how the law can be powerless in face of those who are determined to worship God in their own ways.

A tinker out of Bedford

John Bunyan was a tinker like his father. During the English civil war he was a soldier for Parliament. When peace returned he was ordained a Baptist preacher at his home village of Elstow in Bedfordshire. After the Restoration of the monarchy vigorous efforts were made to suppress anyone who, like Bunyan, strayed from the doctrines and rituals of the established church. He lost the right to preach in church, but continued to minister to his congregation in the fields around the nearby village of Harlington.

Arrested and brought before magistrate Wigton at Harlington House, Bunyan was offered his freedom if he agreed to stop preaching. He refused and was committed to the county gaol. A month later the magistrate sent his clerk to ask the preacher whether he would agree to conform. Bunyan refused again and was committed in custody to quarter sessions.

Quarter sessions were as reluctant to imprison Bunyan as magistrate Wigton and begged him again not to preach. He replied, 'If you release me today, I will preach tomorrow'. It left the court with no alternative and Bunyan was gaoled for three months for 'pertinaciously abstaining' from attending Anglican church services and for preaching at unlawful meetings and conventicles.[18] His wife and friends presented several petitions to the judges, but they were refused, even by the merciful Lord Chief Justice, Sir Matthew Hale.

At the end of his sentence Bunyan continued to preach, with the result that he spent most of the next eleven years in and out of Bedford prison. During this time he wrote and

---

[18] A conventicle was a non-conforming congregation of five or more.

published his spiritual autobiography, *Grace Abounding to the Chief of Sinners*. In 1672 he was released under King Charles' Declaration of Religious Tolerance and became minister of his community at a barn licensed for their meeting-place. The following year Parliament pressured the king into repealing his Declaration and Bunyan found himself once more incarcerated in the County gaol (not the little lock-up on Bedford bridge as was formerly thought). It was there that he wrote his masterwork, *The Pilgrim's Progress*. Published in 1678, it is said to be the second most popular book after the Bible and has never been out of print.

Ten years later Bunyan caught a fever and finally received his reward. 'So he passed over, and all the trumpets sounded for him on the other side.'

Schoolchildren are still told of the simple minded folk who protested at the calendar reform of the eighteenth century which they believed would cut their lives short by ten days, but did the protests really happen?

The calendar riots

The strange thing about the Calendar riots is that there were none; but the legend persists.

Man has struggled for centuries to bring the calendar into line with the days and months which are determined by the forces of nature. Julius Caesar did a good job, but by 1582 the calendar had once again got out of synch with earth time and Pope Gregory had to step in. His reform is known as the Gregorian calendar.[19]

Britain was characteristically slow to adopt this Continental novelty, and only got round to it nearly two centuries later. The effect of the new law was that the day after Wednesday the second of September 1751 became Thursday the fourteenth.

---

[19] Named after Pope Gregory XIII.

There is a persistent story that on hearing of the change simple folk were panicked into rioting in the belief that they would lose twelve days of their lives. It is a delightful tale, but is simply not true. Th most likely origin of the story is Hogarth's painting, *An Election Entertainment*, which depicts a group of Tory opponents to the Whig candidate in the Oxfordshire elections of 1754. On the floor is a campaign banner bearing the words 'Give us our Eleven days'.

Though it barely figures in folk memory today, large areas of London were reduced to flaming ruins by rioters in the late eighteenth century. The supposed author of the disturbances escaped conviction, but his life thereafter was to be ruined by litigation.

London's burning

Fear of and antipathy towards Roman Catholicism had long been endemic in this country when in 1780 the Prime Minister, William Pitt embarked upon a course aimed at bringing about religious harmony. His modest proposals for reform met with widespread opposition, the natural leader of which was the head of the influential Protestant Association, Lord George Gordon.

On 2 June that year Gordon called a protest meeting in St George's Fields near what is now Waterloo station in order to demonstrate the extent of public anger at the proposed relaxation of the anti-Catholic laws. It started in a sedate enough manner, but when the crowd marched across the Thames they were joined by a disorderly element which attempted to invade the Palace of Westminster leading to violent scuffles around and even inside both Houses. Over the next few days riots erupted all over the capital, fires were started and fifty seven buildings burned down. Catholic chapels and the homes of prominent people like the Lord Chief Justice, Lord Mansfield were targeted. Newgate and a number of other prisons were burned or wrecked and their inmates released, many still in chains, to add to the mayhem. Before the rioting was put down by the army some 700 hundred people were dead and countless more had been injured.

Eighty five people were tried at the Old Bailey for serious offences of riot and violence arising from the riots. Forty three of them were acquitted. Of those who were convicted thirty five were condemned to death. Gordon himself was tried separately at the bar of the King's Bench for treason, but got off with the assistance of two able counsel, Lloyd Kenyon, later to become Lord Chief Justice, and his junior, Thomas Erskine, later to become Lord Chancellor. One by one the two advocates destroyed the prosecution witnesses in cross-examination, but it was Erskine's closing speech that was considered to have won the day. His client, he rightly argued, was to be judged, not from the consequences of his actions, but from 'causes and designs', that is to say, his intent: there was very little evidence that Gordon had incited or otherwise intended the riots to take place; they had simply got out of hand.

Nevertheless, Gordon's reputation was in tatters and he became a social outcast.

Some years later when Gordon's restless mind had turned to penal reform he made the mistake of libelling both the Queen of France and Her Majesty's judges. This time there was to be no mistake. He was convicted on charges of criminal libel, but absconded to the continent before he could be sentenced. When he eventually returned to English soil he was arrested by a Bow Street runner, brought before the court and fined £500 for the libel. He was also bound over to find two sureties of £2,500 each for his future good behaviour. Not being able to find the sureties, Gordon was committed to prison in default, where he remained - in relative comfort - for the rest of his days.

During his absence abroad the one time leader of the Protestant Association had converted to Judaism under the adopted name of Israel bar Abraham. He died in the now rebuilt Newgate prison at the age of forty two.

The Gordon riots were to inspire Charles Dickens' novel, *Barnaby Rudge*, the sub-title to which is '*A Tale of the Riots of Eighty*'.

The 1790s were a heady time for English radicals who saw the revolution across the Channel as something which could with advantage be imported here. Some of them belonged to the misleadingly titled London Corresponding Society for Reform of Parliamentary Representation, and went around calling each other 'Citizen'.

In 1794 three men were charged with treason and acquitted. The Society continued to flourish and the king was stoned in public. The government were jittery, and with good reason.

The Pop Gun conspiracy

In September 1794 three members of the Society went to a brassfounder's shop in London where they asked for a three foot long smooth bored tube to be made to specific dimensions, but would not say what it was intended for. They made similar inquiry at two further shops.

The men were Thomas Upton, a watchmaker, Peregrine Palmer, an attorney and Robert Crossfield, a gentleman surgeon, all members of the London Corresponding Society. Whatever their common purpose, like many plotters, they found it difficult to work together in harmony. At the next meeting of the society the mercurial, but lame Upton took offence at a reference to his having 'hopped off' from the last meeting, and went to the authorities. He thereupon vanished, never to be seen again. (People were naturally suspicious of his disappearance, and indeed he had died, but it seems to have been nothing more sinister than a boating accident.) While the Society's activities may have been comical its intentions were not. Upton left behind him a drawing of an air gun, together with wooden patterns for its construction. The proposed weapon was designed to fire an arrow which on impact would activate two forks, attaching it to the victim and releasing poison from a glass tube. Compressed air guns had been a reality since the mid-seventeenth century and were quite capable of delivering a poisoned arrow a fair distance. In this case their intended victim appears to have been the king.

The authorities acted swiftly. A number of people were arrested and examined by the Council but had to be released on bail for insufficient evidence. One of the released men, John Smith, impudently had a sign made to hang over his shop, 'At the Pop Gun, Portsmouth Street'. Crossfield was a different case: he got a job as a ship's doctor and left the country. To his dismay, the vessel he was in was captured by the French and when he finally returned to England he was arrested. On the way to gaol he tried to bribe the constables to release him.

Despite the weakness of the evidence against him it was decided to prosecute Crossfield, and he duly appeared before Chief Justice Eyre at the Old Bailey charged with compassing, along with three others, the death of the King. The others were Thomas LeMaitre (or John Peter le Maitre), a watchcase maker, John Smith, a bookseller and George Higgins, a druggist. After Crossfield pleaded Not Guilty Peregrine Palmer, who was one of the three who had gone to the brassfounders, was called as a witness for the Crown. He was obviously uneasy in this role, insisting that he had been outside the shops and knew nothing of what passed inside. However, an expert witness confirmed that Upton's plans would have produced a workable gun operated by compressed air. And some of Crossfield's fellow prisoners of the French gave evidence of his having revealed an intention to kill the king at the theatre - and Prime Minister Pitt too if the occasion arose. Crossfield brushed off these admissions as unwise words spoken in drink.

It all ended in anti-climax. Although the judge summed up in favour of a conviction the jury returned verdicts of Not Guilty against all defendants. Shortly after, the London

Corresponding Society and similar organizations were made illegal by Act of Parliament.

To this day no one knows how serious the Pop Gun conspiracy was, but it could as easily have ended in tragedy as farce.

> *By the early nineteenth century political dissent no longer attracted the barbaric penalties of days gone by, but the experience of prison could still seem pretty shocking to someone with the sensibilities of a poet.*

The critic as dissident

(James Henry) Leigh Hunt was a distinguished critic and poet whose anti-establishment views eventually got him into hot water.

Leigh Hunt founded and edited a political journal, *The Examiner* which he used to belabour anyone he disapproved of. With the help of the radical lawyer, Henry Brougham he had narrowly escaped a conviction for publishing an article on military flogging. But he pushed his luck too far in 1812 when he described the Prince Regent as, 'a violator of his word, a libertine over head and ears in disgrace, a despiser of domestic ties, the companion of gamblers and demireps,[20] a man who has just closed half a century without one single claim on the gratitude of his country, or the respect of posterity!'

With the benefit of hindsight these were far from wholly unjustified comments. Nevertheless, Hunt and his brother, John (who published *The Examiner*) were arrested, charged with libel and found guilty. Passing sentence, Mr Justice Le Blanc condemned the two of them for 'destroy(ing) the bonds of society, by holding up the government to disgrace and contempt'. (Difficult to imagine that nowadays.) Both were

---

[20] A demirep was a woman of doubtful reputation.

sentenced to two years' imprisonment and a £500 fine, as well as being bound over for their good behaviour.

The poet, Keats indignantly apostrophized the Prince Regent:

> What though, for showing truth to flatter'd state,
> Kind Hunt was shut in prison, yet has he,
> In his immortal spirit, been as free
> As the sky-searching lark, and as elate.

And so on.

Hunt was to claim that he 'never thoroughly recovered the shock given my constitution.' In fact, the conditions in Horsemonger gaol, where he served his term, were far from harsh. Hunt himself described how he 'papered his prison-walls with roses, and painted the ceiling like a sky; he furnished his room with a piano, with bookshelves, with his wife and all his children, and turned a little yard into an arbour of summer loveliness by the help of flowers and paint.'

He was even able to continue editing *The Examiner*.

> *At the beginning of the nineteenth century the flames of revolt in England were fanned by the rising price of food and the inequalities of the archaic electoral system. A political demonstration in Manchester turned into tragedy when a botched attempt was made to disperse it by the forces of law and order.*

'Peterloo'

On 16 August 1819 a huge crowd had assembled in St Peter's Fields, an as-yet unbuilt-up part of Manchester,[21] to demand abolition of the Corn Laws and Parliamentary reform. The principal speaker was to be Henry ('Orator') Hunt, one of the

---

[21] The site was in front of where the Convention Centre known as Manchester Central now stands.

more moderate of the radicals of his day. Hunt arrived shortly after 1pm to an enthusiastic welcome. The crowd were carrying banners reading, LIBERTY AND FRATERNITY, EQUAL REPRESENTATION and (in curious anticipation of the Beatles) LOVE. Although the intention was to hold a peaceful demonstration the banners were ominously topped with the red cap of liberty, symbol of the bloody French revolution of only a generation before.

The day was hot and the local magistrates were keeping an eye on the crowd from a house at the edge of the field. They were determined to maintain a pathway between them and the speakers so as to be able to nip any disorder in the bud. But their intention was frustrated when the mob formed a human barrier in front of the speakers. A magistrate 'read the riot act'[22] from a window at about 1.35 pm. It was probably inaudible to most of the crowd, and those who could hear ignored it.

Having only 400 constables at their disposal to deal with a crowd of some 80,000, the chief magistrate concluded that 'the town was in great danger' and issued a warrant for the arrest of the organizers. When the chief constable refused to execute it unaided the magistrate, 'considering the civil power wholly inadequate to preserve the peace' summoned the assistance of the Manchester and Salford Yeomanry and the regular army Hussars who were waiting nearby. The Yeomanry were the nearer and arrived first. The Chief Constable asked their commanding officer to take his men to the hustings to allow the speakers to be removed in accordance with the warrant. When the cavalry began moving forward 'Orator' Hunt misread the situation and called for the crowd to 'Stand firm. This is a trick.' The mob reacted by linking hands and pelting the Yeomanry with bricks and stones. Believing they had no option but to force their way through, the 60 strong force of part-time cavalrymen laid about them indiscriminately with their sabres, causing horrifying injuries, even death. Hunt and the other speakers surrendered peace-

---

[22] An Act of 1714 allowed a justice or mayor to proclaim a crowd of twelve or more persons to be a riot, thus allowing its forcible dispersal.

fully, but the panicking crowd had difficulty in leaving the square because one of its exits was blocked by infantry.

Then the Hussars arrived. When their commander asked for his orders the chief magistrate replied, 'Good God, Sir. Do you not see how they are attacking the Yeomanry. Disperse the crowd.' In the course of the ensuing action one hussar officer was heard to shout to the Yeomanry, 'For shame! For shame! Gentlemen: forbear, forbear! The people cannot get away!' Within ten minutes it was all over, though disorders continued in surrounding streets. When the next day dawned some 11 to 15 were found dead and 600 people wounded on the field, including a disproportionately large number of women and children. (Precise figures were hard to get.) Three of the dead were special constables, two of them being killed unintentionally by the cavalry. Sixty-seven cavalrymen and 20 horses had been injured by missiles from the crowd.

Critics were to claim that the inadequately trained Yeomanry had been affected by drink and were out of control; they replied that their horses were frightened by the mob. We will never know the full truth since the government refused to order an inquiry, but there seems little doubt that the Yeomanry intervened ineffectively and with unwonted violence. Four of them were prosecuted for their conduct, but acquitted by juries consisting of respectable householders with much to lose from disorder. The Manchester and Salford Yeomanry was disbanded a few years later.

Nine people were charged with sedition. Four were acquitted, but Hunt and some of the other speakers were convicted and sentenced to terms of imprisonment.

The Manchester tragedy became known as the Peterloo massacre, a term coined by the *Manchester Observer* as a conflation of St Peter's Fields and Waterloo. Few events have done so much for the radical cause.

Extreme radicals had little time for Orator Hunt's policy of peaceful protest.

The Cato Street conspiracy

Arthur Thistlewood was one of those men who, having failed to make much of his own life, nevertheless believed himself qualified to order the affairs of others.

Born of a prosperous family and well educated, Thistlewood trained as a land surveyor, but did not like the work. After a few years as an army officer he tried his hand as a farmer but could not make a success at that either. He found a purpose in life only when he moved to London in 1811 and fell in with a radical crowd known as the Spencean Philanthropists. (Thomas Spence was a schoolteacher who argued that, 'if all the land in Britain was shared out equally, there would be enough to give every man, woman, and child seven acres each.')

Travel in America and France left Thistlewood with the conviction that revolution was the only way to remedy England's ills. In 1816 he was one of the organizers of a mass demonstration at Spa Fields, Islington aimed ostensibly at electoral reform, but secretly intended as a springboard for revolution. The result was hours of rioting while Thistlewood led a small force to demand the surrender of the Tower of London. The 'uprising' ended in failure the government suspended habeas corpus and issued warrants for the arrest of the organizers. Thistlewood decided to emigrate with his wife and child, but was caught as he boarded ship for America. Released without trial, he cheekily wrote to the Home Secretary, demanding reimbursement of the cost of the tickets he had purchased for the trip. Lord Sidmouth failed to respond and Thistlewood challenged him to a duel. This resulted in a twelve months prison sentence for breach of the peace. When released, he complained about prison conditions.

Determined to see no repetition of the Spa Fields and Peterloo riots the government introduced the Six Acts of 1819 which made almost any political meeting treasonable. Thistlewood and a small group of revolutionaries decided that the time had come for direct action. The government crisis following the death of King George III seemed to them an opportune moment to strike.

Their plan was to murder the Prime Minister, Lord Castlereagh and the whole of his cabinet while dining at the home of Lord Harrowby in Grosvenor Square. (Harrowby was Lord President of the Council.) Thistlewood described his intention of,

> 'going to the door with a note to present to Earl Harrowby; when the door is opened, the men will rush in directly, seize the servants that are in the way, present a pistol to them, and directly threaten them with death, if they offer the least resistance or noise. This done, a party will rush forward to take command of the stairs. One man is to have fire arms and he will be protected by another holding a hand grenade; a couple of men will take the head of the stairs leading to the lower part of the house. If any servants attempt to make a retreat these men with the hand grenades are to clap fire to them, and fling them in amongst them. All these objects are for the securing of the house and those men who are to go in for the assassination are to rush in directly after.'

Once the house had been secured the plotters intended to decapitate the diners and exhibit their heads on Westminster bridge. Immediately afterwards they would burn down the cavalry barracks and seize its cannon. A provisional government would be set up in the Mansion House, and the Bank of England was to be occupied. The revolutionaries' password was 'but' and their countersign 'ton'. A house in Cato Street was rented for their base, just around the corner from where the dinner was to be held.

What the conspirators did not know was that Thistlewood's first lieutenant was a police spy and that the dinner was a fiction put about by the government with the sole purpose of provoking the radicals to action. The government's intelligence was good, but the operation to arrest the plotters was clumsily carried out.

On 23 February 1820 a magistrate, accompanied by twelve Bow Street Runners, was standing ready to execute a warrant for the plotters' arrest. They were meant to be supported by soldiers from the Coldstream Guards, but the Guardsmen had been given the wrong address and arrived late. The magistrate decided to press on without them and entered the hayloft of the Cato Street building. When one of the Runners moved to arrest him Thistlewood picked up a sword and ran him through. He died on the spot. The plotters hastily extinguished the candles and tried to make their escape. In the confusion four of them managed to do so, only to be captured soon after.

Eleven of the plotters were put on trial. Charges against two were dropped when they agreed to turn King's evidence. One of the accused, a coffee shop owner by the name of James Ings, was asked what he wished to say before sentence was passed. After accepting that what he had intended to do was 'of a most disgraceful and inhuman nature' he went on:

> 'On the other hand, his majesty's minsters conspire together and impose laws to starve me and my family and fellow countrymen; and if I was going to assassinate these ministers I do not see it is so bad as starvation, in my opinion my lord. The Manchester yeomanry rode in among, and cut down men, women and children. They had their swords ground, and I had a sword ground also. I shall suffer no doubt; but I hope my children will live to see justice done to their bleeding country.'

All eleven were found guilty of treason and sentenced to be hung, drawn and quartered, but only Thistlewood, Ings and three others were hanged, one of them the son of the black Attorney General of Jamaica. (By that date the gruesome business of drawing and quartering had been dispensed with.) The rest had their sentences commuted to transportation for life.

> *The last armed rebellion in Britain took place in Newport, Monmouthshire (now Gwent). It resulted in the last sentences of hanging, drawing and quartering ever to be pronounced in this country.*

Civil war (nearly) breaks out in Wales

In the early hours of 4 November 1839 thousands of armed men descended on the town of Newport under the impression that they were the spearhead of a national revolution.

The Chartists, for such they were, had begun as a loose collection of working men's associations which shared radical ideals. The charter which gave them their name had objectives which seem moderate and reasonable by today's standards - universal suffrage, lower and fairer taxes, higher pay and better representation in Parliament. Parliament's contemptuous refusal even to receive their demands led to scattered outbreaks of violence throughout the country, but the Newport Chartists were the only ones to act.

Chief of the Newport Chartists was John Frost, a former Mayor of the town and Justice of the Peace. Earlier that year he had attended a national Chartist convention in London and was asked to be a local 'missionary' for the cause. Though he declined the offer it led to his name being removed from the Commission of the Peace. His plan was for three columns of men to converge on the town at daylight from different directions, one led by himself, another by Zephaniah Williams, a coal miner and innkeeper, and the third by William Jones, an actor. Each of the leaders was to ride on horseback at the head of a column five abreast led by pikemen, followed by musketmen, while the rear would be covered by 'irregulars'. Their intention was to seize the town and then Cardiff, where they expected to be joined by fellow Chartists from other parts of Britain.

The plan began to fall apart, however, even before daylight. In the pouring Welsh rain the revolutionaries were delayed by unplanned visits to local hostelries which offered both drink and relief from the wet, as well as by diversions to local farms designed to force householders to join their ranks. Six and a half hours later than planned the host finally assembled in Newport square, wet and exhausted and having lost the advantage of surprise.

Warned of the threat at the last moment, the Mayor and other local bigwigs had fortified themselves in the Westgate hotel in the city centre, protected by a company of soldiers consisting of two sergeants and 28 men under command of a Lieutenant. Facing them outside were some 3,000 armed rebels. Under the impression that some of their comrades were imprisoned inside the building, the rebels demanded their release. A shot was fired and the Chartists forced their way into the hotel, pushing the soldiers back room by room. Others were not so courageous. At the first sound of firing most of the host beat a hasty retreat. Those inside the hotel, unaware of the disappearance of their fellows, continued their efforts to storm the building, but were eventually driven off.

Within twenty minutes it was all over. Twenty Chartists were dead and many more injured. The mayor and a sergeant of militia were badly wounded. About 150 weapons were collected from in front of the hotel. They included guns, pistols, blunderbusses, swords, bayonets, daggers, pikes, spears, billhooks, reaping hooks, hatchets, cleavers, axes, pitchforks, knife blades, scythes and saws fixed in staves; long iron rods, sharpened to a point; bludgeons, hand and sledge hammers, and mandrils.[23] Later in gaol a remorseful Frost spoke for many when he conceded, 'I was not the man for such an undertaking, for the moment I saw blood flow, I became terrified and ran.'

Dozens were arrested, tried and convicted of minor offences, but the three ringleaders were tried for high treason before a Special Commission chaired by Lord Chief Justice Tindal. They were convicted and sentenced to the only penalty allowed by law, to be hung, drawn and quartered.

---

[23] A mandril was a rod round which metal or glass could be shaped.

The jury made a recommendation for mercy and the sentences were commuted to transportation to Australia for life. All three were later pardoned and permitted to return to Britain. Williams declined the offer and chose to remain in Van Dieman's Land (now Tasmania) where he made a fortune in coal. Jones too declined to return, and died in poverty in Australia. The only one to reach home was Frost, who continued to agitate for reform. He is remembered today by the John Frost Square in Newport.

By the early nineteen-twenties Germany was in a mess. The Mark was in free fall, unemployment was rife and resentment was felt at the swingeing reparations imposed by the Peace Treaty. There was also a real threat of the country being taken over by the Communists.

One man was convinced he had the answer. He began his rise to power with an almost farcical attempt at revolution. It failed and he went to prison. By his lights he put the time to good use by writing an autobiography which also set out a statement of his political philosophy. Its title was originally:

'Four Years of Struggle against Lies, Stupidity and Cowardice'

It was unlikely that a turgidly written political and racist rant with a title like this would ever have achieved much notice. Its success was guaranteed, however, when a canny publisher altered the title to '*Mein Kampf*' ('My Struggle'). The book was written under curious circumstances.

The Bürgerbraükeller was a famous Munich beer cellar. On 8 November, 1923 a meeting of businessmen and politicians was being held there when Adolf Hitler, the leader of the NSDAP[24] decided that the time had come to strike. His plan was to kidnap the members of the Bavarian government

---

[24] German National Socialist Workers' Party.

and force them at gunpoint to accept him as their leader. He surrounded the beer hall with troops of his para-military organization, the SA (*Sturmabteiling* or 'Storm Division', better known as the brownshirts) and declared that 'the national revolution has broken out', adding untruthfully that the army and police barracks had been taken. After a number of rousing speeches he ordered the rounding up of the Jews and the whole of the city council. But little of consequence was achieved that night.

Next day the respected wartime general, Erich Ludendorff took control and announced that they would 'march' - but without any clear idea of where to. The 2,000 strong mob wandered the streets aimlessly until shortly after mid-day when, near the German war ministry, they found themselves confronted by a detachment of one hundred soldiers and a few policemen. Shots were exchanged and the Nazis fled, leaving sixteen marchers and three policemen dead on the ground. Hitler himself received a dislocated shoulder, though exactly how is unclear. It was the end of his abortive coup. But not his career.

The Nazi leader was charged with high treason. The proceedings were quite the opposite of a show trial. The judges were selected by a Nazi sympathizer and the accused was allowed to address the court at length and to cross examine as he saw fit. 'I alone bear the responsibility,' he declaimed, 'but I am not a criminal because of that.' Throughout the trial Hitler's words were reported prominently in all German newspapers.

They also impressed the judges who would agree to the five year prison sentence only after the president assured them that the accused would receive early parole. He did; Hitler spent only eight months in luxurious accommodation in Landsberg prison before being pardoned and released by a sympathetic government.

The Fuhrer dictated his rambling credo to his Deputy, Rudolf Hess, who also edited it. When published, the book set out frankly Hitler's intentions to ignore treaties, to dominate the world by force and to eliminate the Jews. The book sold so well in Germany that it made Hitler a rich man. Pity that it wasn't studied as carefully abroad.

Ten years after emerging from prison Hitler became Germany's Chancellor by democratic means.

> *Wolfe Tone was a traitor who died, not at the executioner's hand, but as a result of the law's delays.*

'Adjutant-general Smith'

Ireland had been a thorn in England's side for centuries. Many good men of all loyalties and persuasions were to die before a foundation for peace was established in the late twentieth century. One of them was the barrister, Wolfe Tone.

Late eighteenth century Ireland was a Catholic country governed by an alien Protestant nation. Not everyone was pleased with the arrangement and when the Society of United Irishmen was founded in 1791 the 26 year old Tone was its natural leader. Tone was the son of a successful coach builder. After taking a BA from Trinity College, Dublin he was admitted to the Bar at the Middle Temple, but instead of practising he turned to political journalism. At first, Tone was prepared to submit to the Society's moderate aims, but in time he led it in a more radical direction:

> 'To break the connection with England, the never-failing source of all our political evils and to assert the independence of my country- these were my objectives. To unite the whole people of Ireland, to abolish the memory of all past dissensions, and to substitute the common name of Irishman in place of the denominations of Protestant, Catholic and Dissenter - these were my means.'[25]

In 1794 Tone was convicted of distributing a seditious address and only escaped imprisonment by betraying a French

---

[25] Tone's *Autobiography*.

agent and agreeing to leave the country After a brief spell in America Tone sailed for France under a forged passport. There, he persuaded the newly installed government, known as the Directory, that he could help them in their war with England by ruining the economy of their mutual enemy through the appropriation of all English property in Ireland.

The French accepted the offer and Tone enthusiastically took part in three abortive French attempts to invade Ireland. He joined the first as 'Adjutant-general Smith', but bad weather and worse seamanship foiled the attempt. The second armada never sailed because of storms off the coast. Tone's role in the doomed third venture was as commander of a naval battery. His vessel was forced to surrender to an English squadron and Tone was captured. Brought before a court-martial for treason, he insisted on wearing his full dress naval uniform. His frank admission of an intent to wage war against England left the tribunal with no alternative but to convict him. No doubt remembering the fate of his brother who had been hanged for a similar abortive 'invasion', Tone asked 'to die the death of a soldier, and that I may be shot.' His request was refused.

A fellow nationalist and lawyer, John Philpot Curran KC made a last minute attempt to stave off the end by seeking a writ of Habeas Corpus from the Court of King's Bench in Dublin. He argued successfully that civilians could not be tried by courts-martial when the ordinary civil courts were sitting. But when the court ordered Tone to be produced the Provost Martial and his commander refused to obey the order. Officers of the court were sent to the prison, but by the time they got there the desperate Tone had already cut his throat with a penknife. He died in agony a few days later.

Tone had very nearly escaped the consequences of his treachery: after the ship he was sailing on was seized he had slipped ashore unrecognized and lived in safety for some time as a French officer until he and a number of other 'Frenchmen' were invited to breakfast by the earl of Cavan. During the meal Sir George Hill, a fellow Middle Temple man, came up to him and said: 'Mr. Tone, I am very happy to see you.' Tone replied: 'Sir George, I am happy to see you; how are Lady Hill and your family?' His cover was blown.

> Roger Casement spent many years as a British Colonial Service officer in the Congo and Peru, where he earned a well justified knighthood for his exposure of the oppression and brutal mistreatment of the native populations. Later in life he espoused the nationalist cause of his native Ireland, but his treasonous role in the Easter Rising was too serious to be ignored.

'Less than love and more than law'

In the early hours of 21 April 1916 Casement was arrested on an Irish beach in the act of running guns into the country from Germany, a country with which Britain was then at war. They were to be used in an uprising which was to take place three days later at Easter. Arrested and put on trial, he pleaded Not Guilty on the ground that his actions were not caught by the fourteenth century Act of Parliament under which he was charged. It was an arguable point of law, but the courts ruled against him and Casement was convicted.

In the end it was not the law, but Casement's impassioned address to the court which was to lodge in peoples' minds:

> 'In Ireland alone in this twentieth century is loyalty held to be a crime. If loyalty be something less than love and more than law, then we have had enough of such loyalty for Ireland or Irishmen. If we are to be indicted as criminals, to be shot as murderers, to be imprisoned as convicts because our offence is that we love Ireland more than we value our lives, then I know not what virtue resides in any offer of self-government held out to brave men on such terms. Self-government is our right, a thing born in us at birth; a thing no more to be doled out to us or withheld from us by another people than the right to life itself - than the right to feel the sun or smell the flowers, or to love our kind. It is only from the convict these things are withheld for crimes committed and proven -

and Ireland, that has wronged no man, that has injured no land, that has sought no dominion over others - Ireland is treated today among the nations of the world as if she was a convicted criminal.'

In an attempt to stifle public sympathy for Casement the British security services secretly released to selected journalists extracts from what came to be known as The Black Diaries. They were Casement's own record of his activities as a predatory pederast. Irish nationalists fiercely denied their authenticity, but in the end they were shown to be genuine. Revealing them to the press during the course of a trial, however, was a disgraceful step for the British to have taken.

Casement received his first and last communion on 3 August 1916. Minutes later he was dead. In 1965 Casement's remains were returned to Dublin where they were given a state funeral.

Casement, as the author has tried to demonstrate elsewhere,[26] was a conflicted character and his case raises the seemingly unanswerable question of what should be done, indeed what realistically can be done, about men of honour who put their loyalty to their native land before their loyalty to a state or faith to which they owe allegiance.

Ezra Pound was and remains an enigma; an unquestionably significant, if notoriously difficult, poet, he was a Jew-hating Fascist, as well as a dyed in the wool traitor who vigorously supported his country's enemies in time of war. His trial was marred, however, by serious failures on the part of America's medico-legal establishment.

The Fascist poet: mad or simply bad?

Ezra Pound was born in Idaho in 1885, but for most of his life he lived abroad in London and Paris and, for twenty

---

[26] *Injustice: State Trials from Socrates to Nuremburg.* Sutton Publishing, 2006.

years, Italy. A major influence in 20th century poetry, Pound's famously difficult 'Cantos' (1925-1962) are regarded by some as his finest achievement.

Pound's political views were a compound of anti-capitalism and anti-Semitism which led him to an admiration of Italy's Fascist dictator, the dangerous buffoon Benito Mussolini. When the war began Pound threw himself into making propaganda broadcasts to America's armed forces over *Radio Roma*. After Germany's capitulation he was arrested and brought to trial in Washington on charges of treason. His agitated state led to his being remanded for psychiatric evaluation to Dr. Winfred Overholser, superintendent of St. Elizabeth's Hospital for the Insane, and three other doctors. They reported that Pound, 'shows a remarkable grandiosity ... believes he has been designated to save the Constitution of the United States for the people of the United States ... has a feeling that he has the key to the peace of the world through the writings of Confucius ... believes that with himself as a leader a group of intellectuals could work for world order ... He is, in other words, insane'. Mmmm.

Faced with this assessment, the court held that Pound was unfit to plead. He was transferred to a more comfortable ward where he was allowed to write, receive visits from literary friends and enjoy sexual relations with his wife and mistresses. Twelve years later Dr. Overholser swore an affidavit declaring that Pound was permanently and incurably insane, but that he was no longer dangerous and that it would be a needless expense for the taxpayers to keep him indefinitely in a government hospital. In 1958 a District Court dismissed the indictment for treason and Pound was released by the same judge who had committed him. He retired to the Continent of Europe, where he died in 1972.

Controversy still surrounds Pound's state of health. Was he really insane? A psychiatrist expressed the view that 'He was eccentric, egocentric, but that didn't mean he was insane.' Others have pointed to the fact that Dr Overholser was an admirer of the poet and a friend of several of his literary supporters. Did this influence his report to the court? The noted American attorney, Alan M. Derschowitz had no doubt about the matter. He described this episode as 'the absolute nadir in the relationship between law and psychiatry.'[27]

When in the nineteenth century a small number of anarchists emigrated from Italy to the United States of America they brought their doctrine of violent revolution with them. Two of their stories demonstrate how people can be moved to do the most wicked things from what they believe to be the noblest of motives.

The anarchists

On 15 April 1920 the local agent of American Express had just delivered the payroll to a firm in a quiet Massachusetts town. Shortly after it had been picked up by the company paymaster and an armed guard shots rang out hitting the guard in the abdomen and severing the artery to his heart. His attacker bent down and picked up the guard's discarded gun, while the other robber fired at the paymaster who dropped the box he was carrying and staggered away across the road. The gunman followed him, bent down and shot him again. The two robbers then returned to the guard, now on his hands and knees and begging for his life. After firing three more shots into him they made their getaway, leaving both men dead on the road.

The robbery was designed to fund a violent anarchist organisation which had brought death and destruction to America. Two Italian immigrants to America, Ferdinando Nicola Sacco and Bartolomeo Vanzetti, were arrested but denied the charges heatedly. Neither had much in the way of education, but their words were nevertheless eloquent.

Sacco, for example, said:

'What is war? The war is not shoots like Abraham Lincoln's and Abe Jefferson, to fight for the free-country, for the better

---

[27] *America on Trial*. Warner Books. 2004.

education, to give chance to any other peoples, not the white people but the black and the others, because they believe and know they are mens like the rest, but they are war for the great millionaire. No war for the civilization of men.'

And Vanzetti:

'I am an Italian, a stranger in a foreign country, and my witnesses are the same kind of people. I am accused and convicted on the testimony of mostly American witnesses. Everything is against me - my race, my opinions, and my humble occupation. I did not commit either of these crimes, and yet how am I ever going to show it if I and all my witnesses are not believed, merely because the police want to convict somebody, and get respectable Americans to testify against us? I suppose a great many Americans think that it is all right to stretch the truth a little to convict an anarchist; but I don't think they would think so if they were in my place.'

Both men were convicted and sentenced to death for the murders. They met their ends bravely in the electric chair. There are still many in the United States who believe them to have been innocent and their trial to have been a flagrant injustice. The better view is that, while Sacco was certainly Guilty, Vanzetti was probably only on the fringes of their violent enterprise.[28]

Soviet communism was even more successful than anarchism in recruiting bright idealists to its insidious cause.

The Rosenbergs

It was March, 1951 and the height of the Cold War when Julius and Ethel Rosenberg were convicted in a New York court of conspiring to pass atomic secrets to the Soviet Union and sentenced to death.

---

[28]See further the author's book, *Injustice: State Trials from Socrates to Nuremburg*. Sutton Publishing, 2006.

Throughout their trial the Rosenbergs had protested their total innocence, but their role as important spies for the Soviet Union was to come out years later. That made it clear that the couple had acted out of principle and not for reward, and the story of their betrayals and deaths cannot be read entirely without sympathy, particularly in light of the passion which they felt for each other.

Julius and Ethel were madly in love, but after their conviction were permitted to see each other only separated by a screen. On the one occasion when they had been allowed any physical contact they:

> 'rushed at each other and embraced tightly, covering each other's faces with fierce kisses. Before anyone knew what was happening, they began pawing one another with wild abandon. They lost all control and wrestled passionately. The witnesses to the scene were stunned by the suddenness and violence of the outburst. They looked on in amazement at the writhing, groaning figures. Finally, the guards and matron recovered. They pounced on them, pulling them apart. Julius was lifted bodily and plumped hard into a chair. Ethel was dragged none too gently. They were still panting... Julius's face was so smeared with lipstick, it looked as if he were bleeding. He laced his hair back with his fingers; Ethel pulled her shirt together in a modest gesture which seemed ludicrous under the circumstances. She pulled her skirt down and demurely patted her dishevelled hair. She could not see the red blotches on her face from her own lipstick smudged off from Julius'... she felt humiliated and began to cry.'[29]

A cynical Communist campaign to secure the Rosenbergs' acquittal failed and husband and wife went to the electric chair within minutes of each other.

It was the anniversary of their wedding.[30]

---

[29] Louis Nizer, *The Implosion Conspiracy*, 1973.
[30] For a more detailed examination of this case see the author's *Injustice: State Trials from Socrates to Nuremburg*. Sutton Publishing, 2006.

> *The career of Ian Robertson Hamilton demonstrates that lawyers can be passionate about issues other than the law and that national autonomy can be advanced by no more serious violence than a cracked stone.*

A Scottish barrister

As a student Hamilton was the leader of a pro-independence group who called themselves the Scottish Covenant Association. Their activities first came to notice on Christmas Eve, 1950 when they stole the Stone of Scone (or Stone of Destiny) from Westminster Abbey. During the theft the stone was accidentally broken into two pieces.

The Stone is a 152 kg block of sandstone which had once been used for the coronation of the Scottish kings. After Edward I's victory over the Scots at Dunbar in 1296 the victorious English took it to London where it was fitted into a purpose-built wooden chair and for centuries was used for the coronation of the English monarchs.

Four months after it was stolen the stone, now repaired, was left on the altar of Arbroath Abbey, from whence it was retrieved and returned to Westminster Abbey. The Prime Minister of the day, John Major, had it taken to Edinburgh Castle where it is still kept except when needed for coronations.

Hamilton and his accomplices were charged in relation to the theft, but never brought to trial.

Three years after the Stone incident Hamilton was called to the Scottish bar, but caused consternation when he refused to swear allegiance to Queen Elizabeth II. His objection was the imaginative one that Scotland had never acknowledged Queen Elizabeth I. The Scottish Court of Session disagreed, holding that the treaty between the two countries contained no provision for the numbering of monarchs, which was a matter for the royal prerogative and not challengeable in the courts.[31]

In 1998 Scotland achieved a devolved Parliament by peaceful means.

In 2009 Hamilton, now Ian Hamilton QC, was given a lifetime achievement award by the Scottish Law Society. Judging by his internet blog, his fires continue to burn not a whit cooler than before.

---

[31] *MacCormick v Lord Advocate*, 1953.

Chapter 5

LIBERTY

Read any red top newspaper and you will discover that most of the woes of the world can be traced to the concept of Human Rights (and the rest to 'Elf and Safety'). Terrorists are let out of gaol because of it. Crooks are allowed to vote because of it. Illegal immigrants can stay in England because of it. Even naughty children threaten their parents with it. While the criticisms are overblown there is some truth in them: judges are now being asked to decide issues that should be the province of politicians, and judges from countries with laws and attitudes towards individual freedom quite different from our own settle issues that should be resolved here. But the idea of human rights – or liberty as it was formerly called – is one of the most emancipating in history. And it all began eight hundred years ago.

In England.

When in 1215 the barons forced King John to agree to the great charter at Runnymede they were not in the least concerned for the liberties of the peasants. Nor could they have imagined that one small clause amongst the many in that document would come to be regarded as the bastion of freedom according to law.

As Rudyard Kipling wrote:

> At Runnymede, at Runnymede,

> Your rights were won at Runnymede!
> No freeman shall be fined or bound,
> Or dispossessed of freehold ground,
> Except by lawful judgment found
> And passed upon him by his peers.
> Forget not, after all these years,
> The Charter signed at Runnymede.

Clause 29 of the Charter, which these lines summarise so accurately, proved in the end to be its most important and is today the only one which remains in force.

But kings and barons did not give up their privileges easily; it took centuries before the rights which hitherto had been enjoyed only by a privileged few were extended to all. It was often a painful process which only the most stubborn and principled were prepared to see through. And this is how it came about.

5.1 FREEBORN ENGLISHMEN

During England's bloody civil war, when others fought for king or Parliament, one man fought for liberty.

'Freeborn John'

John Lilburne was the third son of a minor Sunderland land owner. He was apprenticed in the cloth trade, but his study of the Bible and *Foxe's Book of Martyrs* launched him on a career as a pamphleteer. From the beginning, Lilburne kicked against conformity, gaining him the title, 'Freeborn John' and the distinction of being one of a small number who could claim to have been imprisoned both by King and by Parliament.

Prosecuted in 1637 for attempting to smuggle Puritan pamphlets, or seditious books as the authorities called them, into England, Lilburne was taken before the Court of Star Chamber. When asked to take the oath he insisted that oaths could not be required of Christians and that, in any case, the particular oath he was required to subscribe to was illegal. For this, he was ordered to be pilloried and whipped. Even in the pillory Lilburne continued to inveigh against the Star Chamber until he was gagged. In the end Parliament declared his punishment to have been illegal and abolished the Star Chamber.

The first English civil war broke out shortly after and Lilburne enlisted as a captain in the Parliamentary cause, becoming in time a colonel of a regiment of dragoons. At one point, frustrated at his commander's lack of fighting spirit, he sought permission to attack a castle, but was refused. He ignored the order and negotiated the castle's surrender. His general was not pleased and claimed the victory for himself.

After the war Lilburne took part in the Putney debates of 1645, that extraordinary conference in St Margaret's church, Putney, where for the first time in history serious people sat down to discuss the future form of society. Cromwell brought the discussions to a swift end when Lilburne and others began flirting with ideas dangerously close to what we think of today as democracy and equality before the law.

In 1646 Lilburne found himself in the Tower of London for denouncing his former commander as a traitor. Three years later he was one of the authors of an influential pamphlet entitled *The Agreement of the Free People of England*. It was smuggled out of the Tower and achieved notoriety by being carried in the hatbands of Leveller soldiers. (Levellers were men opposed to the enclosure of land but who in time had bolder aspirations.) Though Lilburne did not see himself as a Leveller his *Agreement* struck chords with that movement by advancing ideas which at the time seemed almost fanciful:

- sovereignty to reside in a democratically elected Parliament;
- people to be free to choose their own religion;

- everyone to be equal under the law;
- no retrospective laws;
- suspects to have the right to silence;
- no imprisonment for debt;
- no capital punishment for petty offences;
- tithes to be abolished; and
- MPs to be personally liable for all monies entrusted to them. (Now, there's an idea!)

After the second civil war Lilburne's attacks on army rule led him to being re-arrested. Put on trial for high treason before a special commission at the Guildhall, he defended himself vigorously and was acquitted to public jubilation. A few years later he was fined heavily and exiled for life for criticizing a notable who had blocked payment of compensation to his uncle.

When the Rump Parliament was dismissed in 1653 Lilburne returned to England, claiming that the order for his exile had been unlawful. At the Old Bailey he argued successfully for his right to see the indictment on which he was being tried (the first person to do so) and was acquitted by a sympathetic jury. A furious Council of State ignored the acquittal and committed Lilburne indefinitely to the Tower of London. Shortly after, he was moved to Mount Orgueil Castle in Jersey, the Governor having been instructed to ignore any writ of habeas corpus. Later he was transferred to Dover castle.

In 1657 at the age of 42 Lilburne was released from prison by order of the Lord Protector, Richard Cromwell. Like many another before him he had been impressed while in custody by the character of a Quaker he had met, and converted to that faith. Shortly after, he died of a fever.

Perhaps the most stirring affirmation of the liberties of Englishmen was made by two Quakers in face of a judge who, clearly, had no idea what they were talking about.

The privileges of Englishmen

William Penn and William Mead were two Quaker preachers. Penn was the son of an Admiral who had been sent down from Christ Church, Oxford for his nonconformist beliefs. He enrolled in Lincoln's Inn, but his studies were interrupted in order that he could accompany his father at sea during the war with the Dutch. Mead was a prosperous linen draper and Trained Band Captain[1]. Neither was the sort of man willing to be bullied, even by a judge.

On 14 August 1670 the two men arrived at their meeting house in Gracechurch Street, London only to find the building locked and the entrance barred by soldiers. When they began to hold their prayer meeting in the street they were arrested, charged with taking part in an 'unlawful, seditious and riotous assembly' and sent to the Old Bailey for trial. The Recorder, Thomas Howell was sitting with two other judges and the lord mayor; he could not have known what he was in for.

When the 26 year old Penn was asked by Howell to plead to the charge the following remarkable exchange took place:

Penn: I desire you would let me know by what law it is you prosecute me, and upon what law you ground my indictment.

Judge: Upon the common-law.

Penn: Where is that common-law?

Judge: You must not think that I am able to run up so many years and over so many adjudged cases, which we call common-law, to answer your curiosity.

---
[1] Trained bands were a sort of local militia.

Penn: This answer I am sure is very short for my question, for if it be common, it should not be so hard to produce.

Judge: The question is, whether you are Guilty of this Indictment?

Penn: The question is not, whether I am Guilty of this Indictment, but whether this Indictment be legal. It is too general and imperfect in answer, to say it is the common-law, unless we knew both where and what it is. For where there is no law, there is no transgression; and that law which is not in being, is so far from being common, that it is no law at all.

Judge: You are an impertinent fellow, will you teach the court what law is? It is Lex non scripta,[2] that which many have studied thirty or forty years to know, and would you have me tell you in a moment?

Penn: Certainly, if the common-law be so hard to understand, it is far from being common; but if the lord Coke in his *Institutes* be of any consideration, he tells us, that Common-Law is common right, and that Common Right is the Great Charter-Privilege'. (He was quoting accurately from Edward Coke's *Institutes*.)

Judge Howell angrily announced that he would instruct the jury in the absence of the prisoners. Penn thereupon turned to the jurymen and, quoting Coke again, said that what was proposed was 'directly opposite to, and destructive of, the undoubted right of every English prisoner.' For this he was ordered into the bale dock, a confined pen at the back of the court.

Mead then took up the cudgel:

You men of the jury, here I do now stand, to answer to an Indictment against me, which is a bundle of stuff, full of lies and falsehoods ... I say, I am a peaceable man, therefore it is a very proper question what William Penn demanded in this case, an oyer of the law,[3] on which our Indictment is grounded.

---

[2] That is, unwritten law.
[3] In this context an oyer was a reading of the charge.

When Mead began to summarize his understanding of the law of riot he too was interrupted by the Recorder who mockingly pulled off his hat and said, 'I thank you, sir, that you will tell me what the law is.'

At the end of the evidence the foreman of the jury was asked for their verdict; he declared Penn to be 'guilty of speaking in Gracechurch Street' and Mead Not Guilty. The furious judge disallowed these verdicts and told the jury that they would be 'lock'd up, without meat, drink, fire or tobacco' until they reached a proper verdict. The foreman stood his ground: 'We have given our verdict and can give no other.' Penn intervened to say: 'The agreement of twelve men is a verdict in law, and such a one being given by the jury, I require the clerk of the peace to record it, as he will answer it at his peril. And if the jury bring in another verdict contradictory to this, I affirm they are perjured men in law.' Turning to the jury he said, 'You are Englishmen, mind your privilege, give not away your right.'

Next morning at 7 o'clock, after what was a hungry and no doubt uncomfortable night, the jury defiantly returned the same verdicts, and were immediately committed to Newgate prison. The following day they returned a different verdict: it was one of Not Guilty. The furious Recorder had no option but to discharge the prisoners, but he wasn't finished with them.

At the beginning of the proceedings Howell had fined the two Quakers 40 marks apiece for contempt of court by reason of their wearing hats in court. (In fact, they had entered the court bareheaded and had been ordered to put their hats on by court officials, no doubt on the orders of the malicious judge who was well aware that Quakers refused to doff their caps to anyone.) At the end of the proceedings the two men refused to pay the fines and were committed to prison. Penn's father forked up the money for both of them and they walked free.

The Recorder then turned his ire on the jury and fined each one of them 40 marks for following 'your own judgments and opinions, rather than the good and wholesome advice which was given you'. When they failed to pay he committed them to prison in default. One of the jurymen, Edward Bushell challenged the order in the Court of Common Pleas by means of a writ of habeas corpus. Lord Chief Justice Sir John Vaughan held that the Recorder's fines were illegal and memorably declared that a judge 'may try to open the eyes of the jurors, but not to lead them by the nose'.[4]

Penn and Mead continued to be persecuted for their faith, but fell out over political differences. Mead devoted himself to his religion and the relief of the poor. Penn emigrated to America where he founded the Province of Pennsylvania (or Penn's woods).

The world's first comprehensive declaration of liberties was written by an English lawyer living in one of England's colonies.

'The Bodie of Liberties'

Nathaniel Ward was the son of a Suffolk minister. He graduated from Emmanuel College, Cambridge and was called to the Bar at Lincoln's Inn. After practising law for ten years he entered the ministry during a sojourn in what is now Germany, before returning to England. Dismissed from his Essex ministry for his Puritan views, Ward emigrated, like so many others, to the New World. While absent from his Massachusetts ministry due to illness he wrote the groundbreaking *Bodie of Liberties* which was adopted by the Massachusetts General Court in December, 1641. Its first paragraph parallels almost exactly clause 29 of Magna Carta (see above). The *Bodie of Liberties* was revoked by King Charles I, but restored by King James.

After the English civil war ended Ward deemed it safe to return to his native land where he became minister of a church in Shenfield in Essex. Sadly, his enlightened views on liberty were marred by his own lack of religious tolerance.

---

[4] *Bushel's Case*, 1670.

(Contrary to American myth, intolerance was a weakness as common among Puritans as among members of the established church.)

But Ward's great work lived on. In 1789, after the American colonists had achieved their independence, the *Bodie of Liberties* formed one of the principal sources of that country's Bill of Rights, as the first eight Amendments to the American constitution are known.

Sometimes liberty has to be seized even from the representatives of the people.

The Freethinker

Charles Bradlaugh was the son of a solicitor's clerk and a nursemaid. After various jobs, including a spell in the Seventh Dragoon Guards he turned to his father's profession, for which he displayed a natural talent. But few knew of his other, altogether more interesting, life.

Bradlaugh had become disillusioned with religion while a Sunday School teacher and became what was then called a freethinker. He wrote pamphlets questioning religious belief under the pseudonym, 'Iconclast' and was soon in demand as a lecturer. In time he formed the National Secular Society, becoming its first president. Though never a socialist, Bradlaugh flirted briefly with the republican movement.

After the death of his wife in 1877 Bradlaugh formed a working partnership with another radical, Annie Besant, the estranged wife of an Anglican clergyman. It was a productive arrangement, but when the pair brought out a book on the subject of birth control they were convicted of publishing an obscene libel, fined and sentenced to six months imprisonment. The convictions were later overturned by the Court of Appeal on the technical ground that the indictment did not identify the allegedly obscene words.

After a number of unsuccessful attempts to get into Parliament Bradlaugh was finally elected MP for Northampton in 1880. He asked to affirm instead of taking the religious oath. However, a Select Committee of the House refused to allow this. He next offered to take the oath 'as a matter of form', but that offer too was turned down. When he attempted to take his seat without being sworn he was arrested and detained briefly in the small cell situated at the foot of Parliament's clock tower. His seat was declared vacant and a by-election declared. The defiant burgers of Northampton then proceeded to re-elect him, not once, but four times.

When in 1883 Bradlaugh again attempted to exercise his vote in the House he was arrested and fined £1,500. Despite support from Gladstone and George Bernard Shaw, attempts to change the law were defeated by the Conservatives and the Church. Finally, in 1886 the new Speaker permitted Bradlaugh to affirm. Two years later he managed to secure the passage of an Act which allowed Members to affirm instead of taking the oath (and clarified the right of witnesses to do likewise).

Bradlaugh died in 1891. His funeral was attended by thousands, including the young Mohandas Gandhi. (Bradlaugh had been known unofficially as the MP for India due to his support for Indian self-government.) The great secularist is commemorated in the city he fought so long to represent by a pub and a curious white statue which stands in a traffic island.

5.2 SLAVERY

The opposite of liberty is slavery. It has a long pedigree. It is referred to throughout the Hebrew Bible. Athens, the world's first democracy, depended upon it utterly, as did the great civilization of Rome. In the Americas it can be traced back at least to the time of the Aztecs. Nearer home, whole Cornish fishing villages were depopulated by the Barbary pirates in search of slaves.

In sub-Saharan Africa slavery had been a way of life for millennia, with tribe raiding tribe for unpaid labour and women. Arabs made the trade commercial by shipping the captured slaves in large numbers to the Middle East and India. When the Portuguese arrived on the west coast they opened up a new market for slaves in the sugar plantations of the Caribbean and the Americas. In time, England and Spain replaced Portugal as the main slaving nations.

It was only in the late seventeenth century that the English became conscious of the abhorrent nature of the institution of slavery. An important spur to the emancipation movement was a decision of the Court of King's Bench concerning a slave brought to England to act as his master's servant.

'Let the black go free'

James Sommersett (the name is variously spelled) was a black African slave owned by Charles Stewart, a customs official of Boston, Massachusetts. When Stewart brought Sommersett to England in 1769 the slave escaped and got himself baptised in the mistaken belief that the ceremony would entitle him to his freedom. Sommersett was reclaimed by his master and put in a ship bound for Jamaica, but before it set sail three people claiming to be his godparents made an application for habeas corpus to the Court of King's Bench on Sommersett's behalf.

The Lord Chief Justice, Lord Mansfield considered the matter for a month before giving a judgment which was to transform the status of slaves in England.[5] According to one report he said,

> 'What ground is there for saying that the status of slavery is now recognised by the law of England? ... Every man who comes into England is entitled to the protection of English law, whatever oppression he may heretofore have suffered and whatever may be the colour of his skin. The air of England is too pure for any slave to breathe. Let the black go free.'

---

[5] *Somerset v Stewart*, sub nom. *Sommersett's Case*, 1772.

The famous last sentence, sadly, was a misattribution. It was in fact Serjeant Davy, who in argument had remarked: 'the air of England has been gradually purifying ever since the reign of Elizabeth... it has been asserted, and is now repeated by me, this air is too pure for a slave to breathe in...'

Exactly what Mansfield did decide is still not clear, but as a result of his judgment some 14,000 to 15,000 slaves then in England obtained their freedom at an average cost to their owners of £50 each.

Less well known that Sommersett's case was the suit brought by a slave trading company against its insurers for the value of slaves lost at sea. The circumstances were appalling, but by no means unique.

Human beings as cargo

'The Zong' was a slave ship sailing from Africa to Jamaica in September 1781. Malnutrition and disease, made worse in the case of the slaves by overcrowding, had killed seven of the crew and some sixty slaves. When contrary winds delayed the ship's progress the captain decided on drastic action: over the next three days one hundred and twenty two sick Africans were thrown overboard to their deaths. The last ten were said to have sprung, 'disdainfully from the grasp of their executioners, and leaped into the sea triumphantly embracing death'.

The slavers claimed on their insurance policy for the value of the 'cargo'. The clause in question read,

'The insurer takes upon him the risk of the loss, capture, and death of slaves, or any other unavoidable accident to them: but natural death is always understood to be excepted: by natural death is meant, not only when it happens by disease or sickness, but also when the captive destroys himself through despair, which often happens: but when slaves are killed, or thrown into thrown into the sea in order to quell an insurrection on their part, then the insurers must answer.'

When the company refused to pay, the owner, a Mr Gregson sued them, claiming £30 a slave. In court the captain asserted that his actions were necessary for the safety of his ship because it had insufficient drinking water on board. The issue of liability was left to the jury who ruled against the insurers, but on appeal Lord Mansfield found that there had in fact been sufficient water aboard and held that it was unnecessary for the slaves to have been killed.[6]

'The Zong' did not, could not, change the law of slavery. However it prompted legislation which made it unlawful to insure against the natural death or ill treatment of slaves or their throwing overboard for any reason whatsoever.

The emancipation movement finally triumphed in 1807 when an Act of the British Parliament banned the trade in slaves throughout the British empire. In 1819 Britain set up a West Coast of Africa Station whose ships came to be known as the 'Preventative Squadron'. Their mission was to suppress the slave trade. The Squadron's operations did not go unchallenged.

'The Preventative Squadron'

One of the principal depots for African slaves were the islands in the mouth of the Gallinas River near the present border between Sierra Leone and Liberia. In 1840 the British Governor of Sierra Leone discovered that two British subjects, a black washerwoman and her child, were being held prisoner by the son of the King of the Gallinas. Commander Joseph Denman RN was ordered to rescue them, which he did successfully. In the process he destroyed or captured the baracoons (or slave sheds), freed 841 slaves and repatriated them to Sierra Leone.

---

[6] *Gregson v Gilbert*, 1783.

Back in Britain, Denman was at first praised and promoted, but the Attorney General advised that his actions were 'not strictly justifiable'. This ill judged opinion encouraged one of the slave masters to sue Denman in the English courts for damages and recovery of the slaves. Denman was put on half pay pending the outcome of the trial and spent the time helping the Admiralty draft its *Instructions for the Suppression of the Slave Trade*. The slaver's suit was finally dismissed by the Court of Exchequer on the ground that the naval action had been authorized by the Foreign Secretary, Lord Palmerston as an act of state.

Commander Denman was the son of Lord Chief Justice Denman and his brother was a High Court judge. He himself went on to become a Rear Admiral. Between 1808 and 1860, the West Africa Squadron seized some 1,600 slave ships and freed 150,000 blacks.

In 1833 England became the first country to free all slaves within its jurisdiction.

The liberties enshrined in the American Bill of Rights seemingly overlooked the three to four million slaves of African descent who lived in that country. When the 'peculiar institution' (as slavery was known) was challenged in the courts the judges ruled almost unanimously in favour of the slave masters.

The Dredd Scott case

Dredd Scott was a farmhand slave in the state of Missouri. When his master died in 1831 he was bought by John Emerson, a surgeon in the U.S. Army, for $500. When Emerson was moved in the course of his duty to the 'free' state of Illinois he took Scott with him. From thence he went to a fort in the territory of Wisconsin (now Minnesota) where slavery was illegal. In 1836 Scott married another slave, Harriett Robinson by whom he had four children, two of them dying in infancy. In 1843 Dr Emerson died and left his estate to his widow. Scott asked to buy his freedom, but Mrs Emerson refused his request and hired him out to her neighbours. With the assistance of two Abolitionist attorneys Scott brought legal proceedings in an attempt to obtain his freedom. He won at first instance, but the ruling was reversed by the State Supreme Court. It was then that Scott appealed to the US Supreme Court.

Seven of the nine judges of the Court supported the 80 year old Chief Justice Taney in his ruling that, as slaves, Scott and his wife had no standing to bring suit. He declared that, 'A free negro of the African race, whose ancestors were brought to this country and sold as slaves, is not a 'citizen' within the meaning of the Constitution of the United States... The only two clauses in the Constitution which point to this race, treat them as persons whom it was morally lawful to deal in as articles of property and to hold as slaves.'[7]

In a dissenting opinion of heroic proportions and formidable scholarship Associate Justice Benjamin Robbins Curtis put the opposite point of view:

> '...it is not true, in point of fact, that the Constitution was made exclusively by the white race. And that it was made exclusively for the white race is, in my opinion, not only an assumption not warranted by anything in the Constitution, but contradicted by its opening declaration that it was ordained and established by the people of the United States, for themselves and their posterity. And as free colored persons were then citizens of at least five States, and so in every sense part of the people of the United States, they were among those for whom and whose posterity the Constitution was ordained and established...'

Disgusted with the majority decision, Curtis resigned from the court. It took another seven years before slavery was finally abolished throughout the USA by the 13th amendment to the constitution.[8] Determined resistance in the South made

---
[7] *Dredd Scott v Sandford*, 1857.
[8] Interestingly, that amendment still permits slavery in America, but only 'as a punishment for crime'.

this reform nugatory and true citizenship only began to be accorded to African Americans in the mid-twentieth century.

Two months after the Supreme Court decision Mrs Emerson, now married to a northern Congressman, turned Dredd Scott over to the sons of his former owner, who immediately gave him his liberty. He was able to enjoy only a year of freedom before his death in 1858.

Roger Brooke Taney's standing as a bit of a legal pariah is not entirely justified. He had been, like most of his class, a slave owner, but had come to regard slavery as 'a blot on our national character'. He freed his slaves, pensioning off those too old to work. By the time of the Dredd Scott case, however, slavery had become an issue which was splitting the nation and Taney saw abolition as a thinly disguised attack on the South. His judgment in the Dredd Scott case was not perverse from a purely legal point of view, as would be expected from a man still widely adjudged to have been a fine lawyer. His reputation derives, not from his prejudice, but from the fact that he lacked the courage to take a bold reforming view of the law when to do so seemed to him to be contrary to the interests of the South.

Update – for the avoidance of complacency

The International Labour Organization (ILO) of the United Nations recently estimated that there are 12.3 million people throughout the world - mainly children - in debt bondage, trafficking and other forms of modern slavery. At the time of writing the first two people have been convicted under a statute of 2010 which was deemed necessary to deal with slavery in contemporary England.

Chapter 6

THE LAWYERS

6.1 THE BENCH

Judges come in all shapes and sizes and it is to be hoped that the contemporary fervour for pressing them all out of one mould does not iron out the individuality that has always been the mark of the outstanding judge.

Here is an eclectic collection of some of the more notable.

An ornament of his profession

William Henry Maule's first love was mathematics. So outstanding were the talents of this senior wrangler[1] that, while still a law student, Maule was offered a chair in that subject. But he turned instead to the law and was admitted a barrister by Lincoln's Inn, taking Silk in 1833.

One story of Maule, the advocate, is that before appearing in the Appeal Committee of the House of Lords he had a heavy lunch of stout and steak; Follett, his leader, who had lunched off sherry and biscuits, asked why he was indulging

---

[1] A senior wrangler is the student who obtains the highest marks among the first class honours in mathematics.

himself so generously. 'To reduce myself to the intellectual level of the Judges', Maule replied.'[2]

As a Judge of the Common Pleas, Maule was renowned for his wit and humanity, both of which are evident in his oft quoted remarks when passing sentence on a hawker convicted of bigamy at the Warwick assizes in 1845:

> 'Prisoner at the bar, you have been convicted of the offence of bigamy, that is to say, of marrying a woman while you have a wife still alive, though it is true she has deserted you, and is still living in adultery with another man. You have, therefore, committed a crime against the laws of your country, and you have also acted under a very serious misapprehension of the course which you ought to have pursued. You should have gone to the ecclesiastical court and there obtained against your wife a decree *a mensa et thoro*. You should then have brought an action in the courts of common law and recovered, as no doubt you would have recovered, damages against your wife's paramour.
>
> 'Armed with these decrees you should have approached the legislature, and obtained an Act of Parliament, which would have rendered you free, and legally competent to marry the person whom you have taken on yourself to marry with no such sanction. It is quite true that these proceedings would have cost you many hundreds of pounds, whereas you probably have not as many pence. But the law knows no distinction between rich and poor. The sentence of the court upon you therefore is that you be imprisoned for one day, which period has already been exceeded, as you have been in custody since the commencement of the assizes.'

In fact, the law report[3] reveals a much less polished judgment and the prisoner was sentenced to four months imprisonment, not one day.

---

[2] Quoted by Richard O'Sullivan, The Spirit of the Common Law, 1965. Like so many good stories, this one is also attributed to other lawyers, notably Brougham and Sir John Millicent.
[3] In *The Times* of 3 April 1845.

The judge who could jump over a cow

Charles Synge Christopher Bowen (1835-1894) was a brilliant scholar and gifted writer, having published verse translations of Virgil's *Eclogues* and the first six books of the *Aeneid*. When young, he was a fine athlete who was said to have been able to jump over a cow standing.

After a shaky start at the Bar Bowen made his name in the Tichborne case. The lengthy and controversial action did nothing for his health and in 1879 he gratefully accepted appointment as a Judge of the Queen's Bench, later becoming a Lord Justice of Appeal and finally a Lord of Appeal in Ordinary, with the title Baron Bowen. Even in his later years when suffering from ill health Bowen was always noted for his courtesy and wit.

In one case he is said to have remarked, 'If, gentlemen of the jury you think that the accused was on the roof of the house to enjoy the midnight breeze, and, by pure accident, happened to have about him the necessary tools of a housebreaker, with no dishonest intention of employing them, you will, of course acquit him.'

Bowen is believed to have been the originator of the Chancery jibe, 'Truth will out, even in an affidavit.' (Others have ascribed it to Chitty LJ). He is also thought to have coined the phrase, 'When I hear of an 'equity' in a case like this, I am reminded of a blind man in a dark room - looking for a black hat - which isn't there'. And it is claimed that he coined the phrase 'the man on the Clapham omnibus'. But perhaps the most well known Bowen story involves the Lord Chancellor, Lord Selborne. In 1882 the judges were asked to present an address to Queen Victoria on the opening of the new Law Courts. On reading a draft of the address Selborne is said to have objected to the phrase, 'Your Majesty's judges are deeply sensible of their own many shortcomings', at least as applying to himself. Bowen with tongue in cheek suggested a compromise wording: 'deeply sensible of the many shortcomings of each other'. (The final version was 'deeply sensible of their own shortcomings'.)

Bowen died in 1892 and the legal world lost one of its brightest talents.

But character failures can ruin the career of even the best judges. The lack of diplomacy of one High Court judge offended some, and his unhappy private life finally led to tragedy.

A judicial tragedy

On 26 April 1933, alone in his flat on circuit, the Hon. Henry Alfred McCardie shot himself. The coroner's verdict was suicide while the balance of his mind was disturbed, but that was only half the story.

In 1916 after an outstanding career on the Midland and Oxford circuits McCardie had been appointed a Justice of the King's Bench Division. It was an unusual honour for a man who had not been to university and was not a Silk.

On the Bench McCardie was admired for his clarity of expression. It was said that 'What McCardie says seems so obvious - after he has said it.' If his judgments did tend towards the prolix, however, his sympathies were always towards the liberal and progressive positions and he was never afraid to break new ground. 'I have no respect', he once declared, 'for a rule of law whose sole claim to esteem is based on its antiquity and its remoteness from everyday life'.

But McCardies' forthrightness and willingness to comment on topics wide and sundry did not appeal to everyone. He was criticized publicly by the Prime Minister, Ramsay McDonald and by Lord Chief Justice Lord Hewart. But it was Lord Justice Scrutton's personal antipathy which hurt most. Allowing an appeal from McCardie's decision in a claim by a husband against another man for enticing away his wife, Scrutton said (in words that were deleted from the official report) that, 'if there is to be a discussion of the relationship of husbands and wives, I think it would come better from judges who have more than theoretical knowledge'. In fact,

McCardie, who was known as 'the bachelor judge', had a long time mistress whom he studiously hid from public gaze. McCardie took the unprecedented step of publicly rebuking Scrutton from the Bench and declaring that he would refuse to supply his files to any panel of the Court of Appeal which included the man. So bitter became the animosity between the two that they are said to have shouted at each other in court before the quarrel was patched up by the Lord Chancellor.

In 1933 McCardie suffered three bouts of influenza while on circuit. He became depressed and was unable to sleep. One of his last cases was a libel action brought by a self-styled medium. During the trial the judge, who was known to dabble in occult matters, received an anonymous letter 'from the spirit world', which was said to have foretold his death. It later came out that he was also burdened with massive gambling debts, for which he was being blackmailed.

McCardie's decision to take his own life was a sad end for a brilliant, generous and reforming judge.

The draper's son

Alfred Thompson Denning was arguably the most loved and admired member of the English Bench in the last century, though not altogether a stranger to controversy.

'Tom' Denning, as he was known at the Bar, was proud to be the son of a Whitchurch draper. After schooling in a National School (for the Education of the Poor) he won an exhibition to Magdalen College, Oxford. When the Great War broke out he was rejected for the army because of a heart murmur. He successfully appealed against the decision and was commissioned in the Royal Engineers, seeing active service in France. Of Denning's four brothers, one was to become a general, another an admiral. The other two died in the Great War. ('They were the best of us', he wrote.) After the war Denning completed his academic career with a first in Mathematical Greats. Deciding to become a barrister, he returned to Magdalen college to study law on a scholarship, achieving a first in all subjects except jurisprudence. He was admitted to Lincoln's Inn in 1920 and called to the Bar three years later, taking Silk in 1938.

After a dramatic rise through the judicial ranks Denning took the unusual step of retiring from the highest court in the land in order to rejoin the Court of Appeal. Even this may not have satisfied him. He liked to tell students: 'When I was a judge of first instance, sitting alone, I could and did do justice. But when I went to the Court of Appeal of three I found that the chances of doing justice were two to one against'.

Denning's robustly libertarian approach to reform of the law of contract, of unmarried partners, and of judicial review, together with his deceptively simple literary style led to his becoming an icon for law students across the world.

Out of court he defended his fundamental approach to the law as follows,

> 'My root belief is that the proper role of the Judge is to do justice between the parties before him. If there is any rule of law which impairs the doing of justice, then it is the province of the Judge to do all that he legitimately can to avoid that rule - or even to change it - so as to do justice in the instant case before him. He need not wait for legislation to intervene; because that can never be of any help in the instant case.'[4]

As Denning once said, 'What is the argument on the other side? Only this, that no case has been found in which it has been done before. That argument does not appeal to me in the least. If we never do anything which has not been done before, we shall never get anywhere. The law will stand still whilst the rest of the world goes on: and that will be bad for both'.[5]

Denning holds the record for the longest tenure of an English judge, 38 years. He died in 1999 at the age of 100. The world is a poorer, greyer place without him.

---

[4] *The Family Story* 1981.
[5] *Packer v Packer*, 1954.

'Ye fearful saints'

Lord Denning was in the not wholly unusual position of being in a minority of one in the Court of Appeal when he sought to re-write the Rules of the Supreme Court, which manifestly failed to do justice in an insurance case:

> 'To wait for the Rule Committee', he said, 'would be to shut the stable door after the steed had been stolen. And who knows that there will ever again be another horse in the stable? Or another ship sunk and insurance moneys here? I ask: why should the judges wait for the Rule Committee? The judges have an inherent jurisdiction to lay down the practice and procedure of the courts; and we can invoke it now to restrain the removal of these insurance moneys. To the timorous souls I would say in the words of William Cowper:
>
>> Ye fearful saints fresh courage take,
>> The clouds ye so much dread
>> Are big with mercy, and shall break
>> In blessings on your head.
>
> Instead of 'saints', read 'judges'. Instead of 'mercy', read 'justice'. And you will find a good way to law reform!'

Sadly, the Appeal Committee of the House of Lords thought otherwise.[6]

Denning's style

Lord Denning's judgments were famous for the simplicity of their style. Here is how one of them began:

> 'Old Peter Beswick was a coal merchant in Eccles, Lancashire. He had no business premises. All he had was a lorry, scales, and weights. He used to take the lorry to the yard of the National Coal Board, where he bagged coal and took it round

---

[6] *The Siskina*, 1977.

to his customers in the neighbourhood. His nephew, John Joseph Beswick, helped him in his business. In March 1962, old Peter Beswick and his wife were both over 70. He had had his leg amputated and was not in good health. The nephew was anxious to get hold of the business before the old man died. So they went to a solicitor, Mr. Ashcroft, who drew up an agreement for them.'[7]

And another:

'Broadchalke is one of the most pleasing villages in England. Old Herbert Bundy, the defendant, was a farmer there. His home was at Yew Tree Farm. It went back for 300 years. His family had been there for generations. It was his only asset. But he did a very foolish thing. He mortgaged it to the bank. Up to the very hilt. Not to borrow money for himself, but for the sake of his son. Now the bank have come down on him. They have foreclosed. They want to get him out of Yew Tree Farm and to sell it. They have brought this action against him for possession. Going out means ruin for him. He was granted legal aid. His lawyers put in a defence. They said that, when he executed the charge to the bank he did not know what he was doing: or at any rate not the circumstances were such that he ought not to be bound by it. At the trial his plight was plain. The Judge was sorry for him. He said he was a "poor old gentleman". He was so obviously incapacitated that the Judge admitted his proof in evidence. He had a heart attack in the witness-box. Yet the Judge felt he could do nothing for him. There is nothing, he said, "which takes this out of the vast range of commercial transactions". He ordered Herbert Bundy to give up possession of Yew Tree Farm to the bank.

'Now there is an appeal to this Court. The ground is that the circumstances were so exceptional that Herbert Bundy should not be held bound.'[8]

Guess which way Denning decided.

And who can forget:

---

[7] *Beswick v Beswick*, 1968.
[8] *Lloyds Bank v. Bundy*. 1973.

'In summer time village cricket is the delight of everyone. Nearly every village has its own cricket field where the young men play and the old men watch. In the village of Lintz in County Durham they have their own ground, where they have played these last 70 years. They tend it well. The wicket area is well rolled and mown. The outfield is kept short. It has a good club-house for the players and seats for the onlookers. The village team play there on Saturdays and Sundays. They belong to a league, competing with the neighbouring villages. On other evenings after work they practise while the light lasts. Yet now after these 70 years a judge of the High Court has ordered that they must not play there any more ... I suppose that the Lintz Cricket Club will disappear. The cricket ground will be turned to some other use. I expect for more houses or a factory. The young men will turn to other things instead of cricket. The whole village will be much the poorer. And all this because of a newcomer who has just bought a house there next to the cricket ground.[9]

Happily, the Lintz cricket club continues to flourish.

Judges are so inured to tales of suffering and woe that it comes as a surprise to find one of them visibly moved by what he heard in court.

Justice struck dumb

Sitting in the Family Division of the High Court recently, Mr Justice Hedley found it necessary to adjourn a hearing when he learned of how two local authorities had failed to agree between them who was responsible for the care of a vulnerable child.

On returning to court the judge declared his surprise at the fact that,

---

[9] *Miller v. Jackson*, 1977.

'neither authority believed that they had any duty to offer even basic support, let alone the extras that a child with special needs requires.' They were, he said, 'present at court not to assist – in fairness they did not even make a pretence at that – but to obtain legal authority to distance themselves from responsibility for this child.' He continued, 'I confess that as I listened to these matters, disbelief was not the only thought or emotion that I experienced. Indeed I found it necessary to adjourn briefly so as to ensure that no wholly improper judicial observations escaped my lips. This judgment has been reserved not because the issues are difficult (they are not) but because I did not trust myself to express my views in a temperate manner. I have always had a high regard for the contribution that social workers make to the family justice system but if in fact we have reached a stage where budget needs trump welfare then we all need to know. Hence my adjourning this judgment into open court.'[10]

According to a report in *The Times* newspaper, the judge himself had an adopted child with special needs.

For some of the ablest lawyers, however, the appeal of the Bench did not last long.

'So utterly boring'

Hugh Laddie had enjoyed a glittering career at the Bar and was co-editor of a leading book on copyright law before being appointed a judge of the Chancery Division of the High Court in 1995.

He resigned from the Bench ten years later; and his reasons for doing so are interesting.

The Lawyer magazine quoted Laddie as saying of his retirement, 'Being at the bench is much more isolated than practising in any other form. It's both lonely and in my view

---

[10] *O & Anor v Orkney Island Council*, 2009.

disorientating. Every day people come into court and bow to you and call you 'My Lord' and laugh at your bad jokes; and even when they disagree with you they don't say that you're wrong, they just say, "with greatest respect, My Lord..." and you can believe it.'

But Laddie went much further and franker. In a lecture to University students he commented that, 'It is neither efficient nor fair on litigants to run a system in which judges are frequently deciding cases outside their area of expertise.' And 'I knew nothing about tax, except that it came as a nasty shock at the end of the year. I have never studied it, nor did it at the bar - nor insolvency.' It would have been better, he added, to use a roulette wheel than to have him deciding. He was to modify these views somewhat later, possibly under pressure from above.

Upon retirement, Laddie became a patent consultant. The following year he was appointed to the chair of Intellectual Property Law at UCL.

The distinguished Law Lord, Patrick Devlin was of a similar mind. When he resigned in 1964 he gave as his reason for doing so the fact that he found the job 'so Utterly Boring'. He told an interviewer, 'I was extremely happy as a judge of first instance. I was never happy as an appellate judge ... for the most part, the work was dreary beyond belief. All those revenue cases!'

Devlin went on to become chairman of The Press Council.

And in 1970 after less than three years as a High Court judge Sir Henry Fisher resigned from the bench, explaining:

> 'I find a Judge's life a dull life, and I have found myself becoming dull as a result. The art of advocacy is a fascinating one to practise, but to sit and listen day after day to other people's advocacy I find a wearisome ordeal.'

Given the undoubted talents of these judges, their disillusionment clearly did not arise from their inadequacy for the task. Perhaps more thought needs to be given to how judges are allocated to the different sorts of work which they are called upon to undertake?

The innovative judge

Jack B Weinstein is a Federal judge in the District Court for the Eastern District of New York. He has long been renowned for his outspoken views and his willingness to adopt novel procedures in court.

A former Columbia Law School Professor and author of a leading work on evidence, Weinstein conducts hearings seated with counsel at a table in the middle of the courtroom, often choosing to wear an ordinary business suit without judicial robes. He has been responsible for innovative methods of tackling mass tort actions, and he is not afraid to risk controversy.

He has, for example, been criticized for being ill disposed towards the tobacco and firearms industries and has recused himself from drugs cases on the ground that he disapproved of the mandatory sentences required by Federal guidelines.

In one of the first decisions concerning the now notorious sub-prime mortgages Judge Weinstein sentenced a securities dealer to five years imprisonment instead of the 45 sought by the government. The blame for this state of affairs, he said, 'is shared not only by individual(s) but also by the institutions that employ them, those who carelessly invest, and those who fail to regulate'.

Nor does the 89 year old judge have much time for the mandatory minimum sentence of five years imprisonment for anyone convicted of viewing child pornography. He did not believe that those who view the images - as opposed to those who produced or sold them - presented a threat to children. 'We're destroying lives unnecessarily... At the most, they should be receiving treatment and supervision'.

6.2 CONTEMPT OF COURT

Courts are usually quiet havens of decorum. When the peace is broken the violence may be directed at the judge.

Judges under fire

In 2009 a defendant threw one of his trainers 30 feet across Court 9 of the Old Bailey, causing Judge Gerald Gordon QC to duck for cover. It missed the judge and hit the wall.

Onochie Madekwe of Nigeria was defending himself on a charge of murdering the son of a former prime minister of Somalia. He explained to the jury, 'I had to throw my shoe in protest because Judge Gordon told me I couldn't do my opening speech. You want me to sit here and be quiet and be convicted? Well I'm not going to do that. I'm innocent.' Later he asked, 'Can I have my shoe back?' Madekwe was acquitted of the murder charge but convicted of violent disorder. No action was taken concerning the incident of the shoe.

Such contempts were viewed less tolerantly in the seventeenth century. A prisoner at Salisbury Assize in 1626 is recorded in a quaint mixture of law French, Latin and English as having *'ject un Brickbat a le dit Justice que narrowly mist.'* The judge, Chief Justice Richardson, had bent down to avoid the missile. Afterwards he said, 'You see now, if I had been an upright judge I had been slain.' The poor man's fate was horrible, because the court *'immediately fuit Indictment drawn per Noy envers le Prisoner, & son dexter manus ampute & fix al Gibbet, sur que luy mesme immediatement hange in presence de Court.'* (An indictment was immediately drawn by Noy against the prisoner, and his right hand was cut off and fastened to the gibbet on which he himself was immediately hanged in the presence of the court.)

But English judges have never had to face violence as serious as that which took place in the Carroll County Courthouse in Hillside, West Virginia at the beginning of the last century.

'Gentlemen. I ain't a-going.'

Floyd Allen was a landowner, storekeeper and occasional officeholder in Carroll County, Virginia. He was also the patriarch of a feuding mountain family, many of whom, like himself, held public office in the area. He had a history of violence, but usually managed to escape the consequences of his actions by intimidating his accusers.

In 1911 two of Allen's nephews were involved in a scuffle outside a schoolhouse where a Baptist service was being held. The pair were charged with disturbing public worship by the Commonwealth's Attorney in nearby Hillsville. Their prosecutor was William M. Foster, a known enemy of Allen. On hearing of this the two men ran off, but were traced to North Carolina and apprehended. On their way back in custody Allen ambushed their captors and released his nephews. He claimed that his intention was only to get the prisoners released from their manacles and, indeed, he did return them later to custody. They were put on trial, convicted and sentenced to short terms of imprisonment.

As a result of his intervention Allen himself was charged with assaulting the officers of the law and on 14 March, 1912 was brought for trial before Judge Thornton L. Massie in the crowded Hillsville courthouse high up in the Blue Ridge Mountains. Allen contested the evidence bitterly, claiming that it came from his political enemies. After he was found guilty Allen said to the Judge: 'If you sentence me on that verdict, I will kill you'. He was a man of his word. When Massie sentenced him to a year's imprisonment Allen rose to his feet and said, 'Gentlemen. I ain't a-going.' It was the cue for the Allen supporters present to pull out their concealed pistols. Court officials, fearful of trouble, had also armed themselves and a hot exchange of fire ensued. When the dust settled fifty bullets were found on the courtroom floor and five people lay dead. They were Judge Massie, Attorney Foster, Sheriff Lew F. Webb, a member of the jury, and a young woman who had been a prosecution witness. Allen himself was wounded in the shootout and arrested. The rest of his clan fled, but were eventually rounded up and brought to trial.

Despite a plea of self-defence Allen was convicted of first-degree murder and sentenced to death. His son Claude received the same sentence. Pleas for mercy were rejected by the State Governor and the two men went to their deaths in the electric chair.

An American judge found himself in hot water when he overreacted to a minor incident in court.

The case of the contemptuous cell phone

The tranquillity of the domestic violence court in Niagara Falls courthouse was disturbed on 11 March 2005 by the ringing of a mobile phone (known in America as a cell phone.)

After the interruption Judge Robert M. Restaino announced:

> 'Now, whoever owns the instrument that is ringing, bring it to me now or everybody could take a week in jail and please don't tell me I'm the only one that heard that. Mr. Martinez, did you hear that ringing?... Everyone is going to jail; every single person is going to jail in this courtroom unless I get that instrument now. If anybody believes I'm kidding, ask some of the folks that have been here for a while. You are all going.'

No one accepted responsibility and, after an unsuccessful attempt by court security to find the offending instrument, the Judge revoked the bail of everyone who had appeared before him that morning and remanded 46 of them into custody. Some were handcuffed and taken to the local prison where they were released in dribs and drabs during the day. The lawyers, court reporters and press representatives were seemingly above suspicion and were left untouched.

Two and a half years later Restaino, was removed from the bench (and his $113,900 a year job) for his 'egregious and unprecedented abuse of judicial power', despite his plea that he had been suffering 'certain stresses in his private life'.

The guilty phone user was never traced.

6.3 HOMER NODDING

> *'I'd rather have been a judge than a miner. Being a miner, as soon as you are too old and tired and sick and stupid to do the job properly, you have to go. Well, the very opposite applies with judges.'*
>
> Peter Cooke

Judges may deserve our admiration for their intellect, their wisdom, or just their ability to get swiftly through a complex list (though the last is a virtue which can be perilously akin to a vice). But, underneath, they are human beings like the rest of us, capable of emotion and, dare I say it, error. But these human frailties pale into insignificance when compared with the judicial vices of days gone by.

The eighteenth century Scottish bench seems to have attracted a more than usual proportion of eccentric and idiosyncratic judges. Henry Lord Cockburn, for example, described how,

> 'At Edinburgh, the old judges had a practice at which even their barbaric age used to shake its head. They had always wine and biscuits on the bench, when the business was clearly to be protracted beyond the usual dinner hour… Black bottles of strong port were set down beside them on the bench, with glasses, carafes of water, tumblers and biscuits; and this without the slightest attempt at concealment.'

Whatever the cause, one does not have to dig deep to discover examples of, shall we say, the individualistic approaches of some eighteenth century Scottish judges.

Kames

(1696 – 1782).

One of the best, if most chilling, stories of the Scottish judiciary concerns Henry Home, Lord Kames. Despite a total absence of formal training in the law, Kames rose to become a judge of the Court of Session and a Lord of Justiciary. He was also a noted philosopher and, as we would put it today, sociologist who was once described by his friend, James Boswell as a 'man of the first distinction in Scotland.'

In 1780 at Ayr Kames found himself trying Matthew Hay, a former chess partner of his, for murder. When the verdict of guilty was returned, he chillingly added, 'That's checkmate to you, Matthew!'

Eskgrove

(1724-1804)

Sir David Rae of Eskgrove, Bart. had risen almost imperceptibly through the ranks of the Scottish judiciary, from Lord of Session, Lord of Justiciary and, finally, Lord Justice Clerk. Yet, wrote the Scottish judge, Lord Cockburn,[11] 'never once did he do or say anything which had the slightest claim to be remembered for any intrinsic merit.' Cockburn went on:

> 'When I first knew him he was in the zenith of his absurdity. People seemed to have nothing to do but to tell stories of this one man. To be able to give an anecdote of Eskgrove, with a proper imitation of his voice and manner, was a sort of fortune in society. (Sir Walter) Scott in those days was famous for this particularly.'[12]

As a judge, Eskgrove displayed a black sense of humour. Once when sentencing a tailor for murdering a soldier by stabbing, he said, 'And not only did you murder him, whereby

---
[11] Not to be confused with the English judge, Alexander Cockburn.
[12] Cockburn. *Memorials of His Time*, 1856.

he was be-reaved of his life, but you did thrust, or push, or pierce, or project, or propel, the le-thal weapon through the belly-band of his regimental breeches, which were His Majesty's'. And he told another condemned man, 'Ye're a very clever chiel, man, but Ye'll be nane the waur o' a hingin'.

Again, when sentencing two prisoners to death, Eskgrove reviewed the nature of their crimes - assault, robbery, and hamesucken - and ended: 'All this you did; and, God preserve us! just when they were sitten down to their denner !'

'Hamesucken' was the crime now popularly known as home invasion.

Hermand

(1743 - 1827)

George Fergusson, Lord Hermand was another eccentric member of the Court of Session, Scotland's supreme civil court. He had a cavalier attitude towards the law and was known to remark: 'A statute! What's a statute? Words, mere words. And am I to be tied down by words? No my laards, I go by the law of right reason.' Striking his chest, he would add, 'I feel the law here, my laards.'

Hermand was a great admirer of his friend and colleague, Sir Walter Scott. Once, when taken by Scott's novel, *Guy Mannering*, he insisted on quoting from it at length during the course of dry legal argument, while the author sat below him in his judicial capacity.

Hermand was a great toper. On one occasion when about to condemn the prisoner to transportation he said, 'We are told that there was no malice, and that the prisoner must have been in liquor. In liquor! Why, he was drunk! and yet he murdered the very man who had been drinking with him! They had been carousing the whole night; and yet he stabbed him! after drinking a whole bottle of rum with him! Good God, my laards, if he will do this when he's drunk, what will he not do when he's sober?'

Braxfield

(1722–1799)

The Scottish judge Robert McQueen Braxfield enjoyed a fine reputation at the Bar. (Boswell penned a short poem which ended, 'And our petition was appointed to be seen/Because it was drawn by Robbie McQueen.') Braxfield is said to have been the last judge to adhere to the old Scottish dialect. Once, when he asked a prisoner whether she desired counsel, she replied, 'No. I only want an interpreter to make me understand what your Lordship says.'

Braxfield was the scourge of eighteenth century radicals. 'Government in this country', he once said, 'is made up of the landed interest, which alone has a right to be represented'. It was an attitude that was all too evident in his trial of the lawyer, Thomas Muir charged with sedition for distributing Tom Paine's book, *The Rights of Man*. The hearing lasted no more than a day before Muir was convicted, helped in part by Braxfield's invention of the novel crime of 'unconscious sedition'.[13] This was not the judge's first innovation: Braxfield once said, 'Let them bring me prisoners, and I will find them law'.

Braxfield is believed to be the model for the cruel judge in Robert Louis Stevenson's unfinished novel, *Weir of Hermiston*.

Monboddo

(1714 – 1799)

James Burnett, Lord Monboddo was a respected member of the Scottish Court of Session and a Lord Commissioner of Justiciary, Scotland's highest criminal court.

An accomplished Greek scholar, controversial linguist and evolutionist, Monboddo was also a bit of an eccentric. Once,

---

[13] Muir was sentenced to fourteen years transportation. He escaped from Australia and made his way to the New World, only to be returned by various vicissitudes to France. His life is said to have inspired Robert Burns' poem, 'Scots Wha Hae'.

after a decision had gone against him concerning the value of a horse, he refused to sit with his brother judges and joined the clerks at their desks below the bench.

On another occasion, on leaving Court and finding it raining, he is said to have put his wig into his sedan chair and walked home.

And one year when Monboddo visited the Court of King's Bench in London part of the ceiling collapsed. People rushed out of the building but the 71 year old judge did not budge. Asked why, he said that he thought it was 'an annual ceremony, with which, as an alien, he had nothing to do'.

Probably the two English judges most notorious for their cruelty are William Scroggs and George Jeffreys, but to what extent are their unsavoury reputations really justified?

Scroggs

Scroggs was elevated to the Bench in 1676, largely as a result of patronage, though he was always careful to condemn the practice. In 1678 he became Lord Chief Justice and was thrust almost immediately into adjudicating on the so-called Popish plot. (See above.) A villain called Titus Oates had put it about that plans were in hand to murder the king and Parliament and massacre all Protestants. As with many conspiracy theories there were reasons for suspecting some such plot, but the reality was far different from the gossip; in this case the gossip was of a malicious and self-serving nature.

Gullibly accepting Oates' claims at face value, Scroggs issued some 40 or 50 warrants of arrest. Within a space of six months he had sent fourteen innocent men to their death for supposed treason, taunting them mercilessly throughout the proceedings. At the trial of a young Catholic banker, for example, Scroggs remarked, 'Now you may die a Roman catholic, and when you come to die, I doubt [not] you will be found a priest too'. Upon learning that the dead man's family were planning an elaborate burial Scroggs ordered his body to be exhumed and his quarters set over the city gates.

It was not until the trial of the Queen's physician, Sir George Wakeman and three Benedictine monks that the mendacious nature of Oates' testimony became clear, even to Scroggs. At the judge's urging and to great public dismay, the four defendants were acquitted. People thought Scroggs had gone mad. A dead dog was thrown into his carriage and demonstrators kept him awake at night. He was even accused of having been bribed by the (Catholic) Queen to secure an acquittal. When attacked in the press the infuriated judge threatened to 'fill all the Gaols in England with [the journalists] and pile them up as Men do Faggots'.

In 1680 Oates and his accomplice, Bedloe sought to silence Scroggs by presenting thirteen articles of high misdemeanours against him to the Privy Council. The ridiculous charges were thrown out, but that was not the end of the judge's troubles. Later the same year he was made the subject of impeachment proceedings for attempting to subvert the fundamental laws, established religion and the government. Scroggs was only saved when the king intervened to dissolve Parliament. Removed from office, he was given a generous pension and his son a knighthood.

Perhaps the most balanced judgement on Scroggs comes from Henry Irving, the famous actor and non-practising barrister, who wrote of him that, 'his mind was intrepid but blatant; he had wit, perhaps, but little humour; and he never seems to have terrified any man, in spite of the violence of his tongue. But he was not a butcher's son[14], and had probably incurred the wrath of posterity more by his folly than his villainy.'[15]

---
[14] The story that Scroggs was the son of a butcher is probably false.
[15] Henry Irving. *The Life of Judge Jeffreys*. 1898.

'Bloody Judge Jeffreys'

Even in his lifetime the name of George Jeffreys, 1st Baron Jeffreys was a by-word for judicial cruelty, based in large measure on his record at the Bloody Assizes of 1685. Here is how he was described in a widely read pamphlet of the time:

> 'A certain barbarous joy and pleasure grinned from his brutal soul through his bloody eyes whenever he was sentencing the poor souls to death and torment...'[16]

But was the reputation justified?

The pamphlet was the work of a small but influential coterie of anti-Jacobites based in Axe Yard, Westminster. Its principal author was John Tutchin. Expelled from school for theft, Tutchin should have been well qualified to write of the Bloody Assize; he himself had been brought before Judge Jeffreys at Dorchester for spreading false news of the success of Monmouth's insurrection. For this, the record shows, he was sentenced to a fine of five marks or imprisonment in lieu and ordered to be whipped. In telling his own story Tutchin inflated his sentence to one of seven years' imprisonment and a yearly whipping throughout all the market towns of Dorset. It was a flagrant lie characteristic of the man's writings. Another of the pamphleteers was the rogue and serial perjurer, Titus Oates, in whose lodgings the coterie were based.

When James II was replaced on the throne by William and Mary Jeffreys was arrested and thrown into the Tower of London where he died of kidney disease at the age of forty four.

With a growing realisation of how much of Jeffreys' reputation is due to his slanderers, attitudes towards the judge have changed in recent times. One historian, for example, described him as 'a great lawyer, a great judge, and a great man...(though) by no means exempt from the defects of the judges of his day...'[17]

---

[16] The Western Martyrology. 1689.
[17] JG Muddiman, *The Bloody Assizes*.

More than any other, the trial of 70 year old Dame Alice Lisle was to seal the reputation of 'Bloody Judge Jeffreys', but a close examination of the facts does not justify the legend.

'A weakness very nearly allied to virtue'

The 'Bloody Assize' of 1685 had been appointed to deal with the rebels who were caught after the defeat of the Monmouth rebellion. Two of them who managed to escape the pursuing King's forces were captured in the Dorset house of Dame Alice Lisle, the widow of one of the regicides (or men responsible for the death of King Charles I). Faced with a charge of harbouring traitors, she pleaded ignorance of their involvement in the rebellion, claiming that she believed them to be only fugitives from religious persecution. After the jury had brought in a verdict of Guilty Chief Justice Jeffreys passed the only sentence allowed by law, namely to be burned at the stake. He nevertheless respited execution in order to allow her to appeal, ordering pen and paper to be provided for the purpose. The King refused clemency, but moderated the manner of Alice's death, and the old lady was beheaded in the market square at Winchester on 2 September.

Though Alice is commonly believed to have been wrongly convicted, her trial was as fair as any in those days and the finding of guilt was well justified on the evidence. The fault lay in her sentence. Alice's crime arose, not from treasonous intent, but from compassion towards men whom she knew to be fleeing for their lives. As Macaulay wrote,

> 'The feeling which makes the most loyal subject shrink from the thought of giving up to a shameful death the rebel who, vanquished, hunted down, and in mortal agony, begs for a morsel of bread and a cup of water, may be a weakness; but it is surely a weakness very nearly allied to virtue, a weakness which, constituted as human beings are, we can hardly eradicate from the mind without eradicating many noble and benevolent sentiments.'

Jeffreys' reputation, in particular the manner in which he conducted Alice's trial, is a far cry from the truth, a fact which, if it were to become generally known, could seriously damage the tourist trade in the West Country.

The judge with a past

There are few judges about whom so many wild tales have been told as Lord Chief Justice Sir John Popham (1531-1607) who presided over the trials of Mary, Queen of Scots, the Earl of Essex, Sir Walter Raleigh and Guy Fawkes.

They begin with Popham the child. Lord Campbell's notoriously unreliable *Lives of the Lord Chief Justices* (1849) repeated an old story that the judge had been stolen by gypsies, disfigured and marked with a 'cabalistic mark which he bore to the grave'. The 'mark', if it ever existed, was probably a tattoo received later in life, but there is nothing to confirm the legend.

More startlingly, John Aubrey's *Brief Lives* (nearly as unreliable as Campbell's *Lives*) recounted how 'for several years Popham had been a highway robber', supplementing the story with much colourful detail. This career is said to have ended only when Popham's wife persuaded him to give up his life of crime and 'stick to the studie of law', urging that 'he could with application make as much money by the law as by highway robbery!' Many years later, when sitting in judgment on one of his companions in crime, Popham is supposed to have inquired about their former associates. 'All the villains are hanged, my Lord', replied the prisoner, 'except you and me!' This extraordinary tale was repeated uncritically by Popham's American biographer, Douglas Walthew Rice as recently as 1942.

Aubrey also repeated an old legend in which Popham has a walk-on part:

'Sir Richard Dayrell of Littlecot in Wilts[ire], (who) having got his lady's waiting-woman with child, when her travell came sent a servant with a horse for a midwife, whom he was to bring hoodwinked. She was brought, and layd the woman; but as soon as the child was borne, she saw the knight take the child and murther it, and burn it in the fire in the chamber. She having done her business was extraordinarily rewarded for her paines, and went blindfold away. This horrid action did much run in her mind, and she had a desire to discover it, but knew not where 'twas. She considered with herself the time she was riding, and how many miles she might have rode at that rate in that time, and that it must be some great person's house, for the room was twelve-foot high : and she should know the chamber if she sawe it. She went to a justice of peace, and search was made. The very chamber found. The knight was brought to his tryall ; and, to be short, this judge had this noble house, park, and manor, and (I think) more, for a bribe to save his life. Sir John Popham gave sentence according to law, but being a great person and a favorite, he procured a *nolle prosequi* [that is a decision not to continue with the prosecution].'

The story of the baby cast into the fire was probably borrowed from other sources. It was given legs by a note to Sir Walter Scott's ballad, *Rokeby*, where the midwife was changed into 'a Friar of orders grey' who murdered the mother instead of the baby. Popham certainly did own Littlecot, but there is no evidence that he received it as a bribe.

The *Dictionary of National Biography* ignores or discounts all these fanciful tales. Instead, it describes Popham as a fine and humane lawyer, conceding only that 'there is more than a whiff of sharp practice about some of his business dealings.' (There are few Elizabethan notables about whom this could not be said.)

Popham died on 10 June 1637 when, according to local legend, he was thrown from his horse and disappeared into what is known as Popham's Pit, a boggy dell in the Blackdown Hills.

Judicial corruption became virtually extinct in England after the eighteenth century. One of the last examples came to light as a result of a financial crash.

When the Bubble burst

Lord Chancellor Thomas Parker, Earl of Macclesfield had for years been supplementing his judicial income by a brisk trade in the sale of judicial offices.

When a vacancy occurred in the office of Master in the Court of Chancery, Francis Elde, a member of the Middle Temple, approached Parker, desiring 'to know if his lordship thought fit to admit me; and I would make him a present of £5,000'. Macclesfield expressed a wish to treat him as a friend, but added, with all due propriety, that he must not make bargains. Elde accordingly approached the Lord Chancellor's man, Cottingham and offered £5,000 for the post. 'Guineas,' the oily Cottingham replied, 'are handsomer.' (For the younger reader, a guinea was worth one twentieth more than a pound.)

Elde promptly went home, stuffed the cash into a basket and took a sedan chair to Macclesfield's house where he handed it over to Cottingham. He was appointed Master the same day.

Some months later he asked for his basket back.

Elde was not the only Master in Chancery who bought his post. Some of them, having paid large bribes for their offices invested heavily in the South Sea Bubble, as the current 'get rich quick' scheme came to be called, in an attempt to recover the expenditure. When the Bubble burst in 1720 nothing was left of their investments, and the ensuing inquiry revealed the Lord Chancellor's 'nice little earner' to have brought in over £100,000 in bribes.

Macclesfield was impeached in 1725 for 'exacting money as the price of appointments to Masterships in chancery and other offices'. In his defence he claimed that the monies were 'presents' freely given in accordance with past practice, and blamed others for any misunderstanding. '[It] never entered his thoughts to make use of, nor did he ever make use of any of the money belonging to the suitors of the court'. Instead, he claimed, he had deposited the monies into court. It cut no ice with the Commons and he was fined what was then the vast sum of £30,000 and imprisoned in the Tower of London until it was paid.

It was a serious downfall for the man who after the death of Queen Anne had temporarily held the office of Regent of Great Britain.

Elde was expelled from the House of Commons. For reasons best known to the Middle Temple, he was rewarded by being made a Bencher of his Inn.

Even nineteenth century judges could be less than admirable people.

The judge who climbed out of the robing room

Alexander James Edmund Cockburn was neither a great lawyer or a paragon of virtue. While a barrister he tried to escape from bailiffs by climbing out of the window of the robing room at Rougemont Castle, Exeter. He was also a notorious womanizer who managed to father two illegitimate children, scandalously introducing one of them into society.

Cockburn was an ambitious man. He was appointed Recorder of Southampton and took Silk before going into Parliament as a Liberal MP. His support for the Foreign Secretary's handling of the 'Don Pacifico' dispute[18] led to him being appointed Solicitor General, later Attorney General. In

---

[18] Don Pacifico was a British subject of Portugese descent and a Jew. While working as the Portuguese consul in Athens his house was ransacked by an anti-Semitic mob. When he appealed for help Palmerston sent a Royal Navy squadron to blockade the port of Piraeus.

1856 he was made Chief Justice of the Common Pleas, automatically becoming the first true Lord Chief Justice when that post was officially recognized.[19] But his morality did not noticeably improve along with his preferment. Lord Palmerstone had promised that Cockburn should have a peerage whenever he wanted it. Many years later when the judge called in the promise the government were informed by the Palace that 'this peerage has been more than once previously refused upon the ground of the notoriously bad moral character of the Chief Justice'.

Though a fine lawyer, critics said of Cockburn that he became a first rate judge only because he sat alongside Justice Blackburn. With his dignified appearance, large head and mellifluous voice Cockburn was prone to self-aggrandizement, constantly exercising the privilege to allocate to himself the more lurid and sensational cases. His great desire, it was said, was to have a page of *The Times* devoted to him every day.

Late in life Cockburn reminisced 'Whatever happens, I have had my whack.' He died in office at the age of 79.

Success at the law does not always guarantee judgement and diplomacy, as the career of a colonial judge demonstrates.

The 'crabby and eccentric' judge

John Walpole Willis was expelled from Charterhouse school in 1809. A few years later he was called to the Bar at Gray's Inn and joined the northern circuit, where his talents secured him a successful career at the Chancery Bar. Unfortunately, diplomacy was not his strong suit.

In 1827 Willis was appointed a judge of the newly created court of equity for Upper Canada. Almost immediately he fell out with the law officers after claiming the right to dictate

---

[19] Before that it was the honorary title of the chief justice of the Common Pleas.

their duties. From the Bench he claimed that the Attorney General (who was his rival for the office of chief justice) had neglected his duty. Within months of his appointment Willis was removed from office by the Lieutenant Governor. He appealed to the Privy Council who at first affirmed the dismissal, but later had to set it aside on the ground that the judge had been denied a hearing before it was made. The secretary of state for the colonies went out of his way to declare that Willis's 'personal honour and integrity were free from reproach'.

In 1831 the British government sought to do justice by Willis by appointing him vice-president of the Court of Civil and Criminal Justice of British Guiana. Despite his diligence in the post he soon fell out with everyone in the legal profession and was removed to a separate judgeship elsewhere in the colony.

Ill health forced Willis to return to England in 1836. After he recovered he obtained another judgeship, this time of the Supreme Court of New South Wales, where he swiftly resumed his old ways; he refused to hear a solicitor who wore a moustache and he rebuked a barrister who advertised the services of his stallion. He is said to have 'quarrelled with the governor, the Executive Council, the judges of New South Wales, the Superintendent of Port Philip, the magistracy, the legal profession, the press, and was distasteful to more than one half the community.' The governor reported that 'for many months the town of Melbourne has been kept in a state of continued excitement by the proceedings of Mr Justice Willis and the extraordinary nature of the harangues, which he is in the habit of delivering from the bench.' He went too far, however, when he cast doubts on the integrity of the Crown prosecutor, and the Bar walked out of court *en masse*. Following objections from over 500 people Willis was removed from office for the last time in 1843.

Although the Privy Council agreed that there were sufficient grounds for the removal of judge Willis, they held once again that, because he had been given no opportunity to comment on the complaints his removal from office was invalid. He was awarded his arrears of salary and costs and went on to enjoy a comfortable thirty year retirement.

'The law west of the Pecos'

Few Justices of the Peace have had as colourful a life as the American, Phantly Roy Bean. When his lady-friend was forced to marry a Mexican officer against her will Bean killed the man in a duel. The dead man's friends captured Bean and hanged him from a tree, but as soon as they left Bean's friends were able to cut him down alive. After serving in the Confederate army during the civil war he took various jobs before moving to a tented village near the Pecos river in Texas, where he was to make his name.

In 1882 Bean was appointed Justice of the Peace and dispensed liquor and what he considered to be justice from his courthouse, which was also his saloon. Over the door was a notice proclaiming, 'The Law West of the Pecos'. And this is how it worked.

Bean was a kindly man, often doing good among the townsfolk, but his administration of the law was rough and ready. Once when an Irishman had been arrested for shooting a Chinese labourer an angry mob surrounded the courthouse and threatened to lynch the justice if their friend was not freed. Bean, who had no formal education, consulted his law book and ruled, 'Gentlemen, I find the law very explicit on murdering your fellow man, but there's nothing here about killing a Chinaman. Case dismissed.'

When the railroad moved on Bean removed himself to the nearby town of Eagles Nest, naming his new saloon 'The Jersey Lilly' in honour of the English actress, Lillie Langtry, who had visited the area (but whom he never met.)

Contrary to legend, Bean was not a great hanger, preferring fines, which he could pocket himself. (The legend probably confused him with Isaac Parker, a District Court judge in Arkansas who is known to have sentenced 160 men and women to death.) Bean only sentenced two to hang, and one of those escaped.

When he failed to get re-elected in 1896 Bean refused to surrender his seal and law book and continued to try all cases north of the tracks. In 1898 when prize-fighting was illegal he circumvented the law by holding the world championship boxing match on a sand-bar in the middle of the Rio Grande River, the boundary with Mexico.

Bean died from a drinking bout in 1903 at the age of 78. Lillie Langtry finally visited his saloon and heard stories about her admirer. 'It was a short visit,' she wrote in her autobiography, 'but an unforgettable one.'

The stellar career of a future Lord Chief Justice, was very nearly wrecked by a financial scandal.

'Gehazi'

In 1913 the French journal, *Le Matin* published an article accusing highly placed members of the British government of corruption in relation to what came to be called the Marconi scandal. Sir Rufus Isaacs, the Attorney General, and Herbert Samuel, the Postmaster General both issued writs for libel which secured an apology and retraction from *Le Matin*, but it was not the end of the matter.

At the root of the story was a government contract which the British Marconi company had been awarded for the setting up of an 'imperial wireless chain' across the world. The contract was criticized as being too generous to the company, and when its shares rose dramatically whispers went round that it had been secured with the help of Godfrey Isaacs, the company's managing director and younger brother of the Attorney General. Herbert Samuel, the Postmaster-General, was also said to have been involved.

Rufus Isaacs assured the House of Commons, 'Never ... have I had one single transaction with the shares of that company' - without making it clear that it was the English and not the American company to which he was referring.

A Select Committee was appointed to look into the affair. It divided in the customary fashion along party lines. The Liberal majority acquitted Samuel of any involvement in the matter and accepted that the others had acted in good faith. The Tory minority, though clearing ministers of corruption, found that Isaacs, Lloyd George and Murray had acted with 'grave impropriety', that their interest had been 'material though indirect', and that they had been 'wanting in frankness'.

During the libel proceedings it had been admitted on behalf of Rufus Isaacs that he, the Prime Minister, Lloyd George and Lord Murray, Treasurer of the Liberal party, had all bought shares in Marconi's American company. What did not come out, however, was that the shares had been made available through Isaacs's brother and at half the price offered when they were floated. Rudyard Kipling in his poem, *Gehazi*[20] justly criticized Isaacs for 'The truthful, well-weighed answer/That tells the blacker lie'. Apart from this unfortunate piece of sophistry, however, Isaacs seems to have acted honourably. Overall, he lost some £1,200 from the transactions; his misjudgement lay in buying the shares in the first place.

But the scandal did not harm Isaac's career. Four months later Isaacs was appointed Lord Chief Justice with the title Lord Reading and went on to become successively Governor General of India and Foreign Secretary.

It is not always possible to foretell from a man's youth where his future will take him.

'F.E.'

William Camp described how a struggling young barrister, known as 'F.E.',

---

[20] See 2 Kings 5:20-5:27.

'who had just begun his career on the Northern Circuit, was on a tram in Liverpool. A young woman sitting opposite him was about to alight when a man boarded the tram and jostled her. 'F.E.' promptly intervened, struck the man on the jaw, and sent him flying into the roadway where he struck his head on the kerb. Instinctively, 'F.E.' knew he was dead. He leaped off the tram and ran as fast as his legs would carry him to a friend in shipping whom he begged to get him out of the country at once. The friend obliged and put him on a boat en route for the Mediterranean.'[21]

After a fortnight at sea the ship called at Malta where F.E. went ashore and picked up an attractive girl who took him home with her. They went upstairs where he removed his boots and trousers. When the infuriated husband came in armed with a knife and a revolver the wife began to protest her innocence. F.E. induced her to keep her husband talking until he got hold of the chamber pot, which he brought down on the man's head. Then he ran all the way back to the ship in his stockinged feet. He later described the incident as one of the most agonizing experiences of his life.

On his return to Liverpool 'F.E.' found, as he feared, that the man on the tram had died, but that the hue and cry had died down with him. The moral of this story, said 'F.E.', was 'Never take your boots off when you're having fun with a woman.'

The man in question was Frederick Edwin Smith (1872-1930), the son of a solicitor. He obtained a scholarship to Wadham College, Oxford where he became president of the Union. After gaining a first in Law and winning the prestigeful Vinerian scholarship, he was called to the Bar by Gray's Inn, coming equal first in the examinations. An early star on the Northern circuit, 'F.E.' was recommended by Marshall Hall KC to the Attorney General. Elected to the Commons in 1906, he moved to London and took Silk. He went on to become the youngest person to hold the office of Lord Chancellor for over two centuries, was created Earl of Birkenhead,

---

[21] *The Glittering Prizes: A Biographical Study of F. E. Smith*, McGibbon & Kee, 1960.

played a leading part in the setting up of the Irish Free State (now the Republic of Ireland) and ended his public life as Secretary of State for India.

Clement Attlee once described 'F.E.' as possessing both a 'brilliant mind' and 'bags of guts.' However, like many driven men he was prone to drink to excess. Towards the end drink began to take its toll, but never his wits. At dinner one night, seated beside a pretentious woman who introduced herself as 'Mrs. Porter-Porter with a hyphen', 'F.E.' replied that he was 'Mr. Whisky-Whisky with a siphon.'

For other examples of 'F.E.'s humour see below.

The 'wicked judge'

Henry Hawkins started his career as a junior in the office of his father's firm. He had to leave because of a practical joke: he had sent a premature report of the death of a local Magistrate to the local newspaper, which had published it.[22]

This inauspicious beginning seems to have been overcome, however, because Hawkins was called to the Bar where he enjoyed a successful career, distinguishing himself in his cross-examination of the Tichborne claimant. In 1876 he was appointed a Judge of the Exchequer Division of the High Court with the customary knighthood. (He had hoped for the recently abolished title of 'Baron' and insisted on being referred to in terms which suggested that he actually bore that distinction.)

On the Bench Hawkins had a reputation for being vain and petty and was described by the great lawyer, R.E. Megarry as 'not lacking in self-esteem'. He admitted to 'a horror of adverse criticism, to which I am perhaps unduly sensitive'. Fearful of being upset on appeal, he went to extreme lengths to prevent cases before him being tried to conclusion.

Hawkins came in for widespread criticism for the conduct of his first murder trial as a judge. Harriet Staunton,

---

[22] Hine, *Memoirs of an Uncommon Attorney*.

a mentally disabled woman, had starved to death in an isolated farmhouse. The dead woman's husband, his mistress, brother and sister in law were all charged with her murder and convicted.[23] According to *The Times*, Hawkins' summing up stressed the motive rather than the issue of legal culpability and referred to the cold hearted indifference with which the accused had witnessed Harriet's lingering death. *The Times* concluded that the judge was unduly influenced by the wish to punish immorality. For his conduct in this case Hawkins earned the contempt of defence counsel, the great Edward Clarke KC, who for forty years insisted on calling him a wicked judge.

Hawkins eventually had to resign from the Bench following complaints of neglect and infirmity, but at his request was raised to the Peerage as Lord Brampton. In this capacity he was able to sit on what was then the highest court in the land, the Appellate Committee of the House of Lords.

A few lawyers find it difficult to make the transition to the Bench, leading them into the temptation to interfere overmuch in the conduct of the case. Lord Denning MR once had to deal with such a complaint in the Court of Appeal.

The ill-tuned cymbal

The accusation was that 'the nature and extent of the judge's interruptions during the hearing of the evidence made it virtually impossible for counsel for the plaintiff to put his client's case properly or adequately or to cross-examine the witnesses ... adequately or effectively.' The judge was Sir Hugh Imbert Periam Hallett MC.

Denning observed:

'Was it not Lord Chancellor Eldon who said in a notable passage that 'truth is best discovered by powerful statements

---

[23] Three of the sentences were commuted to life imprisonment and the fourth defendant pardoned.

on both sides of the question' ... and the Master of the Rolls, Lord Greene, who explained that justice is best done by a judge who holds the balance between the contending parties without himself taking part in their disputations? If a judge, said Lord Greene, should himself conduct the examination of witnesses, he, so to speak, descends into the arena and is liable to have this vision clouded by the dust of the conflict...

'The judge's part in all this is to hearken to the evidence, only himself asking questions of witnesses when it is necessary to clear up any point that has been overlooked or left obscure; to see that the advocates behave themselves seemly and keep to the rules laid down by law; to exclude irrelevancies and discourage repetition; to make sure by wise intervention that he follows the points that the advocates are making and can assess their worth; and at the end to make up his mind where the truth lies. If he goes beyond this, he drops the mantle of a judge and assumes the robe of an advocate; and the change does not become him well. Lord Bacon spoke right when he said that: "Patience and gravity of hearing is an essential part of justice; and an over-speaking judge is no well-tuned cymbal."'[24]

After this criticism the Lord Chancellor arranged that Judge Hallett would resign after a decent interval of time.

A few judges are inclined to be dilatory in the writing of their opinions, sometimes with disastrous results.

The tardy judge

A farmer sued a chartered accountant for damages in a case which came before Mr Justice Harman in June 1994. After a five week trial the judge reserved judgment. But it was what followed, or failed to follow, that was to give rise to concern.

In January the following year the parties were told that the judge was in the middle of drafting his judgment which

[24] *Jones v National Coal Board*, 1957.

was at the forefront of his attention. In July they inquired as to progress, but received no reply, possibly because the judge had had to have surgery. During the Michaelmas term the parties were given an informal indication that they could expect judgment by mid-November. Not having received it by January the following year they wrote to the Vice Chancellor.

When Harman's judgment was finally handed down more than 20 months after the end of the hearing it dismissed the claim for damages. The plaintiff naturally appealed to the Court of Appeal on the ground that, by the time he came to deliver his judgment, the judge, who had lost his trial notes, had forgotten large parts of the evidence in the case, and that he had no clear recollection or impression of the demeanour of the witnesses of fact or their credibility. Directing a re-trial, the Court observed:

> A judge's tardiness in completing his judicial task after a trial is over denies justice to the winning party during the period of the delay. It also undermines the loser's confidence in the correctness of the decision when it is eventually delivered. Litigation causes quite enough stress, as it is, for people to have to endure while a trial is going on. Compelling them to await judgment for an indefinitely extended period after the trial is over will only serve to prolong their anxiety, and may well increase it. Conduct like this weakens public confidence in the whole judicial process. Left unchecked it would be ultimately subversive of the rule of law. Delays on this scale cannot and will not be tolerated. A situation like this must never occur again.[25]

It was a crushing rebuke. Harman resigned from the bench shortly afterwards.

---
[25] Goose v Wilson Sandford & Co. and another.

> *The written judgment of a Hong Kong judge was not only delivered late, but concluded with a decision quite contrary to that originally announced.*

'The correct version'

Mr Justice Pang of the Hong Kong Bench heard an appeal in 2007 against the conviction of a company for failing to provide and maintain a safe silk screen printing machine. The appeal was allowed with reasons to be handed down later. 'Later' turned out to mean just over seven and a half months later, when to everyone's surprise the written judgment *dismissed* all grounds of appeal.

Counsel for the company immediately wrote to the Judge's clerk reminding him that the Judge had earlier allowed the appeal. At a hearing later that day, Pang said that the written judgment was 'the incorrect version' and that he was now handing down 'the correct version'. He asked the parties to return their copies of the first judgment and then handed down a second written judgment. Its contents were essentially the same as those of the first, except for one paragraph.

The prosecutor's appeal was rejected under what is appropriately known as the slip rule and the judge was reprimanded for his delay in dealing with the case.[26]

> *Litigants can sometimes be difficult, but judges are unwise to respond in kind.*

'You want a piece of me?'

Albany City Judge William A Carter made a crude comment from the Bench in 2004 'in which he appeared to encourage

---
[26] *HKSAR v Tin's Label Factory Ltd.*, 2008.

a police officer to use violence against a defendant'. The defendant responded with an offensive gesture and the judge told the officer: "If you are so upset about it, why don't you just thump the shit out of him outside the courthouse, because I am not going to do anything about it.'"

An earlier incident involving Judge Carter was even more dramatic. The defendant became agitated and refused to participate in the proceedings which, he claimed, were unlawful. The Judge 'angrily left the bench, threw off his glasses and judicial robes, and proceeded rapidly towards the defendant, saying, 'You want a piece of me?'

Judge Carter, a former State Trooper, was found guilty of misconduct by The New York Commission on Judicial Conduct, censured and warned that any future ethical lapses would be viewed with severity. Two members of the Commission had wanted to remove the judge from office, but were out-voted.

At the time of writing the judge still sits in Albany courthouse.

The hypocritical judge

William ('Wild Bill') Douglas, as he was proud to be called, served as an Associate Justice of the US Supreme Court longer than any other (1939 to 1975). He was a rugged individualist and outdoorsman who delighted in being thought of as a libertarian. But his private life was less than an example.

Douglas' first wife had seen him through law college and had born him two children before she divorced him in 1953, on the ground that he left her 'abandoned and alone' while working and travelling abroad. It was the Court's first divorce in more than a century and a half's existence. But more was to come. Six months after his divorce Douglas married his 18 year old research assistant who had left her husband in order to live with him. Throughout his life he was to have affairs, both in and out of the Supreme Court building.

Nine years this marriage his second wife obtained a divorce from Douglas on the ground of cruelty, which he did not contest. Five days after the decree was made absolute he married his third wife, a 22 year old with whom he had been having an affair for at least two years. It caused a hubbub in Congress with talk of impeachment, but Douglas managed to ride it out. That marriage too came to an end in 1966 when at the age of 68 he married a 22 year old student he had met while she was working as a cocktail waitress. They were to remain together until his death fourteen years later.

Douglas might legitimately ask why his personal difficulties should tarnish his judicial record; after all, many other judges have had chaotic private lives. It is probably his hypocrisy that offends most. Shortly before he divorced his third wife Douglas described the benefits of marriage from the Bench. It is, he said, 'a coming together for better or for worse, hopefully enduring, and intimate to the degree of being sacred.'[27] Needless to say, this 'Father of the Year', as he had once been named, had no time for his children.

Mischievous humour from the Bench can sometimes go too far.

The judge and the Fibonacci numbers

Mr Justice Peter Smith issued a 71 page judgment in 2006 rejecting a claim that Dan Brown's best-selling novel, *The Da Vinci Code* breached the copyright of an earlier non-fiction book. A few weeks later he revealed to reporters that,

> 'if you pluck all the italicized letters out of the text [of his judgment], you find that the first 10 spell "Smithy Code," an apparent play on "Da Vinci Code." But the next series of letters, some 30 or so, are a jumble, and this is the mystery that needs to be solved to break the code.'

A typographical error, he added, had been inserted deliberately in order to 'create further confusion'. Apparently, the

---

[27] *Griswold v. Connecticut*, 2006.

judge's code was based on the Fibonacci number sequence, which is used by characters in the Dan Brown novel.[28]

The judge's message was unravelled by Daniel Tench, a lawyer and *Guardian* journalist. Decoded, it read:

'"Smithy Code" Jackie Fisher who are you Dreadnought.'

Reference to *Who's Who* revealed Judge Smith to be an admirer of Admiral Jackie Fisher, the man who introduced the Dreadnought to the British Navy.

The Court of Appeal upheld Judge Smith's decision in the copyright case despite an erroneous ruling on a point of law, but his judgment attracted criticism. Lord Justice Lloyd observed that it was, 'not easy to read or to understand. It might have been preferable for him to have allowed himself more time for the preparation, checking and revision of the judgment.'

One of Judge Smith's decisions was challenged in the Court of Appeal the following year when the criticism was more serious. The judge had declined to recuse himself in a case which involved a partner in a firm in which he had recently sought employment (without success). His behaviour in the case was described by the Court of Appeal as 'intemperate" and "somewhat extraordinary'. Judge Smith issued a press release seeking to justify his conduct, but the Office for Judicial Complaints concluded that it amounted to misconduct and the Lord Chief Justice issued a reprimand.

This time, Judge Peter Smith made no public reaction, coded or otherwise.

> *No one could guess that the indictment of a former Chilean President by a Spanish magistrate on ninety four counts of torture and assassination would lead to serious embarrassment for a respected member of the highest court in the United Kingdom.*

---

[28] The Fibonacci sequence is one in which each number is the sum of the previous two.

The embarrassment of a judge

In 1998, six days after the Spanish indictment, General Augusto Pinochet flew from his native country to London for medical treatment. He had given significant assistance to the United Kingdom during the Falklands conflict and may have assumed that this would afford him immunity from arrest on the Spanish warrant. In this he was mistaken: on landing at Heathrow he was immediately detained by police.

Pinochet claimed immunity as a head of state, a claim which eventually found its way to the Appeal Committee of the House of Lords, where it was rejected.

But for once this was not the end of the matter. Following an anonymous tip-off, Pinochet's law team challenged the Lords' ruling on the ground that Lord Hoffmann, one of the committee members, was a Director and Chairman of Amnesty International. Amnesty, had campaigned vigorously against Pinochet and had intervened in the earlier proceedings to support the case for extradition. Furthermore, the judge's wife, Lady Hoffmann had worked as an administrative assistant for the international arm of the charity. There was no suggestion of actual bias on the judge's part, but the Law Lords nevertheless considered that they had no option but to set aside their earlier decision and direct a re-hearing before a differently constituted committee.

The judge's error of judgement did not affect the outcome: the second committee confirmed the view that crimes such as torture could not attract head of state immunity. But it was a deep humiliation for Hoffman personally.

In March 2000, before extradition could take place, Pinochet was released from prison on medical grounds and immediately left for Chile. When his plane landed at Santiago airport the elderly general got up from his wheelchair to the acclamation of his supporters. He was to live six years more, and was never brought to justice for his vile crimes.

Lord Hoffmann retired from the Bench in 2009 with his reputation as one of the more brilliant holders of high judicial office undimmed.

6.4 THE PRACTITIONERS

On being told by Lord Erskine that the Inns of Court Yeomanry consisted entirely of lawyers King George III said with a smile, 'Call them the Devil's Own', a title the Corps has borne ever since. The occasion was the King's 67th birthday parade in Hyde Park in 1799. A story went around that when the order, 'charge' was given, every member of the Corps produced a note-book and wrote down 'six and eight-pence'.

Lawyers are accustomed to being criticized, but few have suffered the fate of John Cook (or Cooke), the only lawyer in this country to suffer death simply for acting as a prosecutor.

The prosecutor

John Cook was a barrister of Gray's Inn and of King's Inn in Dublin. He had travelled widely before making his name in 1646 as counsel for John Lilburne, or 'Freeborn John', later becoming even more widely known as a pamphleteer for radical causes.

Following the defeat of the royalists in the civil war Cook was appointed Solicitor General to the Commonwealth. In this capacity he was invited to act as joint prosecutor of King Charles, becoming sole prosecutor when the other man fell out. As we all know, the trial resulted in the king being sentenced to death.

After the Restoration Cook was arrested and prosecuted for treason, along with the remaining members of the court. He made a spirited defence based on the fact that he had done no more than any lawyer acting for a client would have done. This was not entirely true. It is the prosecutor's task to present the prosecution case dispassionately. This does not seem to have been the case with Cook who was heard to declare, 'He [the king] must die and monarchy must die with him.'

About Cook's high ideals there can be no doubt. Shortly before he met the gruesome death reserved for traitors, he wrote,

> 'We are not traitors or murderers or fanatics, but true Christians and good Commonwealthsmen, fixed and constant in that noble principle of preferring the universality before particularity. We fought for the public good and would have enfranchised the people and secured the welfare of the whole groaning creation, if the nation had not more delighted in servitude than in freedom.'[29]

Prolixity can be a professional fault in lawyers. A seventeenth century Lord Chancellor knew how to deal with it.

The loquacious lawyer

Thomas Egerton, 1st Viscount Ellesmere was annoyed to learn that a plaintiff's answer to a bill in equity (known as a replication) was 'six score sheets of paper' long, 'yet all the matter thereof which is pertinent might have been well contrived in sixteen sheets of paper.' It had been prepared, he was told, not by counsel, but by counsel's son, Richard Mylward, also a barrister.

Ellesmere announced angrily that 'such an abuse is not in any sort to be tolerated, proceeding of a malicious purpose to increase the defendant's charge, and being fraught with much impertinent [ie irrelevant] matter not fit for this Court.' He ordered:

> 'that the Warden of the Fleet [prison] shall take the said Richard Mylward, alias Alexander, into his custody, and shall bring him into Westminster Hall, on Saturday next, about ten of the clock in the forenoon, and then and there shall

---

[29] For a sympathetic biography of Cook see Geoffrey Robertson, *The Tyrannicide Brief: the story of the man who sent Charles I to the scaffold.* Chatto & Windus, 2005.

cut a hole in the myddest of the same engrossed replication (which is delivered unto him for that purpose), and put the said Richard's head through the same hole, and let the same replication hang about his shoulders, with the written side outward; and then, the same so hanging, shall lead the same Richard, bare headed and bare faced, round about Westminster Hall, whilst the Courts are sitting, and shall shew him at the bar of every of the three Courts within the Hall, ... '

Mylward was also ordered to pay a fine of £10 to the Crown and 20 nobles to the defendant for his costs.[30]

O tempora. O mores!

Judges can usually rely on the advocates appearing before them to arrive at agreeable compromises on procedural matters; when such an agreement was not forthcoming in an American court recently the judge resorted to unusual measures.

Rock, paper, scissors

After the attorneys in an insurance case were unable to agree between themselves the location for deposing a witness U.S. District Judge Gregory Presnell ordered:

'Upon consideration of the Motion – the latest in a series of Gordian knots that the parties have been unable to untangle without enlisting the assistance of the federal courts – that said Motion is DENIED. Instead, the Court will fashion a new form of alternative dispute resolution, to wit: at 4:00 P.M. on Friday, June 30, 2006, counsel shall convene at a neutral site agreeable to both parties. If counsel cannot agree on a neutral site, they shall meet on the front steps of the Sam M. Gibbons U.S. Courthouse, 801 North Florida Ave., Tampa, Florida 33602. Each lawyer shall be entitled to be accompanied by one paralegal who shall act as an attendant and witness. At that time and location, counsel shall engage

---

[30] *Mylward v Weldon*, 1695.

in one (1) game of "rock, paper, scissors." The winner of this engagement shall be entitled to select the location for the 30(b)(6) deposition to be held somewhere in Hillsborough County during the period July 11-12, 2006. If either party disputes the outcome of this engagement, an appeal may be filed and a hearing will be held ... '

The problems were soon resolved without recourse to the judge's novel form of dispute resolution.[31]

Advocates sometimes have to stand up to authority in defence of their client, even if it means offending a judge.

The independence of the English Bar

When the radical journalist, Tom Paine was charged with sedition by reason of the comments in his book, *The Rights of Man* Thomas Erskine KC agreed to act for him, well realizing that by doing so he would be risking his reputation and livelihood. His client was convicted, but the world remembers Erskine's bold declaration:

'I will for ever at all hazards, assert the dignity, independence and integrity of the English Bar without which impartial justice, the most valuable part of the English constitution, can have no existence. From the moment that any advocate can be permitted to say that he will or will not stand between the Crown and the subject arraigned in the court where he daily sits to practise, from that moment the liberties of England are at an end. If the advocate refuses to defend, from what he may think of the charge or of the defence, he assumes the character of the judge; nay, he assumes it before the hour of judgment; and in proportion to his rank and reputation, puts the heavy influence of perhaps a mistaken opinion into the scale against the accused, in whose favour the benevolent

---

[31] *Avista Management v. Wausau Underwriters*, 2006. Rock, paper and scissors is said to date back to the Chinese Han dynasty of the third dynasty BC.

principle of English law makes all presumptions, and which commands the very judge to be his counsel...'[32]

For his defence of Paine Erskine lost the profitable office of Attorney to the Prince of Wales, as he feared he would. Fourteen years later he was appointed Lord Chancellor in Grenville's Ministry of All the Talents.

The privilege of an advocate

Five years after *The Rights of Man* trial (see above) another of Tom Paine's works gave rise to criminal proceedings. A bookseller by the name of Thomas Williams was prosecuted for blasphemy for selling Tom Paine's latest book, *The Age of Reason*. This seminal work put forward a deist view of Christianity sceptical of miracles and much of the more primitive tales in the Bible. The trial took place before a special jury at the Court of King's Bench. Erskine was the prosecuting counsel. Stewart Kyd of the Middle Temple acted for Williams.

Kyd's argument was that the test for blasphemy should be whether the author was seriously examining his topic or whether he had a 'wanton and malevolent intent to do mischief'. In the course of it he had to repeat Payne's demolition of some of the more ludicrous stories in the Bible. It was all too much for the judge, Lord Kenyon who said 'I cannot sit in this place and hear this kind of discussion'.

Kyd replied:

My lord, I stand here on the privilege of an advocate in an English court of justice: this man has applied to me to defend him; I have undertaken his defence; and I have often heard your lordship declare that every man had a right to be defended; I know no other mode by which I can seriously defend him against this charge, than that which I am now pursuing; if your lordship wish to prevent me from pursuing

---

[32] *R v Paine*, 1792.

it, you may as well tell me to abandon my duty to my client at once.[33]

Kenyon churlishly responded, 'Go on, Sir.'

Bookseller Williams was convicted and sentenced to a year's hard labour for 'sapping the foundation of our holy religion', but at least his advocate had been allowed his say.

The offence of blasphemy was abolished in 2008

Advocates must always beware of getting too involved with their client's interests, as Scotland's most famous biographer discovered.

Boswell's first case

On 16 May 1763 the young James Boswell met Dr. Samuel Johnson for the first time at Tom Davies's bookshop in Covent Garden and one of the world's most famous literary friendships was born. Three years later Boswell was called to the Scottish Bar and for most of the first decade of the two men's acquaintance remained in Edinburgh practising law, sometimes with curious results.

Boswell's first criminal case was that of John Reid, accused in 1774 of sheep stealing. After the jury had spent some time in retirement they let it be known that they would bring in a verdict of Guilty. Boswell thought fit to join them in their pre-conviction celebrations in a local tavern, drank a great deal - at public expense - and bathed in compliments on his courtroom performance. ('I was in such a frame as to think myself an Edmund Burke', he wrote.) He finally got home about one in the morning. A few hours later he pleaded, unsuccessfully, for his client's life and afterwards helped his client compose his valedictory speech.

So convinced was Boswell of his client's innocence that he resolved to make off with the body after it was hanged and

---

[33] *R v Williams*, 1792.

attempt to revive it. (Hanging was a very imperfect science in those days.) But his client's remarks on the gallows changed his mind. The biographer-to-be recorded how Reid declared to the assembled crowd:

> '"Take warning. Mine is an unjust sentence." Then his cap was pulled down and he went off. He catched the ladder; but soon quitted his hold. To me it sounded as if he said, "just sentence"; and the people were divided, some crying, "He says his sentence is just." Some: "No. He says unjust." Mr. Laing, clerk to ... one of the town clerks, put me out of doubt, by telling me he had asked the executioner, who said it was unjust. I was not at all shocked with this execution at the time. John died seemingly without much pain. He was effectually hanged, the rope having fixed upon his neck very firmly, and he was allowed to hang near three quarters of an hour; so that any attempt to recover him would have been in vain. I comforted myself in thinking that by giving up the scheme I had avoided much anxiety and uneasiness.'

After comforting the newly made widow Boswell went on:

> 'It was now about eight in the evening, and gloom came upon me. I went home and found my wife no comforter, as she thought I had carried my zeal for John too far, might hurt my own character and interest by it, and as she thought him guilty. I was so affrighted that I started every now and then and durst hardly rise from my chair at the fireside. I sent for [a friend], but he was not at home. I however got Dr. Webster, who came and supped, and he and I drank a bottle of claret But still I was quite dismal.'

After Johnson's death in 1784 Boswell moved his family to London where he was called to the Bar at the Inner Temple. His Southern practice never flourished. It was just as well for the most famous biography in the English language, which was published just three years later.

Few advocates have had such beneficial effects on forensic advocacy and the way cases are tried as William Garrow, yet until recently his achievements were known only to a few.

'Garrow's Law'

William Garrow was the son of an Anglican clergyman who was called to the Bar at Lincoln's Inn in 1783. His intellectual and rhetorical powers, coupled with a brilliant and often aggressive approach to cross-examination, made him the most admired defender of his day. Three years after Call he is recorded as acting in 117 out of the 192 Old Bailey trials in which counsel was named. It has been suggested that his assumption of such a pro-active stance in court had the unexpected effect that judges were able to begin assuming their modern role as independent arbiters, rather than inquisitors.

Garrow, who also played a part in establishing the principle that a man is presumed innocent until proved guilty, was a champion of the underdog and an opponent of slavery and animal cruelty. His efforts on his clients' behalf did not go unrecognized. On one occasion when his wife Sarah was robbed by a highwayman the robber, who by then had realized who his victim was, followed the coach and returned his booty to her - but not to the other passengers.

Garrow was much in demand as a public speaker, first in the then fashionable debating societies and later in the House of Commons as the Member for Westminster in the Whig interest. In 1793 he was created a KC and was employed by the government to prosecute a number of prominent cases. In time he was appointed successively Solicitor General (when he received the customary knighthood) and then Attorney General. In 1817 he was named a puisne Baron (or judge) of the Court of Exchequer. He was not an outstanding success in any of these roles, but his brilliant and innovative style as a young advocate altered forever the nature of the criminal trial process in the common law countries.

Garrow's achievements only came to the attention of the general public with the 2010 television series, *Garrow's Law*.

The Victorians favoured a floridly dramatic style of courtroom advocacy. Its foremost expositor was Edward Marshall Hall KC.

'The Great Defender'

Called to the Bar in 1883, Marshall Hall soon made a name for himself, taking Silk only five years later. No one would describe him as a great lawyer. Indeed, if a point of law arose he would often ask his junior to deal with it. It was as a court-room performer that Marshall Hall excelled.

One of his earliest cases concerned Marie Hermann, a prostitute charged with the murder of a client. Addressing the jury in tears Marshall Hall said, "Women are what men made them. This woman was at one time a beautiful and innocent child. Gentlemen, I almost dare you to find a verdict of murder. Look at her, gentlemen of the jury, look at her! God never gave her a change, won't you?' (She got away with a conviction for manslaughter which saved her neck.)

On another occasion Marshall Hall was acting for the artist, Robert Wood, who was accused of the brutal Camden Town murder. It was touch and go whether he should call his client to give evidence, but he elected to do so against the advice of his instructing solicitor.[34] Paradoxically, it was the young man's weak and foolish demeanour that had persuaded the solicitor that he should not be put into the witness box that convinced the jury that he was incapable of murder. Marshall Hall was instructed in a number of other high profile cases such as that of Frederick Seddon, the poisoner and George Joseph Smith, the 'brides in the bath' murderer. He refused to take on Crippen after the doctor rejected Marshall Hall's

---

[34] It was the first time since the passing of the Criminal Justice Bill of 1905 that the accused in a murder trial was able to give evidence on his own behalf.

advice that he should run the defence of accidental death after having administered an overdose of anti-depressant.

Like all good advocates, Marshall Hall understood the benefit of conceding everything against his client which could not be refuted: 'My client is not on trial for enjoying strong drink. He is not on trial for abandoning his ill wife and his three young children, though perhaps he should be.' But he was not universally loved. Lord Justice Mathew, with whom Marshall Hall had often fallen out, criticized as inflammatory his address to the jury in the case of an actress who was suing the *Daily Mail* for libel. As a result, the flow of briefs diminished, but not for long.

Despite ill health Marshall Hall successfully defended the solicitor, Harold Greenwood who was accused of poisoning his wife with arsenic. His closing speech in that case was described as 'the finest ever heard at the English bar'.[35]

Marshall Hall was a long time sufferer from haemorrhoids, but the great thespian managed to turn even this to his advantage. When he entered court, his clerk would bring a large inflatable rubber ring for him to sit upon. If the case was going against him he would remove the rubber ring from beneath him and reflate it, thus ensuring the sole attention of the jury.

As Marshall Hall later explained, 'My profession, and that of an actor are somewhat akin except that I have no scenes to help me and no words are written for me to say. There is no backcloth to increase the illusion. But, out of the vivid, living dream of somebody else's life, I have to create an atmosphere; for that is advocacy.'

---

[35] Gerald Sparrow, quoted in Edward Marjoribanks, *The Life of Sir Edward Marshall Hall*, Victor Gollancz Ltd, London 1929.

> *The demands of modern advocacy are far removed from those of Marshall Hall and call for entirely different qualities.*

A record speech?

Nicholas Stadlen QC sat down in court 73 of the Royal Courts of Justice in 2005 after 119 days spent delivering his opening address for the Bank of England in its defence of an £850m compensation claim brought against it by creditors of the failed bank, BCCI.

The speech, which may have been the longest in English forensic history, exceeded substantially the opening address of the liquidators' counsel, Gordon Pollock QC, which lasted a 'mere' 86 days. When Mr Stadlen rose to reply he memorably began: 'After six months the Empire strikes back.'

The liquidators finally abandoned their action after 12 years of litigation and a hearing of 256 days. Their legal costs were said to have amounted to some £38m.

Mr Pollock's conduct of the liquidators' case attracted trenchant criticism from the judge, Mr Justice Tomlinson.

Mr Stadlen was appointed a High Court judge in 2007.

> *Skill in the courtroom does not guarantee success in that far more testing arena, life.*

'Gorgeous George'

George Alfred Carman's glittering career at the Bar was in sharp contrast with what little we know of his private life.

After a brief flirtation with the church Carman took a good first at Balliol. Called to the Bar at Lincoln's Inn as the King George V Coronation Scholar, he practised from chambers in

Manchester, taking Silk in 1971. A few years later he moved to Gray's Inn, where his career really took off.

The roll call of Carman's clients was unequalled for his time: Lord Kagan, the Gannex raincoat manufacturer charged with tax offences, Geoffrey Prime the government cryptographer accused of treason, the Maxwell brothers who were charged with fraud, Jeremy Thorpe who was accused of murder, and the comedian, Ken Dodd who had fallen foul of the tax laws. (In gratitude for getting him off the comedian is said to have named one of his Diddymen after Carmen.) But the QC's halcyon days were as a libel lawyer, acting for or against such 'celebrities' as George Best, Richard Branson, Marco Pierre White, Imran Khan, Tom Cruise, Elton John, Gillian Taylforth, Norman Tebbitt, Mohamed Al Fayed and Jonathon Aitken.

Apart from his surgical-like skills as a cross-examiner Carman was noted for his memorable turns of phrase. He said of David Mellor, for example, that if a politician 'behaves like an ostrich and puts his head in the sand, thereby exposing his thinking parts, it may be that a newspaper is entitled to say so'. He described the former MP, Neil Hamilton as 'on the make and on the take'. Of Ken Dodd he remarked: 'Some accountants are comedians, but comedians are never accountants.' In one case he suggested that one of the prosecution witnesses had regarded the 10 commandments as an exam paper with only seven out of the 10 to be answered. And in another, that 'Entrusting Arthur Scargill with upholding civil liberties is as dangerous as trusting Satan to abolish sin.'

'Gorgeous George', as he was sometimes known, died of prostate cancer in 2001. His private life had not been a happy one. Each of his three marriages had ended in divorce. A posthumous biography by his son by an earlier marriage depicted Carman controversially as a heavy drinker and gambler. But whatever the character of Carman the man, in his day Carman the lawyer was unequalled as a fighting advocate.

A single case can put an end to an advocate's career.

'The Claimant'

The story of the nineteenth century Tichborne claimant nearly beggars belief. An unexpected consequence of the litigation was the disgrace of one of the counsel involved.

Roger Charles Doughty was the eldest son of Sir James Tichborne, tenth baronet. When at the age of 25 he went missing at sea his distraught mother, the dowager Lady Tichborne refused to accept her son's death. Eleven years later a man by the name of Thomas Castro was 'discovered' in Wagga Wagga, Australia claiming to be the long lost Tichborne, which, if true, would make him heir to the Tichborne estates and fortune. Castro bore a striking facial resemblance to Tichborne. However, at 18 stone he was much more heavily built than the slim, effete youth who had gone missing at sea. And a tattoo which was on Roger was absent on the claimant. Nevertheless, the gullible Lady Tichborne had the claimant, as he was known, brought to Europe where she 'recognized' him immediately as her son and fastened on him a yearly annuity of £1,000. She was not alone in the identification: about a hundred others were also to attest to the claimant's noble birth.

Orton brought a claim for 'his inheritance' in the Court of Common Pleas in 1871. Before the trial began Lady Tichborne died, leaving the claimant penniless. The action failed and Orton was arrested on the orders of the judge and put on trial for perjury, where he was defended by Edward Kenealy QC.

Kenealy was an odd character. Brought up an Irish Catholic, he had become a Protestant mystic. As a young man he had served a prison sentence for cruelty to his illegitimate child.

Despite a flourishing criminal practice, Kenealy never managed to master the mass of documentary evidence in the

Tichborne case. During the proceedings he made accusations against prosecution witnesses for which he could seldom find evidence, and he defamed the Jesuits and the French over matters altogether irrelevant to the trial. Kenealy had a short fuse and clashed dramatically and repeatedly with the judge, Chief Justice Cockburn.

At ten months duration, the Tichborne case became the longest trial at nisi prius on record.[36] In the end the Claimant was convicted and sentenced to fourteen years penal servitude. He served only just over ten. After being released he appeared on the music halls in a desperate bid for cash to further his claim. He died in 1898 and was buried in a pauper's grave.

In his summing up to the jury Cockburn accused Kenealy of mis-stating evidence, perverting facts, and making imputations against innocent people. The jury added to the condemnation by censuring him for his language. None of this stopped the barrister from continuing to make his views known out of court in the bluntest of terms. As a result, he was dispatented (that is stripped of the title of Queen's Counsel), disbarred and expelled from the Oxford circuit. In disgust with his fellow members he threw their records out of a train.

Kenealy became a Member of Parliament and spent his remaining years continuing to assert Orton's spurious claim.

The general view today is that the claimant was one, Arthur Orton, a former butcher's boy from Wapping, but there are unanswered questions that make some commentators wonder if there might have been a glimmer of truth in Orton's story.

---

[36] That is, a trial before a court of first instance.

A nineteenth century advocate rose to the top of his profession on both sides of the Atlantic, but his career may have concealed a dramatic secret.

Was England's most celebrated lawyer Lincoln's assassin?

Judah Philip Benjamin, a British subject of Jewish descent, was the son of parents who emigrated to the USA from the West Indies when he was five years old. After being admitted to the Louisiana Bar he rose to become one of the new Republic's foremost lawyers and was offered, but declined, appointment to the Supreme Court. In 1842 he was elected to the Louisiana House of Representatives and to the US Senate a decade later. The American poet, Stephen Vincent Benet described him at this time as a 'Seal-sleek, black-eyed, lawyer and epicure,/Able, well-hated, face alive with life' and 'with [a] slight Perpetual smile'.

Despite having once challenged Jefferson Davies to a duel, the two men became good friends and during the short lived Confederacy when Davies was President of the Confederate States Benjamin served as his Attorney General, and later Secretary for War, a post which he had to resign following the loss of Roanoke island to the North. He was then appointed Secretary of State, in which role he was responsible for the Secret Service of the Confederacy and helped to secure England's support for the Confederate cause. As soon as the war was over Benjamin fled to England in an open boat fearful that he would be tried for the assassination of Abraham Lincoln. (Though the Confederacy secret service were certainly implicated in the President's death, Benjamin's personal involvement was never proved.)

Arriving in this country, Benjamin joined Lincoln's Inn. His pupil master was the great C.E. (later Baron) Pollock. Called to the Bar in 1866, Benjamin took chambers in Caesar's Building in the Middle Temple. By 1877 he had become so successful it was said that he would accept no case for a fee of less than 300 guineas, a vast sum in those days. Benjamin was raised to the rank of Queen's Counsel in 1872 and retired in 1883, when the Bar gave an almost unprecedented banquet in his honour. His book, *Benjamin's Sale of Goods* is still in print.

After his retirement Benjamin left for Paris, where he died. He is buried in the Père la Chaise cemetery.

Like many an ambitious man, America's most celebrated advocate was prepared to stop at nothing in his early years.

'Attorney for the Damned'

Clarence Seward Darrow (1857-1938) was in his time the most outstanding criminal defender in America. What is not generally known is that he was twice prosecuted for corrupt practices, only escaping conviction by the skin of his teeth.

Before turning to the criminal law in which he was to make his name Darrow began his career, first as a corporate lawyer and then as a workers' advocate. In 1912 he was acting for three anarchists charged with a bombing in which 21 newspapermen died. A private enquiry agent hired by Darrow to investigate jurors offered money to two jurymen if they agreed to vote for acquittal of his client. The police got to hear of it and set up a 'sting' operation. Darrow arrived at the scene just as the money was being passed over. In court the agent pleaded guilty to jury tampering, and implicated Darrow in the process. Two months later the attorney was himself indicted for attempted bribery. He retained the most capable defender in the country and was acquitted after a thirteen week trial in which he declaimed somewhat hypocritically: 'I am not on trial for having sought to bribe a man named Lockwood. I am on trial because I have been a lover of the poor, a friend of the oppressed, because I have stood by Labor for all these years.' Two months later Darrow was put on trial again for attempting to bribe another juryman.

When Darrow's attorney withdrew from the second trial through illness Darrow chose to defend himself. He handled this own case badly, as lawyers often do, and the judge declared a mistrial after the jury voted 8 – 4 in favour of conviction. The District Attorney agreed not to retry the case if Darrow promised never to practise law in California again. Darrow agreed and walked free.

The case caused Darrow to lose all credibility with organized labour which had hitherto paid his bills, and he turned to the criminal courts. It was an arena he was to dominate for many years.

One of Darrow's most famous cases concerned a doctor charged with murder.

Vintage Darrow

A gynaecologist, Dr Ossian H. Sweet moved with his wife and two year old daughter into a quiet neighbourhood of Detroit, Michigan in 1925. The only problem was that the area was predominantly white and he was black. The resulting confrontation was to lead to a trial which laid bare the racial prejudice then so prevalent in America.

The night after Dr Sweet moved in an antagonistic crowd of several hundred appeared in the street outside. In the house with Sweet were his two brothers, Otis, a dentist, and Henry, a student who had already experienced hostile crowds at an earlier address. Stones were thrown at the building all evening and at about ten o'clock a dozen shots were fired from the ground and upper floors of the house. One man in the crowd was killed and another injured. The doctor and all the other adults in the house were arrested and charged with first-degree murder. At his trial Dr Sweet testified: 'When I opened the door and saw that mob, I realized in a way that it was that same mob that had hounded my people through its entire history. I realized my back was against the wall and I was filled with a peculiar type of fear - the fear of one who knows the history of my race.' The trial ended with a hung jury and a fresh trial was ordered.

At the retrial Henry Sweet was represented by Clarence Darrow. Instead of accusing the prosecution of prejudice he charged the jury with suffering from it themselves:

> A child is born into this world without any knowledge of any sort. He has a brain which is a piece of putty; he inherits nothing in the way of knowledge or of ideas. If he is white, he knows nothing about color. He has no antipathy to the black. The black and the white both will live together and play together, but as soon as the baby is born we begin giving him ideas. We begin planting seeds in his mind. We begin telling him he must do this and he must not do that We tell him about race and social equality and the thousands of things that men talk about until he grows up. It has been trained into us, and you, gentlemen, bring that feeling into this jury box.
>
> You need not tell me you are not prejudiced. I know better. We are not very much but a bundle of prejudices anyhow. We are prejudiced against other people's color. Prejudiced against other men's religions; prejudiced against other people's politics. Prejudiced against people's looks. Prejudiced about the way they dress. We are full of prejudices. You can teach a man anything beginning with the child; you can make anything out of him, and we are not responsible for it. Here and there some of us haven't any prejudices on some questions, but if you look deep enough you will find them; and we all know it.
>
> All I hope for, gentlemen of the jury, is this: that you are strong enough, and honest enough, and decent enough to lay it aside in this case and decide it as you ought to.

The jury brought in a verdict of not guilty.

Even the most distinguished of counsel can sometimes display a surprising ignorance of contemporary society.

Do lawyers live in the ordinary world?

One of the most seminal events in the moral history of the twentieth century was the prosecution of Penguin Books for publishing D.H. Lawrence's novel, *'Lady Chatterley's Lover'*. While opening the case for the prosecution Mervyn Griffith-Jones QC memorably asked the jury:

> 'Would you approve your young sons, young daughters – because girls can read as well as boys – reading this book? Is it a book you would have lying around in your own house? Is it a book you would wish even your wife or your servants to read?'[37]

More than any other aspect of the proceedings this question exposed the yawning gulf between the generations.

'Penguin' were acquitted and sales of the book mushroomed. Four years later Griffith Jones was appointed Common Serjeant (or judge) of the City of London.

It is unfair to take as an exemplar of the solicitor's branch of the legal profession a man, however interesting, who chooses to describe himself as an 'Uncommon Attorney', but the life and writings of Reginald L. Hine are too fascinating to omit.

The Uncommon Attorney

Hine was an antiquarian, bibliophile and collector of curious information and anecdotes, particularly about his beloved town of Hitchin. His principal legacy was the eccentric, but

---

[37] *R v Penguin Books*, 1960.

delightful memoir, *The Confessions of an Uncommon Attorney*, in which he described the law office of Hawkins & Co. of Hitchin that he had entered as an articled clerk in 1901:

> 'Like most lawyers' offices (but why, why, why!) the rooms - littered with files, the dust of ages upon them - looked dishevelled and untidy. The wallpapers were of the mock varnished and grained pine in favour a century before, though if you explored with a penknife you might light upon five or six other specimens, each more attractive than the one above. The windows were made to open; but a ponderous legalistic atmosphere hung about the chambers: a curious conglomerate of parchment, sealing wax, corroding ink, calf bindings, stale tobacco, escaping gas, and myriad decaying matters. But very soon one became 'part and parcel' of all this; one accepted, one even liked one's surroundings; they were all of a piece with the antiquity of the firm; one was proud to be able to smell one's way back to Elizabethan times.'

Hine died in 1940. One moment he was talking calmly with a fellow traveller on Hitchin Railway Station; the next he had stepped in front of the Cambridge train. It was only a fortnight after he had retired suddenly from his practice and he had been suffering from depression. Hine's ashes were scattered in the supposedly haunted Minsden Chapel which he had been busily researching.

Chapter 7

'THE DUSTY PURLIEUS OF THE LAW'

7.1   THE COURTS

In the earliest days the king's courts followed their master wherever he went around the country, but in 1215 Magna Carta required the Court of Common Pleas to be permanently based in the Palace of Westminster, where it was soon joined by the Courts of King's Bench and Exchequer. And that is where the courts remained for most of the next eight hundred years.

The courts sat in the four corners of William Rufus' Great Hall, vying for space, and audibility, with the law stationers and other stall holders who surrounded them, as well as with each other. Until 1739 they were separated by a number of low barriers which were in time replaced by a Gothic screen. Between 1822 and 1827 the growth of judicial business was such that seven new buildings had to be erected between Westminster Hall and St Margaret's Street to accommodate it. They were built to the design of John Soane (who had yet to receive his knighthood).

The Great Hall had a narrow escape on 16 October 1834. The Exchequer had decided to replace its old tally sticks by paper records. Some wanted to give the wooden sticks to the poor, but for reasons of confidentiality it was decided to burn them. It was not a wise economy: the stove was not up to the task and a fire broke out in its chimney. Soon, the whole Palace of Westminster was reduced to flames, the only surviving parts being the Jewel Tower, the crypt of St Stephen's Chapel, the old cloisters and the Great Hall. The courts were homeless and had to move into temporary accommodation.

In 1866 Parliament decided to consolidate the scattered courts into one new building to be erected on a run-down site just off the Strand. It resolved that the architect should be chosen by competition, but the enterprise did not get off to an auspicious start.

The smell of justice

Despite much deliberation the judges could not decide between the merits of two architects, Charles Barry, who had designed the Houses of Parliament and proposed a building in the Greek revival style, and George Edmund Street, who was the great Gothicist of his day. Barry's plan was considered more convenient, Street's more visually striking, so the judges came up with the idea of a joint design. It proved impracticable and led to about a year's delay before Street was given the sole commission. The size of the enterprise is thought to have contributed to the architect's early death in 1881.

The first brick of the new building was laid on the last day of April, 1874 at the junction of Bell Yard and Carey Street. When a strike by the masons halted construction German workers were brought in, only causing further delay. The 1,000 room building was finally opened by Queen Victoria on 4 December 1882; it had cost about £1.45m, about half of which was paid for out of the estates of intestates.

A nineteenth century writer described the new Law Courts as having a smell of their own:

> 'It is an amalgamated effluvium, a reek of stuff gowns, dog-eared papers, mouldy parchment, horse-hair wigs, imperfectly washed spectators, police constables and witnesses,

with a bracing whiff of ammonia from the wood pavement in the Strand outside, to which, on days when a sensational trial is in progress, must be added the Araby the Blest gusts from the scent-bottles and the perfumed handkerchiefs of the gaily-dressed ladies who have flocked to listen, with the greediest of ears, to the scandalous details of a crapulent case...'[1]

The English courts were created ad hoc with varying degrees of success. The Court of Star Chamber came to have a terrifying reputation. It did not start that way.

An oppressive court

The Court of Star Chamber got its name from the *camera stellata*, or room decorated with stars in Westminster Palace. It began as the judicial arm of the King's Council and was made a separate court by Henry VIII in 1487.

At first, most of the business of the Star Chamber involved property rights and cases of official and judicial corruption. It offered to people groaning under the powerful nobles remedies not available in the ordinary courts, later extending its work to any petition for redress of grievances.

The court sat in secret without a jury, was prepared to act on rumour and used torture to extract evidence. Though it could not order the death penalty, the court could impose unlimited fines, pillorying, branding and whipping. It was the Tudors who realized the potential of such a court as an instrument of religious and political oppression, and the Stuarts continued its misuse.

One of the first acts of the Long Parliament (1640-1648) was to abolish the now hated Star Chamber. The room in which it sat was demolished in 1806. Its ceiling can still be seen in Leasowe castle hotel in the Wirral.

---

[1] *London Up to Date*, by George Augustus Sala, 1895.

One of England's most successful courts was created to deal with the aftermath of a national disaster.

The Fire Court

For three days in September 1666 fire swept through the mediaeval capital of England destroying over 13,000 of its old wooden houses, along with old St Paul's cathedral and 87 parish churches. Amazingly, only six people were killed. The fire started in Pudding Lane and, 'as every schoolboy knows', ended in Pie Corner.[2]

Determined to avoid any repetition of the disaster, Parliament passed the Rebuilding Act 1667 which required new buildings to be constructed of brick or stone without any projections over the street. Rules were made for street widening and the building of a 'column or pillar' to commemorate the fire, known ever since as The Monument. The cost of all this was to be paid for by a coal tax.

But problems arose over the rental contracts which made tenants liable to repair and rebuild in the event of damage to their houses: how were such disputes to be resolved? The answer was a court created specially for the task. It came to be known as 'The Fire Court' and sat at Clifford's Inn under the chairmanship of Sir Matthew Hall, Chief Baron of the Exchequer, and seventeen other judges. The judges worked for free, three to four days a week, usually giving their verdict within a day. Disputes were settled on the principle of ability to pay.

The Fire Court was wound up in 1672 after dealing with some 1,500 cases. The artist, John Michael Wright, was commissioned to paint portraits of all the judges who had sat in it. The result of his labours can be seen in the Guildhall Art Gallery.

---

[2] It is really meaningless to speculate on where the fire 'ended'. It is however commemorated by a figure in Cock Lane near Pie Corner known as the golden boy.

Matthew Hall went on to become Lord Chief Justice.

Many countries boast a supreme court. The United Kingdom has had two.

The Supreme Court

The newly created Supreme Court of the United Kingdom held its first substantive hearing in 2009 in the reconstructed building of the former Middlesex Guildhall. It is not the UK's first Supreme Court, though it is the first to deserve that title.

A Supreme Court of Judicature had been established by an Act of 1873. It comprised the High Court and the Court of Appeal. The court got its name because the Act was originally intended to abolish the appellate jurisdiction of the House of Lords, thus making the Court of Appeal the supreme court in the land.

But it was not to be. Following a change of government it was decided to retain the judicial role of the House of Lords, so until recently England was left in the anomalous position of having a Supreme Court which was not supreme.

7.2 THE INNS OF COURT

The training of barristers has long been in the hands of four societies of lawyers known as the Inns of Court. Two of them are located in a part of the City of London known as The Temple.

The Temple and its church

The Temple is so called because it was formerly the English headquarters of the Knights of the Military Order of the Temple of Solomon in Jerusalem who moved there from Holburn in the twelfth century. The Temple's association with the law began when Henry III directed that a number of law schools, and their hostels, should be moved to the Western borders of the City. In the sixteenth century the Temple area was confiscated by the Crown as part of the dissolution of the monasteries and given to two self-governing societies of lawyers, known respectively as the Inner and Middle Temples. (The Inner Temple was so-called because it was located on the side of the Temple nearer to the City centre.)

It is a condition of the charter (strictly speaking, letters patent) given to the Inner and Middle Temples by king James I that they maintain the Temple church, which is one of only four round churches in the country.[3] Constructed in 1185 as part of a large monastic compound, the Temple church is a 'royal peculiar', or extra-diocesan, church. It once contained within its walls a cell 4'6" high by 2' 9" wide which was known for obvious reasons as 'Little Ease'. It was there that Walter le Bacheler, Knight, Grand Preceptor of the Order of the Templars in Ireland, was starved to death as punishment for financial malpractice. The cell was destroyed by bombing during the second world war.

The Temple gardens are one of the hidden delights of London. Tradition has it that the wars of the roses received their name at a meeting in the Temple gardens between Richard Plantagenet and John Beaufort. Sadly, the story is a fiction of Shakespeare in his play, *Henry VI*, Part I.

The Temple was once described by one who lived in it as 'the most elegant spot in the metropolis. What a transition for a countryman visiting London for the first time - the passing from the crowded Strand or Fleet-street, by unexpected avenues, into its magnificent ample squares, its classic green recesses!'[4]

---

[3] Legend says that they are round because they were modelled on the Church of the Holy Sepulchre in Jerusalem.
[4] Charles Lamb. *The Old Benchers of the Inner Temple.* Charles and his sister, Mary, the authors of *Lamb's Tales from Shakespeare*, were born at 2 Crown Office Row. Their father, John Lamb, was a Hall waiter and clerk to Samuel Salt, the Under-Treasurer.

The four Inns

As well as the two Temple Inns there are two other Inns of Court, Gray's Inn off Holburn and Lincoln's Inn off Chancery Lane. The four Inns vie with each other as to which is the most ancient. Gray's got its name from the owner of the manor of Purpoole, Sir Reginald de Grey, Chief Justice of Chester who died in 1308. Lincoln's inn takes its name from Henry de Lacy, third Earl of Lincoln, who died in 1311. The Inner Temple and the Middle Temple were first mentioned by name in a manuscript yearbook of 1388. But the teaching of law did not necessarily start at those dates. In truth, there is little to choose between the four Inns so far as antiquity is concerned.

The sixteenth century was the golden age of the Inns of Court, and Queen Elizabeth its tutelary deity. It is said that the Bench tables in Gray's Inn Hall were the gift of Queen Elizabeth who once gave a magnificent banquet there. On every grand night the Inn drinks a toast to 'the glorious, pious, and immortal memory of Queen Elizabeth'. Another delightful tradition, sadly unsupported by any evidence, has it that the Queen made a Christmas pudding for the members of Gray's Inn with her own hands, and that part of the pudding has been inserted in the following year's repast ever since.

Wherever the Queen went, there followed her players. The first night of *The Comedy of Errors* was put on at Gray's Inn in 1594. This is how it was recorded in the Inn's *Gesta Grayorum* (1688):

> 'The next grand Night was intended to be upon Innocents-Day at Night; at which time there was a great Prefence of Lords, Ladies, and worfhipful Perfonages, that did expect fome notable Performance at that time... a Comedy of Errors (like to Plautus his Menechmus) was played by the Players. So that Night was begun, and continued to the end, in nothing but Confusion and Errors; whereupon, it was ever afterwards called, The Night of Errors.'

Shakespeare himself was not among the players: he was performing that day before the Queen at Greenwich.

The first recorded performance of Shakespeare's *Twelfth Night* took place in the Great Hall of the Middle Temple on Candlemas day 1602, the culmination of the Inn's Twelfth Night Revels. The student barrister, John Manningham noted in his diary,

> 'At our feast we had a play called "Twelve Night, or What You Will", much like 'The Comedy of Errors' ... A good practice in it to make the steward believe his lady-widow was in love with him, by counterfeiting a letter as from his lady, in general term telling him what she liked best in him and prescribing his gesture in smiling, his apparel, etc. and then, when he came to practice, making him believe they took him for mad.

The revels were an outstanding feature of the Inns in Tudor times. Gray's was then the largest Inn, renowned for the unruly revels of the imaginary Prince of Purpoole. The Inner Temple Revels of 1561 celebrated the appointment of Robert Dudley, Earl of Leicester as the 'Christmas Prince' in gratitude for his intervention in a dispute with the Middle Temple over the now defunct Lyon's Inn. The Parliament and Governors of the Inn swore never to take a case against Dudley and to offer him their legal services whenever required.

Walking through all four Inns of Court (which can easily be accomplished with barely a step into the real world) one is struck by the antiquity of the buildings. The Elizabethan Great Hall of the Middle Temple, for example, is one of the finest example of its type in the country. The Cup Board [or table] at which newly called barristers stand to enter their names in the Inn's books is made from the forehatch of Drake's vessel, *'The Golden Hind'*, the lantern of which hung in the entrance to the Hall until it was destroyed in bombing in 1941. In like manner the 'Armada' screen in Gray's inn hall is believed to have been made in part from the timbers of the Spanish ship *"Nuestra Senora del Rosario"* and donated by Howard of Effingham who commanded the English fleet against the Spanish.

Queen Victoria opened the Great Hall of Lincoln's Inn in 1845. It is the largest of any of the Inns of Court. Inside there is displayed an oil painting by Norman Hepple, R.A. entitled 'Short Adjournment'. It commemorates the occasion when six out of the nine members of the Court of Appeal (shown without robes) were benchers of the Inn. While it was being painted one of them was elevated to the House of Lords, where he was restyled Lord Denning. Appropriately, his figure is shown moving towards the door.

Lincoln's inn is surrounded by a wall built in 1562. Tradition has it that Ben Jonson helped lay the brickwork.[5] Oliver Cromwell is thought to have occupied the rooms above the gatehouse when he was a law student there in 1617, though the Inn has no record of his attendance.

Lincoln's Inn was for centuries the home of the Court of Chancery. By Dickens' time that court was in urgent need of an overhaul. Here is how the novelist described it in his novel, *Bleak House*:

> 'London. Michaelmas Term lately over, and the Lord Chancellor sitting in Lincoln's Inn Hall. Implacable November weather...... Fog everywhere. Fog up the river, where it flows among green aits[6] and meadows; fog down the river, where it rolls defiled among the tiers of shipping, and the waterside pollutions of a great (and dirty) city...... And hard by Temple Bar, in Lincoln's Inn Hall, at the very heart of the fog, sits the Lord High Chancellor in his High Court of Chancery.'

Dickens and the law

Charles Dickens was as familiar as any lawyer with the Inns of Court and their inhabitants. At the age of fifteen he joined the Holburn offices of Ellis and Blackmore, attorneys as a clerk at number 1 South Square, Gray's Inn. He does not seem to have enjoyed the experience. 'Indeed', he wrote in *The Uncommercial Traveller*, 'I look upon Gray's Inn... as

---

[5] Before he was a dramatist Jonson was a soldier. Before that he was, like his father, a bricklayer.

[6] An 'ait' or eyot is a long island in a river.

one of the most depressing institutions in brick and mortar, known to the children of men.'

Dickens was later to recount how Mr Pickwick was once assailed in a tavern by a little yellow, high-shouldered man with a shrivelled face, a fixed grim smile, skinny hands with nails of extraordinary length, and ragged gray eyebrows, who burst into an animated torrent of words concerning days gone by when young barristers in chambers,

> 'shut themselves up in those lonely rooms, and read and read, hour after hour, and night after night, till their reason wandered beneath their midnight studies; till their mental powers were exhausted; till morning's light brought no freshness or health to them; and they sank beneath the unnatural devotion of their youthful energies to their dry old books? ... Look at them in another light-their most common-place and least romantic. What fine places of slow torture they are! Think of the needy man who has spent his all, beggared himself, and pinched his friends, to enter the profession, which is destined never to yield him a morsel of bread. The waiting-the hope-the disappointment-the fear-the misery-the poverty-the blight on his hopes, and end to his career-the suicide perhaps, or the shabby, slipshod drunkard. Am I not right about them?'

(*Pickwick Papers* was published in episodes in 1836, but is set a decade earlier.)

In an attempt to relieve his tedious labours Dickens learned shorthand and used the skill to became a reporter for the Chancery Court and Doctors' Commons. But the future novelist had even more ambitious plans. It is not widely known that in 1839 Dickens joined the Middle Temple as a student member and ate dinners, though he was never called to the Bar. He explained his ambitions to a friend:

> 'I am (nominally, God knows!) a Law student, and have acertain number of 'terms to keep' before I can be calledto the Bar; and it would be well for me to be called asthere are many little pickings to be got pretty easilywithin my reach - which

can only be bestowed on Barristers.'[7]

The enigmatic phrase, 'little pickings' was a reference to the post of stipendiary magistrate (now deputy judge) which he unsuccessfully applied for. The world is the richer for the failure of the great man's ambition.

> Over the centuries a number of Inns of court and Inns of Chancery fell by the wayside. One of them was Clement's Inn.

The Inn that time forgot

Clement's Inn was a minor Inn of Chancery located where the Royal Courts of Justice and the London School of Economics now stand. Inns of Chancery were originally institutions for the training of clerks of the Court of Chancery. Later, they became training centres for the Inns of Court, each one being attached to a particular Inn. As an association of lawyers Clement's Inn probably dated back to the reign of king Edward IV, but a nineteenth century Royal Commission found it curiously difficult to uncover more of its history.

Thomas Gregory, the Inn's steward, told the Commission that some of its papers had been lost by fire, and 'some of them we can't read.' The inn, he believed, was formerly a monastery, and took its name from St. Clement. It had once had a connection with the Inner Temple, 'except,' he added, 'that a Reader comes once a term, but that was dropped for twenty years - I think till about two or three years ago, and then we applied to them ourselves, and they knew nothing at all about it; the under-treasurer said he did not know anything about the Reader, and had forgotten all about it.'

It was apparently the custom for the Inner Temple to submit three names to the ancients; and, said the witness, 'we chose one; but then they said that the gentleman was out of

---

[7] Letter dated 17 April 1846 to Mme. De La Rue. It was no idle fancy. Three years before he had indicated his ambition to be a police magistrate to Lord Brougham.

town, or away, and that there was no time to appoint another.' The cause of legal education does not appear to have suffered, for it appears that all a Reader had ever done was to explain some recent Act of Parliament to the 'ancients' (or Benchers) and commoners, there being no students.

Clement's Inn continued its slow and sorry decline until it was finally dissolved in 1903. The building was sold in 1934.

Chapter 8

LAWS AND LAW MAKING

The law has long been criticized as being inaccessible and written in arcane language. At least the ancient Greeks tried to do something about it.

Inaccessible laws

All too aware of the inaccessibility of their laws, the citizens of the ancient city of Athens asked Draco, one of their magistrates, to put them into a code to be inscribed on rotatable wooden posts readable by all.

Draco's efforts were a great success, but it backfired on him. If legend is to be believed, when the code was completed a reception was thrown in honour of the author. So enthusiastic were the invitees that they 'threw so many hats and shirts and cloaks on [Draco's] head that he suffocated, and was buried in that same theatre.' (The use of a guest as a cloakroom was apparently regarded in Athens as the height of compliments.)

The Romans had the most sophisticated laws of the ancient world. Over time, however, they grew so complex that the sixth century emperor Justinian had the laws gathered together and simplified into a single work. *The Codex*, as it was called, was accompanied by a students' primer (*The Institutes*) which began with this pithy statement:

> 'The maxims of the law are these: to live honourably, to hurt no one, to give every one his due.'[1]

Modern day lawmakers could learn from this succinct style. Listen to Lord Justice MacKinnon on the Trade Marks Act 1938:

> 'In the course of three days hearing of this case I have, I suppose, heard section 4 [of the Act of 1938] read, or have read it for myself, dozens if not hundreds of times. Despite this iteration I must confess that, reading it through once again, I have very little notion of what the section is intended to convey, and particularly the sentence of two hundred and fifty three words, as I make them, which constitutes sub-section 1. I doubt if the entire statute book could be successfully searched for a sentence of equal length which is of more fuliginous obscurity.'[2]

The Act was not repealed until 1994.

> *Until recently the lawyers' occasional use of Latin and a sort of Anglicized French, served as an extra barrier between the profession and those they aimed to serve.*

Arcane language

The first attempt to flush foreign words out of the courts was made by an Act of 1730.[3] It was not a success and had to be repealed. Today, while English is firmly established as the language of the law,[4] French and Latin still appear in a number of legal terms which the lawyers insist on pronouncing as if they were in their own tongue. The former Lord

---

[1] The phrase was lifted from Cicero's treatise, *'On Law'*.
[2] *Bismac Ltd. v. Amblins (Chemists) Ltd.*, 1940.
[3] The Proceedings in Courts of Justice Act.
[4] In Wales the Welsh language enjoys equal status with English.

Chief Justice, Lord Woolf urged 'the abolition of Latin and the adoption of simple English when rewriting our Rules of Procedure and, indeed, in our courts'. He anticipated the opposition that might ensue. 'How, it was complained, were you to make an ex parte interlocutory application *in terrorem* for an interim order of *certiorari* when the court needs to be assisted by an *amicus curiae* if there is no guardian *ad litem* or any *pro bono* representative?

Woolf's bold proposals have had much success. However, some French or Latin words are in such common use that it would be futile to remove them. Others represent concepts that cannot easily be replaced by a single word. And the substitution of 'claimant' for 'plaintiff' has bemused many people living on benefits.

As a matter of principle the law should apply to everyone equally, but in this country the monarch has always enjoyed special privileges. Not all of them have disappeared with time.

The Queen's corset and the King's feast

According to an Act of 1322,[5] '... the King shall have ... throughout the realm, whales and great sturgeons taken in the sea or elsewhere within the realm, except in certain places privileged by the King.'

It used to be said that when a whale was captured in the seas adjoining the coast the head belonged to the King and the tail to the Queen. The great jurist, Blackstone remarked: 'The reason for this whimsical division, as assigned by our ancient records, was to furnish the Queen's wardrobe with whalebone. The reason is more whimsical than the division, for the whalebone lies entirely in the head'.[6]

And from ancient times the Sovereign has enjoyed special privileges over swans. All white swans which are wild and

---

[5] The *Prerogativa Regis* ('Of the King's Prerogative')
[6] *Commentaries on the Laws of England*.

unmarked are the property of the Crown by virtue of the royal prerogative. However, a subject may own an unmarked swan in his manor or private waters and, if it escapes, may reclaim the bird, provided it has not escaped to nature.[7]

By custom, cygnets belong equally to the owner of the cock and the owner of the hen swan, 'For the cock swan holdeth himself to one female and is the emblem of an affectionate and true husband to his wife above all other fowls'. (Sadly, the legend of the swan's lifelong fidelity is a myth.)

Nowadays, the Queen exercises her rights only on certain stretches of the Thames and its surrounding tributaries.

When in 1991 an Act of Parliament abolished the royal privilege over wild creatures generally an exception was made with regard to 'royal fish and swans'.

The Scots have a legal system of their own. It is a blend of laws from various sources, including elements of the common law, even Roman law. And it continues to develop, as the following story of a drunken brawl that went wrong demonstrates.

The wounded puddings

A Mr Carnegie of Lour in Angus, Scotland had the unhappy task of burying his daughter. He invited a number of friends to the event on 9 March 1728. Among them were Charles Lyon, sixth Earl of Strathmore, Carnegie's own brother, James Carnegie of Finhaven and a Mr John Lyon of Bridgeton. After the interment the party went to a tavern, drank freely and began to quarrel. From there they went to the house of Carnegie's sister, but had to be persuaded to leave. Back in the street, Lyon taunted Carnegie of Finhaven and pushed him into a ditch. After his servants had pulled him out covered with mud Carnegie drew his sword and ran at his attacker. The Earl jumped between the two men and received

---

[7] *The Case of Swans*, 1592.

the full force of the blow, the sword passing right through his body 'wounding his puddings in three parts', as the report quaintly describes it.[8] He died two days later of his wounds.

Charged with murder, Carnegie admitted that he had been 'mortally drunk' and protested that he, 'would much rather that a sword had been sheathed in my own bowels'. Carnegie's counsel, Robert Dundas (who went on to become Solicitor General of Scotland) urged the jury to assert its 'ancient right' to bring in a verdict of Not Guilty, but was overruled by the judge. The jury disregarded his ruling and brought in a verdict of Not Guilty.

Scottish juries have enjoyed the right to bring in a verdict of Not Guilty ever since.

Britain's empire may have faded away, but its most lasting memorial is the common law which still holds sway over large parts of the world. If there is one man who expressed the spirit of the common law better than any other it was the first Vinerian professor of law at Oxford.

'The poetry of the law'

William Blackstone was a member of the Middle Temple who on 24 October 1758 delivered the first of a series of lectures which for the first time gave expression to the common law in language easily understandable by anyone.

The lectures were later reduced to book form as Blackstone's *Commentaries on the Laws of England*. The introduction contains a stirring declaration of English liberties when it refers to:

> 'A land, perhaps the only one in the universe, in which political or civil liberty is the very end and scope of the constitution. This liberty, rightly understood, consists in the power of doing whatever the laws permit; which is only to be effected

---

[8]'Puddings' or 'puddens' was a Scottish word for intestines.

by a general conformity of all orders and degrees to those equitable rules of action by which the meanest individual is protected from the insults and oppression of the greatest. As therefore every subject is interested in the preservation of the laws, it is incumbent upon every man to be acquainted with those at least with which he is immediately concerned; lest he incur the censure, as well as inconvenience, of living in society without knowing the obligations which it lays him under.'

Jeremy Bentham described Blackstone as having, '... taught jurisprudence to speak the language of the scholar and the gentleman; put a polish upon that rugged science, cleansed her from the dust and cobwebs of the office and, if he has not enriched her with that precision which is drawn only from the sterling treasury of the sciences, has decked her out to advantage from the toilet of classical erudition, enlivened her with metaphors and allusions and sent her abroad in some measure to instruct.' US Federal judge John Marshall expressed a similar sentiment when he described the *Commentaries* as 'the poetry of the law'.

Blackstone was appointed in turn a judge of the Court of Common Pleas and King's Bench, in which offices he achieved no special distinction.

The judges developed the common law over the centuries. But it was only when carefully written reports of their decisions started to be produced that it was possible for a coherent body of law to develop. Before that, court reporting was patchy at best and misleading at worst.

Good reports

Isaac Espinasse was a member of Gray's Inn who in the early years of the nineteenth century produced a set of reports of cases in the Court of King's Bench. Like many another early reporter his works were not well regarded; Chief Baron

Pollock said of Espinasse, that 'he only heard half of what went on and reported the other half.'

But for all their quirks and quiddities the old law reporters could be charmingly human. The present Lord Chief Justice, Lord Judge, speaking to the ICLR[9] recently recalled a 15th century yearbook,

> 'when Mr Justice Yelverton, a great pal of the Paston family, made a comment – a mere dictum of course - in that wonderful Latin Norman French about the right to kill someone who "va molesté votre très chere compagnon", and there is an accompanying observation from a law reporter about how the judge smiled as he thought of his wife, his very dear companion.'

Good reporters can have a hidden influence on the law. The nineteenth century Lord Chief Justice, Lord Campbell was frank concerning his own practices as a law reporter:

> 'When I was a nisi prius reporter[10] I had a drawer marked 'Bad Law,' into which I threw all the cases which seemed to me improperly ruled. I was flattered to hear Sir James Mansfield, C.. J. say, 'Whoever reads Campbell's reports must be astonished to find how uniformly Lord Ellenborough's decisions were right.' My rejected cases, which I had kept as a curiosity - not maliciously - were all burnt in the great fire in the Temple when I was Attorney General.'[11]

The great strength of the common law is that it is founded on real situations, not academic theory. Take the case of the sailors who killed and ate the cabin boy. Should the law allow them to plead self-preservation as a defence to a charge of murder? There was no Act of Parliament to answer this question, so the judges had to make up their own rules.

---

[9] Incorporated Council of Law Reporting.
[10] That is, a reporter of trials at first instance.
[11] *Campbell's Lives of the Chancellors.*

Cannibalism and the law

The crew of the yacht *Mignonette* faced an agonising decision when on 5 July 1884 their yacht was badly damaged in a gale off the Cape of Good Hope.

Before the vessel went down some members of the crew managed to launch the lifeboat. On board were Tom Dudley, the captain, and crewmen Edwin Stephens and Edmund Brooks, as well as Richard Parker, the cabin boy. Apart from two tins of turnips and a turtle which they managed to catch, they had nothing to eat and little to drink. Just over a week later the boy Parker fell ill, probably from drinking sea water. When he became comatose his desperate companions debated what they should do. Next day they plucked up courage and used a penknife to open his jugular vein. When all signs of life were gone the quick fed hungrily upon the dead.

A sail was finally sighted on 29 July and the survivors were picked up by a German sailing barge and taken to Falmouth harbour. Here, they told the authorities their story and candidly admitted the extremities to which they had been driven in order to stay alive. They were arrested, brought before the magistrates and remanded in custody. Despite considerable public sympathy, the Home Secretary, Sir William Harcourt decided, after consulting the Attorney General, to prosecute Dudley and Stephens, and to use Brooks as a witness for the Crown.

The trial of the two men began at Exeter Assizes before Baron Huddleston. He pushed the jury into accepting what was called a special verdict, which would leave the question of whether the killing could be justified to be decided by a panel of judges. When the issue came before a Divisional Court of the Queen's Bench under Lord Coleridge the judges held that the common law offered no defence of necessity to a charge of murder on the ground that it could become a 'legal cloak for unbridled passion and atrocious crime'. Dudley and Stephens were each sentenced to death with a recommendation for mercy.[12] The sentences were later commuted to six months' imprisonment without hard labour.

Of the men's plight and sincerity there was no doubt. How, it must be wondered, did the court expect them to have acted in their hour of need?

The fate of the *Mignonette* was commemorated by W.S. Gilbert in his poem, *'The Yarn of the Nancy Bell'*. It tells the story of 'an elderly naval man' whose ship, the Nancy Bell was wrecked. The ten survivors ate each other one by one. The narrator goes on to explain how in these circumstances he became,

> 'At once a cook, and a captain bold,
> And the mate of the Nancy brig,
> And a bo'sun tight, and a midshipmite,
> And the crew of the captain's gig.'

The defence of necessity continues to develop. In the year 2000 it was accepted by the court as a defence to the surgical separation of conjoined twins and at the time of writing it has recently been rejected in relation to the mercy killing of a man with 'locked-in' syndrome.

Judges indignantly deny that they are law makers, but they are sometimes willing to bend the meaning of an Act of Parliament to accommodate the justice of a case. Take for example the law of cremation. It is a heartening story that begins with a Welsh mystic and ends with a Hindu ex-squaddie.

Burnt offerings

William Price was a Welsh doctor who suffered from mental illness. Whether as a result of that or otherwise, he was a nationalist, a Chartist, a naturist, a supporter of trade unionism

---
[12] *R v Dudley and Stephens*, 1884.

and a vegetarian. He also single-handedly resurrected his own version of the long forgotten religion of the Druids.

After Dr Price's marriage in 1883 his wife was delivered of a boy whom he named 'Jesu Grist'[13] as an act of defiance against the Christian religion. When the boy died at the age of five months Price burned his body on a hillside overlooking his home town of Llantrisant in order, as he saw it, not to pollute the earth. Local people were angered at this and Price had to be rescued from them by the police. He was subsequently prosecuted for what the police believed to be the criminal act of cremation. At his trial before Mr Justice Stephen Dr. Price successfully argued that, while cremation was not specifically authorised by law, it was not actually prohibited.

When Price died in 1893 this friend of the miners was cremated on two tons of coal. An extraordinary life size statue of the man stands in the centre of Llantrisant.

In 1902 Parliament resolved to regularise the practice of cremation and set up rules to govern it. It was in this way that the modern crematoria were born. But our legislators failed to anticipate the results of mass immigration. Over a century later a 70-year-old Hindu, Mr Davender Kumar Ghai, wished for his remains to be cremated – when the time came - on a hill in Northumberland in order, according to his beliefs, to liberate his soul after death. He was refused permission by the local council acting upon their understanding of the 1902 Act.

Mr Ghai took the case to court and in 2010 the Court of Appeal ruled in his favour according to the principle that an ambiguous criminal statute should be interpreted in favour of the accused. The Cremations Act did not prevent open air cremations, the judges held, provided that they were in a 'building', generously interpreted, and did not contravene environmental regulations.

After the decision Mr Ghai, a former British soldier, declared, 'I never wanted to be divisive or offend anyone - the

---

[13] The Welsh form of Jesus Christ.

> There is a report of an Arkansas Supreme Court decision concerning the effect of legislation that, startlingly, purported to repeal all previous laws.

Poisson d'Avril

The Arkansas Supreme Court described the Arkansas' Act 17 of 1945 as probably the most radical piece of legislation any court has had to consider. It provided that: '*All laws and parts of laws, and particularly Act 311 of the Acts of 1941, are hereby repealed.*'

The report describes how the appellant had claimed that this Act had repealed, among others, the Statute of Frauds (an early Act of Parliament which gave protection against certain types of oral contracts) and that, therefore it was possible for him to enforce a contract for the sale of land which was not in writing. His argument had been rejected by the court below and he had appealed.

Giving the judgment of the Supreme Court, Associate Justice George Rose Smith revealed how the court had 'devotedly worked our law clerks to the bone and, indeed, have lost some sleep ourselves.' They could find no precedent for the repeal of all laws, save the opinion of Montaigne, 'that it would be better for us to have no laws at all than to have them in so prodigious numbers as we have.' But, as the Court pointed out, the word, 'laws' could have two meanings.

> 'After much anxious study we have concluded that the legislature intended for the [clause] to apply only to statutes, not to the common law. We are simply unable to believe that the General Assembly would do away with judge-made law... It is essential that the common law be preserved if we are to avoid anarchy - that state of society where there is no law. The statutory law is not equally essential. Indeed, it will

be found that the statutes which were on the books when the [clause] was adopted in 1945 can, for the most part, be spared. This is true simply because the common law, always fluid in nature, will at once seep into the temporary vacancy left by the evaporation of the statutes and keep the ship of state safely on the right track.'

By contrast, the court observed, 'in nearly every instance the purposes served by the [clause] (ie the repeal of all statutes) are praiseworthy and beneficent.' The court had in mind particularly the abolition of the sales tax and the income tax. The appeal was allowed.

Sadly, the case of *J. R. Poisson v. Etienne d'Avril* turned out to be a hoax. It was a fictitious opinion written by Justice Smith as a joke. The name of the imaginary case, 'Poisson d'Avril' (literally 'April Fish') was a hint: it is the French term for April Fool, the very day on which the 'judgment' claimed to have been delivered.

But what if?

Divorce nowadays is a fairly simple matter, legally speaking at any rate; it was not always so. In the nineteenth century an ingenious official is said to have adopted a most imaginative work-around to the problem, as it would now be called.

The Town Clerk's marriage

The story of a highly unlikely divorce was given credence by Lord Jenkin of Roding. Speaking in the House of Lords, he said,

'There is a case that appears in all legal storybooks about the Local Government Act, which was a private Act of Parliament hundreds of pages long that provided a huge amount of power to the local authority promoting it. It was so long that nobody read it the whole way through. The town clerk had successfully slipped into the Act, where nobody would look, a provision that the town clerk's marriage shall hereby be dissolved. The Bill was enacted, and he got his divorce. That happened before the Divorce Act. Such incidents could happen; therefore, the wording of Bills should be limited so that a permanent secretary cannot get a divorce by inserting a provision in the order without anyone noticing.[14]

A more detailed version of this story was given by R.E. Megarry QC, as he then was:

'More than 100 years ago, when, divorce in the modern sense was possible only by Act of Parliament an unhappily married Town Clerk was promoting a Waterworks bill for his town; and in clause 64, mingled with something technical about filter beds and stopcocks, appeared the innocent little phrase "and the Town Clerk's marriage is hereby dissolved"... In due course the Royal Assent was given and the Town Clerk lived happily ever after."'[15]

So far as the present writer is aware, no one has been able to establish exactly what, if any, statute was involved. Might the town clerk's divorce be no more than an urban myth?

People sometimes say that England has no constitution. They are wrong; we do have a constitution, but it is not contained in a single document like those of America or France. Instead, it consists of a number of disconnected texts, together with what are called the conventions of the constitution. But this was not always the case.

England's written constitutions

At the end of the second English civil war the victorious Parliament had to decide how the country should be governed without a king. There was no precedent for this, so in 1653 after much debate Oliver Cromwell and his Council of Officers adopted an *Instrument of Government*. The *Instrument*

---
[14] *Hansard*, 17 March 2003.
[15] *Miscellany at Law*, Stevens and Sons, 1955.

devolved executive power to an elected Lord Protector in consultation with a permanent Council of State of between thirteen and twenty-one members. The Lord Protector was required to call triennial parliaments which were to sit as a single house for a minimum of five months. Checks and balances were included in the *Instrument's* detailed provisions in order to prevent any part of government from overriding the other. Cromwell was named Lord Protector for life.

The *Instrument of Government* was never formally endorsed before it was replaced four years later by the *Humble Petition and Advice* of the second Protectorate Parliament. Unlike the *Instrument of Government*, which had been written by army officers, this was drafted by Parliamentarians and was intended to avoid disasters like the recent oppressive rule of the major generals. (John Lilburne, see above, is said to have contributed to the drafting of both constitutions.) The Crown had been offered to Cromwell, but it was declined. Instead, the Lord Protector was given power to appoint his successor. The *Humble Petition* also introduced a second chamber, consisting of people nominated by the Lord Protector and approved by Parliament, which would have power of veto over legislation.

The new constitution also had a short life, vanishing with the Restoration. It was to be England's last written constitution - so far.

Those tempted to pine for the constitutional certainties of a written constitution would do well to ponder the words of one of America's founding fathers:

> 'Some men look at constitutions with sanctimonious reverence, and deem them like the ark of the covenant, too sacred to be touched. They ascribe to the men of the preceding age a wisdom more than human, and suppose what they did to be beyond amendment. I knew that age well; I belonged to it, and labored with it. It deserved awell of its country. It was very like the present, but without the experience of the present; and forty years of experience in government is worth a century of book-reading; and this they would say themselves, were they to rise from the dead. I am certainly

not an advocate for frequent and untried changes in laws and constitutions. I think moderate imperfections had better be borne with; because, when once known, we accommodate ourselves to them, and find practical means of correcting their ill effects. But I know also, that laws and institutions must go hand in hand with the progress of the human mind. As that becomes more developed, more enlightened, as new discoveries are made, new truths disclosed, and manners and opinions change with the change of circumstances, institutions must advance also, and keep pace with the times. We might as well require a man to wear still the coat which fitted him as a boy, as civilized society to remain ever under the regimen of their barbarous ancestors.'[16]

---

[16] Thomas Jefferson to his friend, Samuel Kercheval, 1816.

Chapter 9

LAW AND THE SUPERNATURAL or, Who can resist a ghost story?

A condemned prisoner once cursed a court with such horrifying effect that it became known as the Black Assize.

The Black Assize

The story goes that in 1577 Rowland Jenkes, a bookbinder and Roman Catholic recusant,[1] was awaiting trial for speaking 'treasonable words, against the queen', when he was allowed by the Under Sheriff, a Catholic sympathiser, to go into town accompanied by a guard. Here, he had an apothecary make up a mixture based on a 'receipt' which he told the chemist was intended to kill rats. After being returned to the dock and having been convicted Jenkins is said to have cursed the court

---
[1] That is, someone who refused to attend the services of the established church.

and the town, got out a tinderbox and lit a wick impregnated with his mixture, whereupon 'A pestilent vapour suddenly arose as to almost smother the court.'[2]

Some six hundred people fell ill immediately, a hundred of them in the outlying villages. Within forty days three hundred were dead. Among them were Lord Chief Baron Sir Robert Bell and another judge, Sir John Banham, as well as counsel, jurors and others who had been present at the time of Jenkes' conviction. No women, children or prisoners were affected. Just over a month later the sickness died out as abruptly as it had begun.

While the curse may well have been made, and the people referred to above certainly did die, the rest is fiction. Jenkes was not sentenced to death, but to have his ears nailed to the pillory. (After serving his sentence he became a baker and went back to his native Belgium.) And the idea that a prisoner could somehow have lighted a wick in the dock is fanciful.

The most likely explanation for the tragedy of the Black Assize is gaol fever, or typhus, which was endemic in the prisons of that day, often killing more than were executed by order of the court. Oxford just happened to be a particularly virulent outbreak.

Oxford castle was abandoned as a seat of justice after the Black Assize. In the year 2004 more than 60 skeletons were discovered buried between the former prison and the castle in the grounds of which the Assize had sat.

Is it a defence to a charge of murder that you believed the victim to have been a ghost?

The case of the Hammersmith ghost

For weeks before Christmas 1803 a number of people reported having seen a ghost in Hammersmith village. The

---

[2] *The Lounger's Commonplace Book.* 1807.

apparition, dressed in white robes, had actually attacked passers-by. According to *The Newgate Calendar*, 'One poor woman in particular, when crossing near the churchyard about ten o'clock at night, beheld something, as she described, rise from the tombstones. She attempted to run; but the ghost soon overtook her, and pressed her in his arms, when she fainted; in which state she remained some hours, till discovered by some neighbours, who kindly led her home, when she took to her bed, from which, alas, she never rose.' The figure was very tall and very white and was assumed to be a man who had cut his throat a year before and was buried (improperly, as a suicide) in the churchyard.

Local people set up armed patrols and on 3 January 1804 at around 11pm a 29 year old excise officer named Francis Smith was in Black Lion Lane armed with a blunderbuss when he saw a figure in white. Smith demanded to know the identity of the apparition and, when the figure moved towards him, Smith, who may have been in drink, shot at it. The 'apparition' turned out to be a 23-year-old plasterer by the name of James (or Thomas) Milwood who was wearing flannel clothing and the white apron of his trade. He died from Smith's shot.

Smith surrendered himself to the constable and was put on trial at the Old Bailey for murder. Lord Chief Baron Macdonald ruled that the charge, if proved, could amount to nothing less than murder. When the sympathetic jury nevertheless returned a verdict of manslaughter the judge refused to accept it and the jury were forced to enter a revised verdict of murder. After sentencing Smith to death the judge reported the case to the king and the sentence was commuted to a year's hard labour.

Exactly why Smith believed that the lead shot with which his weapon was loaded would kill a spectre was never explained.

After the trial, an elderly shoemaker called John Graham came forward and admitted having pretended to be a ghost by using a white sheet to frighten his apprentice for having read ghost stories to his children.

A 'ghost', presumably of the innocent plasterer, is said to haunt the Black Lion pub at Hammershith where Milwood's body was taken after he had been shot.

Spiritualism, or the supposed art of communicating with the dead, was particularly popular during the Second World War when folk at home were anxious for the safety of their loved ones abroad. The authorities became disturbed, however, when a 'spiritualist' was thought to have exposed a naval secret.

The spiritualist and the Naval secret

The battleship, HMS Barham was torpedoed and sunk off Egypt by a German U Boat on 25 November 1941 with the loss of over 800 lives. It was a great setback at such an early stage of the war and news of the tragedy was withheld so as not to damage morale and in order to keep the Germans in the dark. To the horror of the Admiralty the fact of the sinking was revealed later that month at a séance held in Portsmouth by a Mrs Helen Duncan, a 62 year old Scottish Spiritualist medium. No action was taken at the time, but three years later another of her séances was raided by police and she was arrested and charged. After an eight day trial at the Old Bailey Mrs Duncan was convicted of being a fraudulent medium under the Witchcraft Act 1735 and of taking 25 shillings a head from her audience under false pretences. It was not her first conviction and she was sentenced to nine months imprisonment.

The Prime Minister, Winston Churchill angrily demanded to know why the Witchcraft Act, which he described as a piece of 'obsolete tomfoolery', should have been used instead of the Vagrancy Act, the more usual ground for prosecuting fraudulent mediums. The answer lay in the fact that the Act of 1735 allowed for imprisonment, which the authorities deemed appropriate for someone who had seemingly disclosed a military secret in time of war, while the Vagrancy Act did not.

To this day, there are those who give credence to Mrs Duncan's claim to have seen the 'ectoplasmic' form of a sailor with the words, 'HMS Barham' on his cap band; but sailors' caps did not bear the ship's name at that time for reasons of security. The most likely explanation is that the 'medium' had heard of the sinking from sailors in Portsmouth, the home of the Royal Navy.

The Witchcraft Act was repealed in 1951, when it was replaced by the Fraudulent Mediums Act. Helen Duncan died five years later, shortly after having been arrested yet again for fraud.

Even in America it must be unusual for a court to hold as a matter of law that a house is haunted, yet that was the conclusion of the Appellate Division of the New York Supreme Court in a recent case.

The legally haunted house

Jeffrey Stambovsky had made a down payment for the purchase of a large Victorian house on the Hudson river in New York, unaware of its supposedly haunted reputation. When a local architect happened to say to him, 'Oh, you're buying the haunted house' Stambovsky tried to back out of the agreement, but the vendor, Helen Ackley, would not let him. Stambowsky went to court asking for an order rescinding the contract for sale.

During the court proceedings it came to light that Mrs Ackley had told the local press and *The Readers' Digest* that there were poltergeists in her house. So notorious had the house become that it was included in a five-home walking tour of the area and had been described in a newspaper article as 'a riverfront Victorian (with ghost).'

The court upheld Mr Stambovsky's application on the ground that, not being a 'local', he could not readily have learned that the house was haunted.

'From the perspective of a person in the position of plaintiff herein', the court said, 'a very practical problem arises with respect to the discovery of a paranormal phenomenon: "Who you gonna' call?" as the title song to the movie "Ghostbusters" asks. Applying the strict rule of caveat emptor to a contract involving a house possessed by poltergeists conjures up visions of a psychic or medium routinely accompanying the structural engineers and [pest control] man on an inspection of every home subject to a contract of sale. In the interest of avoiding such untenable consequences, the notion that a haunting is a condition which can and should be ascertained upon reasonable inspection of the premises is a hobgoblin which should be exorcised from the body of legal precedent and laid quietly to rest.'[3]

Mrs Ackley, the court held, had not only taken unfair advantage of the buyer's ignorance but had created and perpetuated a condition about which he was unlikely to even inquire. She was therefore estopped from denying the existence of the ghosts, 'and, as a matter of law,' said the judge, 'the house is haunted.' Of course, the Court was not declaring that the house *was* haunted, merely that in the particular circumstances the seller could not in law deny that it was haunted.

Unfortunately, the court could not resist adding that, as agent for the seller, the real estate broker [or estate agent] was 'under no duty to disclose to a potential buyer the phantasmal reputation of the premises and that, in his pursuit of a legal remedy for fraudulent misrepresentation against the seller, plaintiff hasn't a ghost of a chance'.

Why juries come to the decisions they do is largely a matter of conjecture, for the courts refuse to allow their deliberations to be subject to academic scrutiny. In one case at least a jury is known to have resorted to a superstitious practice.

---

[3] *Stambovsky v. Helen V. Ackley* 1991.

The jurymen and the Ouija board

An insurance broker by the name of Stephen Young was convicted at Hove Crown Court in 1994 of the murder of a newly married couple and sentenced to life imprisonment. It later came to light that four members of the jury, while staying at a hotel, had consulted what was described by the press as an Ouija board.[4]

There was in fact no board; instead, letters of the alphabet had simply been written on scraps of paper and placed on a table. Each of the jurymen put a finger on an upturned wineglass, which then moved between the letters. Asked whom they were speaking to, the letters spelled out the words, 'Harry Fuller', the name of one of the victims in the case. After that, they spelled out the message, 'Vote guilty tomorrow...'. Some of those present were disturbed by the experience and threw away the papers. They all agreed not to reveal to anyone what they had done and retired to their rooms.

Over breakfast the next day the four revealed to their fellow jurymen what had taken place, one of them adding that, 'Walther PPK' had been spelled out by the letters. (It was a type of pistol mentioned in the case.) When the defendant appealed against his conviction the Court of Appeal said the incident could not be laughed off as merely a drunken game. What mattered was not whether the jury were really in contact with the deceased, but whether they believed themselves to be so or whether they might have been influenced by the 'answers' they received.

Concluding that there was a real danger that what had occurred during the Ouija session might have influenced some jurors and might thereby have prejudiced the trial their Lordships allowed the appeal and ordered a retrial.[5]

---

[4] The OED suggests that the word, 'Ouija' is a conflation of the French and German words for 'yes', but this is contested.

[5] *R v Young*, 1995. Ouija boards are thought to work by unconscious muscle movements known as ideomotor action, that is action unconscious to the subject which is caused by suggestion or expectation.

At the second trial Young was convicted again and gaoled for life.

Chapter 10

LAUGHTER IN COURT

Courtrooms can be boring places at the best of times and judges are sometimes tempted to lighten the mood by comments which, to the jaded legal mind at least, might seem humorous. They would do well to bear in mind the comments of Murray Gleeson, Chief Justice of Australia who referred to 'what might generously be described as judicial humour'. 'Most litigants and witnesses', he said, 'do not find court cases at all funny.'

It was a sentiment that inspired the barrister, WS Gilbert in his comic opera, *The Mikado* to have the Lord High Executioner list among his targets for execution 'that Nisi Prius Nuisance...the Judicial Humorist. (He never will be missed.)'

As with most things, attitudes towards courtroom humour have changed with the times.

Sir Edward Hall Alderson was one of the ornaments of the early nineteenth century bench. As an advocate he was a formidable cross-examiner who once reduced the engineer, George Stevenson to jelly. Alderson's commercial judgments were widely admired and in matters criminological he was ahead of his time. His summing up to a Northampton jury is a good example of his forthright wit.

The shortest summing up?

Alderson was trying a man for stealing a pair of shoes. Asked what he had to say to the charge, the prisoner replied,

> 'My Lord, I only took them away as a joke.'

Alderson: As a practical joke?

Prisoner: Yes, My Lord.

Alderson: How far did you convey them?

Prisoner: A mile and a half, My Lord.

Alderson: I think that's carrying a joke a bit too far. (Addressing the jury) What do you say, Gentlemen?

Foreman, after consulting the jury: Guilty, My Lord.

Alderson: Three months imprisonment with hard labour.

Brilliant, but doubtful whether a judge would get away with such conduct nowadays.

The shortest judgment?

Lord Hewart was Lord Chief Justice of England throughout the 1920s and 1930s. A stout believer in the jury system, he was also the originator of the adage that 'Not only must justice be done, but should manifestly and undoubtedly be seen to be done.'[1]

Hewart was capable of paring a judgment down to its essentials. In one case he addressed counsel for the respondent as follows:

> 'We need not trouble you, Mr Valentine. Mr Meston has put his case, such as it is, very clearly. It really comes to this, that if his case were different from what it is he might succeed, but as his case is what it is this appeal must succeed.'[2]

---

[1] *R v Sussex Justices, ex parte McCarthy* (1924).
[2] *Sidcup Building Estates Ltd. v Sidery*, 1936.

His brother judges agreed and the appeal was dismissed.

Robert Thompson was the class clown in the 1980s California Court of Appeal.

The offensive footnote

One of Thompson's drolleries was a seemingly bland footnote appended to the majority opinion he delivered in a prosecution for possessing obscene films. It read:

'We feel compelled by the nature of the attack in the dissenting opinion to spell out a response:

1. Some answer is required to the dissent's charge.

2. Certainly we do not endorse "victimless crime."

3. How that question is involved escapes us.

4. Moreover, the constitutional issue is significant.

5. Ultimately it must be addressed in light of precedent.

6. Certainly the course of precedent is clear.'

A correspondent in the *Los Angeles Times* spotted that the first letters of the footnotes spelled out a 'Yiddish vulgarism defined by *Webster* as a "contemptible or foolish person; jerk."' Another definition referred to a portion of the male anatomy. As soon as the dissenting judge got to hear of it he publicly condemned the opinion's 'lack of propriety, collegiality and judicial temperament'. Thompson denied any intent to criticize and claimed disingenuously that the footnote was only meant to show that a word can have differing meanings.[3]

The footnote was vulgar and not particularly funny. Its only mitigation was that it offended no one except another judge.

[3] *People v. Arno*, 1979.

What is Golf?

Judges are sometimes faced with issues that seem to invite a light-hearted approach. This is Associate Justice Scalia of the US Supreme Court:

> It has been rendered the solemn duty of the Supreme Court of the United States... to decide 'What Is Golf?'
>
> I am sure that the Framers of the Constitution, aware of the 1457 edict of King James II of Scotland prohibiting golf because it interfered with the practice of archery, fully expected that sooner or later the paths of golf and government, the law and the links, would once again cross, and that the judges of this august Court would some day have to wrestle with that age-old jurisprudential question, for which their years of study in the law have so well prepared them: Is someone riding around a golf course from shot to shot *really* a golfer? The answer, we learn, is yes. The Court ultimately concludes, and it will henceforth be the Law of the Land, that walking is not a "fundamental" aspect of golf.[4]

One judge was notorious for his unintended humour.

Arabin

William St Julien Arabin (1773–1841) was a deputy Common Sergeant (or judge) at the Old Bailey. A 'thin, wizen-faced old man' both short sighted and deaf, he was renowned for his often mangled use of language, of which these are examples:

- 'If there ever was a case of clearer evidence than this of persons acting together, this case is that case'.

- (Referring to the residents of Uxbridge:) 'They will steal the very teeth out of your mouth as you walk through the streets – I know it from experience.'[5]

---

[4] *PGA v Martin*, 2001.
[5] Both quoted by Sir R. Megarry in *Arabinesque at Law*, 1969.

- 'Prisoner, God has given you good abilities, instead of which you go about the country stealing ducks.'[6]
- No man is fit to be a cheesemonger who cannot guess the length of a street.[7]

Such was Arabin's limited understanding of what was going on in court that counsel could play verbal games with him. After a conference between court and counsel concerning a plea Arabin said, 'Mr Philips. You must distinctly understand that I know nothing of this arrangement.' Counsel replied, 'Yes, My Lord. It is thoroughly understood that your Lordship knows nothing.'[8]

Humour is usually more acceptable when it comes from the Bar rather than the Bench. One barrister who pushed the privilege to its limits was Frederick Edwin Smith KC, generally known as 'F.E'.

'F.E.'

In and out of the courtroom F.E. gave an impression of effortless superiority and could be intolerant of slower minds, but his wit was coruscating, as the following examples demonstrate.[9]

Judge Willis (addressing F.E.): Mr Smith, you must not direct the jury. What do you suppose I am on the bench for?

'FE': It is not for me, your honour, to attempt to fathom the inscrutable workings of Providence.

***

---

[6] Quoted in *'Notes and Queries'*.
[7] Theobald Matthew, *Arabiniana; or, The Remains of Mr Serjeant Arabin*, 1843.
[8] *The Bar and the Old Bailey, 1750 – 1850* by Allyson Nancy May.
[9] Some of them taken from *Frederick Edwin, Earl of Birkenhead* by Frederick, Second Earl of Birkenhead, 1933.

Master of the Rolls (addressing FE): Really, Mr Smith, do give this Court credit for some little intelligence.

'F.E.': That is the mistake I made in the Court below, My Lord.

***

Judge: Are you trying to show contempt for this court, Mr Smith?

'F.E.' No, My Lord. I am attempting to conceal it.

***

'F.E.' to witness: So, you were as drunk as a judge?

Judge (interjecting): You mean as drunk as a lord?

'F.E.': Yes, My Lord.

***

Judge: I have read your case, Mr Smith, and I am no wiser now than I was when I started.

'F.E.': Possibly not, My Lord, but much better informed.[10]

***

Mr Justice Ridley: 'Well, Mr Smith, I have read the pleadings and I do not think much of your case'.

'F.E.' 'Indeed, my Lord, I'm sorry to hear that, but your Lordship will find that the more you hear of it, the more it will grow on you.'

And of course:

'FE Smith's worst insults were reserved for Judge Willis, a worthy, but sanctimonious county court judge, full of kindness which he was wont to express in a patronising manner. FE had been briefed for a tramway company which had been sued for damages for injuries to a boy who had been run over.

---

[10] Quoted in London Letter by Francis Cowper in the New York Law Journal.

The judge was deeply moved. 'Poor boy, poor boy', he said. 'Blind. Put him on a chair so that the jury can see him.'

F.E. said coldly: 'Perhaps your honour would like to have the boy passed round the jury box.'

'That is a most improper remark', said Judge Willis angrily.

'It was provoked', said F.E., 'by a most improper suggestion.' There was a heavy pause, and the judge continued, 'Mr Smith, have you ever heard of a saying by Bacon - the great Bacon - that youth and discretion are ill-wed companions?'

'Indeed I have, your Honour; and has your Honour ever heard of a saying by Bacon - the great Bacon - that a much talking judge is like an ill-tuned cymbal?'

The judge replied furiously, "You are extremely offensive, young man'; and F.E. added to his previous lapses by saying: 'As a matter of fact we both are; the only difference between us is that I'm trying to be and you can't help it.'"

'No reference to fun in any Act of Parliament'

One of the most notable judgments of Lord Chief Justice Lord Light concerned the appeal of a Mr Haddock who had been convicted of various charges arising out of his having jumped off Hammersmith bridge during the regatta. In his defence he claimed that he had done so 'for fun'. His appeal against conviction was famously rejected by the Court of Criminal Appeal with these words:

> 'The appellant made the general answer that this was a free country and a man can do what he likes if he does nobody any harm... It cannot be too clearly understood that this is *not* a free country, and it will be an evil day for the legal profession when it is. The citizens of London must realize that there is almost nothing that they are allowed to do. Prima facie all actions are illegal, if not by an Act of Parliament, by Order of Council, or if not by Departmental regulations or Police regulations, or bye-laws. They may not eat what they like,

drink where they like, walk where they like, drive where they like, sing where they like or sleep where they like. And least of all may they do unusual actions "for fun". People must not do things for fun. There is no reference to fun in any Act of Parliament. If anything is said in this court to encourage a belief that Englishmen are entitled to jump off bridges for their own amusement the next thing to go will be the Constitution.'

The remarks of the learned Chief Justice came under criticism from an American jurist in a 1967 study published in *The Lawyers* when he smugly remarked, 'No such opinion could be written by an American court.' While the writer was no doubt correct in this conclusion, he was mistaken in the assumption behind it. The case of *Rex v Haddock* was in fact a figment of the fertile imagination of Alan Patrick Herbert, or 'A.P.H.', as he was widely known.

Alan Herbert had a distinguished career. After taking a first in jurisprudence he was called to the Bar at the Inner Temple, but never practised. When the Great War broke out he joined the Royal Navy, serving with distinction as a petty officer at Gallipoli. After the war he turned to politics, becoming independent MP for Oxford at a time when that university enjoyed separate constituency status. He was personally responsible for a major reform of the divorce laws in 1937 and was knighted in Winston Churchill's resignation honours.

A.P.H. was the author of a series of fictional law reports entitled *Misleading Cases*, the first of which appeared in 1910. Many of them featured the doughty litigant, Albert Haddock. To this day they continue to give pleasure to many, sometimes even being quoted in court.[11]

---

[11] See for example Mr Justice Sedley in the case of *Lilley v Carter & Ors* (1999).

Chapter 11

VALEDICTORY

In ending we should remember the words of a great American judge who reminded us that legal rights alone are insufficient to guarantee our freedom.

The spirit of liberty

It was 1944 and 150,000 newly naturalised citizens of the United States of America had assembled in Central Park, New York, to swear the oath of allegiance to their newly adopted country. Before leading them in this ceremony Billings Learned Hand,[1] Chief Judge of the United States Circuit Court of Appeals for the Second Circuit, made this brief speech.

> 'We have gathered here to affirm a faith, a faith in a common purpose, a common conviction, a common devotion. Some of us have chosen America as the land of our adoption; the rest have come from those who did the same. For this reason we have some right to consider ourselves a picked group, a group of those who had the courage to break from the past and brave the dangers and the loneliness of a strange land.

---

[1] 'Learned' was his mother's maiden name.

'What was the object that nerved us, or those who went before us, to this choice? We sought liberty; freedom from oppression, freedom from want, freedom to be ourselves. This we then sought. This we now believe that we are by way of winning.

'What do we mean when we say that first of all we seek liberty? I often wonder whether we do not rest our hopes too much upon constitutions, upon laws and upon courts. These are false hopes; believe me, these are false hopes. Liberty lies in the hearts of men and women. When it dies there, no constitution, no law, no court can save it. No constitution, no law, no court can even do much to help it. While it lies there, it needs no constitution, no law, no court to save it.

'And what is this liberty which must lie in the hearts of men and women? It is not the ruthless, the unbridled will. It is not freedom to do as one likes. That is the denial of liberty, and leads straight to its overthrow. A society in which men recognize no check upon their freedom soon becomes a society where freedom is the possession of only a savage few; as we have learned to our sorrow.

'What then is the spirit of liberty? I cannot define it; I can only tell you my own faith. The spirit of liberty is the spirit which is not too sure that it is right. The spirit of liberty is the spirit which seeks to understand the minds of other men and women. The spirit of liberty is the spirit which weighs their interests alongside its own without bias. The spirit of liberty remembers that not even a sparrow falls to earth unheeded. The spirit of liberty is the spirit of Him who, near two thousand years ago, taught mankind that lesson it has never learned, but has never quite forgotten: that there may be a kingdom where the least shall be heard and considered side by side with the greatest.

'And now in that spirit, that spirit of an America which has never been, and which may never be; nay, which never will be, except as the conscience and the courage of Americans create it; yet in the spirit of that America which lies hidden in some form in the aspirations of us all; in the spirit of that America for which our young men are at this moment fighting and dying; in that spirit of liberty and of America I ask you to rise and with me to pledge our faith in the glorious destiny of our beloved country - with liberty and justice for all.'

Two weeks after this speech the first Allied troops landed in Normandy prepared to give their lives in order to rescue Europe from dictatorship.

It is not without reason that Billings Learned Hand has been called the greatest American judge never to sit on the Supreme Court bench.

Index

Ackley, Helen, 345
Adams, John, 182, 183
Adams, John Quincy, 89
Addison, Joseph, 124
Affair of the Poisons, 133
Agreement of the Free People of England, 237
Air Loom Gang, 66, 69
Aitken, Jonathan, 37
Albert, Prince, 37, 174, 175
Alderson, Sir Edward Hall, 349
Aldington, Lord, 192
Allen, Floyd, 263
Alsatia, 9, 10, 69
Alwyne, Bishop of Winchester, 4
Amnesty International, 178, 292
Amos, Andrew, 100
Animals, prosecutions of, 2
Annan, Beulah, 91
Arabin, William St Julien, 352
Arabinesque at Law, 352
Archer, Jeffrey, 37
Arkansas Supreme Court, 335

Armagh, Archbishop of, 33
Armstrong TD, Major Herbert Rowse, 50
Armstrong, Eliza, 143, 144
Armstrong, Herbert Rowse, 50
Armstrong, Major, 51
Ashford, Mary, 106
Ashley-Cooper, Anthony, 101
Ashmolean Museum, 103
Atkin, Lord, 114, 186
Atkins, Samuel, 101
Aubrey, John, 206, 274
Avery, Mr Justice, 123

Babbacombe Lee, John, 71
Bacon, Lord, 286
Baker v Bolton, 119
Ball, John, 198
Bampton, Thomas, 197
Banham, Sir John, 342
Barber, Judge Paul, 40
Barham, HMS, 344, 345
Barnaby Rudge, 211
Barrett, Michael, 24
Barrow, Eliza, 53
Barry, Charles, 314
Bean, John William, 175
Beck, Adolf, 74, 76, 77

Beecher, Henry Ward, 156
Bell, Lord Chief Baron Sir Robert, 342
Bell, Mr Justice, 124
Benet, Stephen Vincent, 129, 307
Benito Mussolini, 228
Benjamin, Judah Philip, 307
Bentham, Jeremy, 330
Bentley, Dereck, 26
Berry, James, 73
Besant, Annie, 243
Bessell, Peter, 152
Beswick v Beswick, 258
Beswick, John Joseph, 258
Beswick, Peter, 257, 258
Bigham, Mr Justice, 55
Bill of Rights, American, 248
Billings, Thomas, 20
Birkenhead, Earl of, 283, 353
Black Assize, 341, 342
Black Bess, 45
Black Tom Tyrant, 62
Blackstone, William, 329
Blakely, David, 92, 93
Bleak House, 321
Bligh RN, Lieutenant William, 183
Bloody Assize, 8, 272, 273
Bloody Code, 23
Blount, Thomas, 99
Bobby Seale, 95, 96
Bodie of Liberties, 242, 243
Boleyn, Anne, 165
Boleyn, Mary, 165

Book Bandit, The, 84
Boswell, James, 267, 298
Bottomley, Horatio, 56, 159
Bow Street Runners, 36, 37, 219
Bowen, Charles Synge Christopher, 253
Bradlaugh, Charles, 243
Brereton, Sir William, 166
Briancourt, Jean-Baptiste, 134
Brooke, Daisy, 146
Brougham KC, Henry, 137, 213
Brown, John, 176
Brunswick, HMS, 185
Bryan, William Jennings, 79
Buckley, Sheila, 58
Bucknill, Mr Justice, 54
Bundy, Herbert, 258
Bunyan, John, 207
Burke and Hare, 47
Burke, Edmund, 298
Burne-Jones, Edward, 162
Burnett, James, 269
Burns, Robert, 269
Burr, Aaron, 87, 88
Butt, Hon. Mr Justice, 141
Byng, John, 65, 66

Cade, Jack, 200, 201
Campbell, Lord, 274, 331
Campbell, Lord Chief Justice, 49
Campion, Edmund, 17
Cantley, Mr Justice, 153
Carbolic Smoke Ball Company, 116

Cardoza, Chief Judge Benjamin, 115
Carlill, Mrs Louisa, 116
Carman QC, George, 153
Carnegie of Finhaven, 328
Carr, Robert, 99
Carter, Benjamin, 107
Casement, Sir Roger, 37
Cassel, Sir Ernest, 122
Castlereagh, Lord, 218
Castro, Thomas, 305
Catesby, Robert, 203
Catherine of Aragon, 165
Cato Street, 217–219
Cecil, Sir Robert, 204
Chains of Slavery, The, 104
Chambre Ardente, 135
Charles I, King, 62, 187, 242, 273, 294
Charles II, King, 32, 206
Chicago Eight, 95
Chicago Seven, 95, 96
Chitty LJ, 253
Christian, Fletcher, 184, 185
Christmas, 119, 232, 319, 320, 342
Christmas Humphreys, 93
Churchill, Winston, 121, 122, 344, 356
Claimant, The, 305
Clarke KC, Edward, 285
Clarke QC, Sir Edward, 147
Clink, The, 9
Clinton, President Bill, 130
Cockburn, Alexander, 173, 267
Cockburn, Chief Justice, 306
Cockburn, Henry Lord, 266
Cockburn, Sir Alexander, 49
Coke, Chief Justice, 22
Cook, John, 49, 293
Corday, Charlotte, 103
Corey, Giles, 10
Cottington, Lord, 63
Cowper, Francis, 354
Craig, Christopher, 81
Crippen, Dr., 37
Cromwell, Oliver, 17, 321, 337
Cromwell, Richard, 238
Cromwell, Thomas, 166
Crossfield, Robert, 211
Curran KC, John Philpot, 225
Curtis-Bennett KC, Sir Henry, 52
Cussen, Desmond, 92

Da Vinci Code, The, xii, 290
Danton, Georges Jacques, 171
Darling, Justice, 52
Darling, Mr Justice, 52, 123
Darrow, Clarence Seward, 308
Davidson, Harold Francis, 160
Davies, Jefferson, 307
Davy, Serjeant, 246
Dawson, Sir Bertrand, 90
Dayrell, Sir Richard, 274

Denman RN, Commander Joseph, 247
Denning, Alfred Thompson, 255
Deodand, 118, 119
Devlin, Patrick, 261
Dickens, Charles, 139, 211, 321
Dilke, Sir Charles Wentworth, 141, 142
Donoghue v Stevenson, 114, 115
Doughty, Roger Charles, 305
Douglas, James, 28
Douglas, Lord Alfred, 121
Doyle, Sir Arthur Conan, 76
Dr. Winfred Overholser, 228
Dredd Scott v Sandford, 249
Dreyfus, Alfred, 69
Drummond, Edward, 172
Dudley, Lord Robert, 98, 320
Duncan, Helen, 344, 345
Dundas, Robert, 329
Duvall, Claude, 44

Edalji, George, 74, 76
Edalji, Shapurji, 74
Edison, Thomas, 29
Edward I, King, 232
Edward III, King, 19
Edward IV, King, 7, 323
Edward the Confessor, 4
Eichmann, Adolf, 188, 189
Elde, Francis, 276

Eldon, Lord Chancellor, 285
Electrocution, 30
Elizabeth I, Queen, 232
Elizabeth II, Queen, 232
Ellenborough, Lord, 67, 118, 331
Ellesmere, Viscount, 294
Ellis, George, 94
Ellis, Ruth, 26, 92
Elyot, Sir Thomas, 147
Emerson, John, 248
Englishry, 1, 2
Epstein, Judge, 130
Erskine KC, Thomas, 296
Erskine, Lord, 293
Erskine, Thomas, 210
Eskgrove, Sir David Rae of, 267
Espinasse, Isaac, 330
Essex, Earl of, 274
Essex, Lady Frances, 100
Ethelred, King, 4
Evans, Richard, 127

Fawkes, Guy, 17, 274
Fergusson, George, 268
Fielding, Henry, 36
Fielding, John, 36
Fiennes, James, 201
Fire Court, The, 316
Fisher, Admiral Jackie, 291
Fisher, Jackie, 291
Fisher, Sir Henry, 261
Fitzherbert, Lady, 136
Fleet Street, 9
Flynn, Billy, 91
Fortunes of Nigel, The, 9
Fouquier-Tinville, Antoine Quentin, 170, 172

Francis, John, 175
Frankpledge, 2
Fraudulent Mediums Act, 345
Freeborn John, 236, 293
Freethinker, The, 243
Frost, John, 220, 222
Fulton, Sir Forrest, 78

Gaertner, Belva, 90
Garnet, Henry, 202, 203
Garrow, William, xi, 300
Gascoigne, 148
Gentleman Jack, 41
George III, King, 218, 293
George V, King, 89, 149, 303
George, Prince of Wales, 136
Gifford, Robert, 137
Goddard, Lord Chief Justice Lord, 82
Godfrey Isaacs, 281
Godfrey, Justice, 103
Godfrey, Sir Edmund Berry, 101
Goetz, Bernhard, 39
Golden Thread, The, 85
Goldman, Ronald, 97
Goldsmith PC, Lord, 194
Goose v Wilson Sandford, 287
Gordon QC, Judge Gerald, 263
Gordon-Cumming, Sir William, 146
Gorgeous George, xi, 303, 304
Graves, Robert, 49, 50
Grayson, Albert, 150

Grayson, Gregory, 150
Great Rumour, The, 196
Gregory XIII, Pope, 208
Gregory, Maundy, 149
Gregory, Thomas, 323
Gregson v Gilbert, 247
Grey, Mr Justice, 127
Griffith-Jones QC, Mervyn, 311
Guillotin, Dr Joseph-Ignace, 27, 28
Gunpowder Plot, 202

Haddock, Albert, 356
Haigh, John, 26
Hailsham, Lord, 14
Hale, Sir Matthew, 207
Halifax Gibbet, 28
Hall, Matthew, 169, 316, 317
Hallett MC, Sir Hugh Imbert Periam, 285
Hamilton, Alexander, 87
Hampshire, HMS, 122
Harcourt, Sir William, 73, 332
Harman, Mr Justice, 286
Harris, Elizabeth, 71
Harrowby, Earl, 218
Harrowby, Lord, 218
Haslam, John, 67
Havers, Mr. Justice, 93
Hawkins, Henry, 284
Hay, Matthew, 267
Hayes, Catherine, 20
Heckington Common, 45
Hedges, John, 132
Hedley, Mr Justice, 259
Heights of Weehawken, 87
Help the Poor Struggler, 26

Henry III, King, 318
Henry IV, King, 201, 318
Henry V, 147
Henry VI, King, 16, 200
Henry VIII, 7, 9, 16, 19, 165, 315
Henry, Major Hubert, 69
Hepple, Norman, 321
Herman, Armand-Martial-Joseph, 170, 172
Hermand, Lord, 268
Hewart, Lord Chief Justice Lord, 254
Heywood, Midshipman Peter, 184
Higgins. George, 212
Hill, Sir George, 225
History of Tom Jones, The, 36
Hitler, Adolf, 126, 222
Hoffman, Abbie, 95, 96
Hoffmann, Lord, 292
Holker, Sir John, 163
Hopkins, Douglas George, 14
Hostetler, Judge David of Coshocton, 30
Hove Crown Court, 347
Howard of Effingham, 320
Howell, Thomas, 239
Hugh White, 181
Hugo, Victor, 38
Human Rights, European Court of, 125, 193
Hunt, Leigh, 213
Hussein, Saddam, 177, 194

Incorporated Council of Law Reporting, 331

influencing engine, 69
Ingoldsby Legends, 25
Ings, James, 219
Inherit the Wind, 80
Inner Temple Revels, 320
Inns of Chancery, 323
Inns of Court, 293, 317, 319–321, 323
Instrument of Government, 337, 338
Irishry, 2
Irving, David, 126
Isaacs KC, Sir Rufus, 53
Isaacs, Rufus, 281, 282
Ito, Judge Lance, 97

Jack the Ripper, 111
James Duke of York, 32
James I of England and VI of Scotland, 3, 60
Jarrett, Rebecca, 143
Jefferson, Thomas, 87, 339
Jeffreys, Judge, 271–273
Jeffreys, Lord Chief Justice, 33
Jenkes, Rowland, 341
Jersey Lilly, The, 280
Jesu Grist, 334
Joan of Arc, 179
John of Gaunt, 198
John, King, 235
Johnson, Dr, 66
Johnson, Dr. Samuel, 298
Joly v Pelletier et al, 130
Jones v National Coal Board, 286
Jones, Paula, 154, 155
Jonson, Ben, 12, 19, 321
Joyce, William, 26, 37, 191
Jungle Book, The, 145

Kemmler, William, 29
Kenealy QC, Edward, 305
Kenyon, Lloyd, 210
Ketch, Jack, 33, 113
Keyse, Emma, 71
Kipling, Joseph Rudyard, 144
Knox, Professor Robert, 46
Kray twins, 37

La Reynie, 135
Laddie, Hugh, 260
Lamb, Charles, 318
Lamb, John, 318
Langtry, Lillie, 280, 281
Laud, Archbishop, 205
Lauterpacht, Professor, 189
Lavegny, 2
Lawrence, D.H., 311
Le Blanc, Mr Justice, 213
Le Bureau des Renseignments, 38
Le Maitre, John Peter, 103, 105, 106
Lee, John Henry George, 71
Leicester, Earl of, 320
Leonard, John, 118
Levellers, 237
Lewinsky, 154, 155
Lewinsky, Monica, 154
Lewis, Sir George, 55
Lewison, Mr Justice, 125
Light, Lord Chief Justice Lord, 355
Lilburne, John, 236, 293, 338
Lilley v Carter, 356

Lincoln, Abraham, 185, 229, 307
Lincoln, Earl of, 319
Lindsay, Sir Coutts, 162
Lintz Cricket Club, 259
Lipstadt, Deborah, 126
Lisle, Dame Alice, 273
Little Ease, 318
Liversidge v Anderson, 187
Lloyd George, 149, 151, 282
Lloyd George, David, 149
Lloyd George, Gwilym, 93
London Stone, 201
Lord Haw Haw, 37, 191
Louis XV, 55
Louis XVI, King, 171
Low, Edward, 120
Lowther, George, 120
Ludendorff, Erich, 223

Macclesfield, Earl of, 276
Macdonald, Lord Chief Baron, 343
MacKinnon, Lord Justice, 326
Maclibel, 124
Magdalen College, 255
Magna Carta, 242, 313
Maiden Tribute of Modern Babylon, The, 142, 143
Manisty, Mr Justice, 72
Manningham, John, 320
Mansfield, Lord, 209, 245, 247
Mansfield, Sir James, 331
Manual of Military Law, 189

Manual of the Law of Armed Conflict, 190
Marat, 104–106
Marat, Jean-Paul, 103, 104
March, Frederic, 80
Marjoribanks, Edward, 302
Marshall Hall KC, Sir Edward, 53, 301
Marshall, Henry, 23
Marshall, John, 88, 330
Martin, Oswald, 51
Mathew, Lord Justice, 302
Matthew, Theobald, 353
Matthews, James Tilly, 66
Maundy Gregory, Arthur, 149
Maybrick, James, 109, 111
Mayo, Gerald, 129
McCardie, Hon. Henry Alfred, 254
McDougal, Helen, 46
McGowan, Cathy, 117
Megarry QC, R.E., 337
Meissonier, Ottilie, 77
Melbourne, Lord, 139
Melford Stevenson QC, 93
Middle Temple, 36, 63, 141, 224, 225, 276, 277, 297, 307, 318–320, 322, 329
Mignonette, 332, 333
Mikado, The, 349
Mildoon, Donald Clive, 59
Miles, PC Sidney, 82
Minories, The, 9
Mme. De La Rue, 323
Monboddo, Lord, 269

Monkeyhangers, 3
Montgomery Hyde, H., 121
Montgomery, Hugh, 182
Monvoisin, Catherine Deshayes, 135
Mount Orgueil Castle, 238
Mrs. May Donoghue, 113
Murdrum, 2
Mylward v Weldon, 295
Mylward, Richard, 294

Neck, Jane, 72
Newgate Calendar, The, 23, 108, 343
Newgate prison, 24, 210, 241
Newport Chartists, 220
Nizer, Louis, 231
Norris, Sir Henry, 166
Norton, George Chapple, 138

Oates, Titus, 32–34, 101, 270, 272
OJ Simpson, 96
Old Bailey, 11, 14, 19, 21, 24, 35, 42, 53, 77, 93, 143, 152, 153, 210, 212, 238, 239, 263, 300, 343, 344, 352, 353
Old Benchers of the Inner Temple, The, 318
Oppenheim, Professor, 189
Oradour sur Glane, 1
Ordeal by fire, 3, 4
Ordeal by water, 3
Orrell, Judge James, 117

Ors v Warner Music UK Ltd, 126
Orton, Arthur, 306
Outlawries Bill, 5
Overbury, Sir Thomas, 99

Packer v Packer, 256
Page, Sir Richard, 167
Paine, Tom, 269, 296, 297
Palgraf, Mrs, 116
Palmer the Poisoner, 48
Palmer, William, 48
Palmerston, Lord, 50, 248, 278
Palsgraf, Mrs Helen, 115
Pang, Mr Justice, 288
Parker, Isaac, 280
Parker, Lord Chancellor Thomas, 276
Parry, Serjeant John Humffreys, 163
Peel, Sir Robert, 172, 173
Peine forte et dure, 10, 11
Pelletier, Nicolas Jacques, 27
Penguin Books, 311
Penn, William, 239, 240
Pepsi Stuff, 117
Pepys, Samuel, x, 101
Perkins KC, Travers, 57
Perrin, Reggie, 58, 59
Peter, Henry, 106
Peter, John, 106, 212
Peterloo, xi, 214, 216, 218
PGA v Martin, 352
Pickwick Papers, 139, 322
Picquart, Lt Col Georges, 70
Pierrepoint, Albert, 26, 93

Pinochet, General Augusto, 292
Plunkett, Oliver, 17, 33
Pollock QC, Gordon, 303
Pollock, Chief Baron, 331
Popham, Lord Chief Justice, 61, 274, 275
Porter-Porter, Mrs., 284
Pound, Ezra, 227
Powis, Mr Justice, 43
Prerogativa Regis, 327
Prerogative Court of Canterbury, 132
Presentment of Welshry, 2
President William Jefferson, 154
Presnell, U.S. District Judge Gregory, 295
Preventative Squadron, 247
Pride, Colonel Thomas, 168
Prime, Geoffrey, 304
Prince of Purpoole, 320
Proceedings in Courts of Justice Act, 326
Prolixity, 294
Prynne, William, 205
Purpoole, Sir Reginald, 319

R v Dudley and Stephens, 333
R v Penguin Books, 311
R v Sussex Justices, 350
R v Williams, 298
R v Young, 347
Radcot Bridge, 8
Radio Buxton, 117

Radio Roma, 228
Raleigh, Sir Walter, 60, 61, 274
Reading, Lord, 282
Reid, John, 298
Resurrectionists, The, 46
Rex v Haddock, 356
Richard Ellman, 121
Richard I, King, 2
Richard II, King, 8, 130, 165, 197, 199
Richardson, Chief Justice, 263
Ridley, Mr Justice, 354
Rights of Man, The, 269, 296, 297
Rinka, 152
Robert Pate, 176
Robertson, Geoffrey, 294
Robinson, Harriett, 248
Robinson, Sir Joseph, 150
Robsart, Amy, 98
Rochford, George, Viscount, 166
Roose, Richard, 15
Rosenberg, Julius and Ethel, 230
Rosenbergs, The, 230
Rosse, Edith, 150
Royal Courts of Justice, 55, 303, 323
Rubin, Jerry, 96
Ruskin, John, 162
Russell QC, Sir Charles, 147
Russell, Edward Southwell, 14
Russell, Lord, 14

Sacco, Ferdinando Nicola, 229
Salisbury Assize, 263
Salisbury Court, 9
Salt, Samuel, 318
Salter Douglas, Mr Justice, 122
Salvation Army, 74, 143
Samuel, Herbert, 281
Sanctuary, 6, 7
Sankey, Lord, 86
Scopes, John Thomas, 79
Scott, Norman, 152
Scott, Sir Walter, 9, 47, 98, 268, 275
Scottish Inner House, 114
Scottish Law Society, 233
Scottish Maiden, 28
Scottish/Irish, 162
Scroggs, Chief Justice, 33, 102
Seddon, Frederick Henry, 53
Sedley, Lord Justice, 9
Sedley, Mr Justice, 356
Selborne, Lord, 253
Serious Organized Crime Agency, 9
Seymour, Jane, 168
Shadwell, Thomas, 9
Shaftsbury, Earl of, 101
Shaw, George Bernard, 244
Sheppard, Jack, 35, 41, 43
Sheridan MP, Richard Brinsley, 5
Sheridan, Caroline, 138
Sidmouth, Lord, 217
Simon, Viscount, 187
Siskina, The, 257

Smeaton, Mark, 166
Smith KC, Frederick Edwin, 353, 354
Smith, Francis, 343
Smith, George Joseph, 301
Smith, Mrs. Ellen, 141
Smith, Peter, The Hon., 290, 291
Smithy Code, 290, 291
Somerset v Stewart, 245
Somerset, Earl of, 99
Sommersett, James, 245
Southwell, Robert, 12
Spa Fields, 217, 218
Sparrow, Gerald, 302
Spence, Thomas, 217
Spencer, Gabriel, 19
St Leonards, Lord, 131
Stadlen QC, Nicholas, 303
Stambovsky, Jeffrey, 345
Star Chamber, 205, 237, 315
Staunton, Harriet, 284
Steele, Helen, 124
Stephen Blumberg, 83
Stephen, Mr Justice James Fitzjames, 110
Stevenson, George, 349
Stone of Destiny, 232
Stone of Scone, 232
Stonehouse, John Thomson, 58
Stow, Archdeacon of, 157
Strafford, Earl of, 62, 63
Street, George Edmund, 314
Stuart, Arbella, 60
Subway Vigilante, The, 39
Sugden, Sir Edward, 131

Sweet, Henry, 310
Swift, Mr Justice, 86

Tale of the Riots of Eighty, 211
Tebbitt, Norman, 304
Temple Bar, 321
Templer, Reginald, 72, 74
Tesimond, Father Oswald, 203
Thatcher, Margaret, 59
Thief-Taker General, The, 35, 42
Thistlewood, Arthur, 217
Thomas Egerton, 294
Thompson, Robert, 351
Thornton, Abraham, 107
Thorpe, Jeremy, 152, 304
Tindal, Lord Chief Justice, 221
Tolstoy-Miloslavsky, Count Nikolai Dmitrievich, 192
Tomlinson, Mr Justice, 303
Tonge, Israel, 32
Topcliffe, Richard, 12
Topsy the elephant, 29
Tresilian, Robert, 8
Turpin, Dick, 45
Tutchin, John, 272
Twelfth Night, 320
Tyburn, 8, 19, 21, 23–25, 35, 43, 44
Tyler, Wat, 198, 199
Tyrannicide Brief, The, 294
Tyrie, David, 17

Uncommon Attorney, The, 311
Upton, Thomas, 211

Valjean, Jean, 38
Vane, Sir Henry, 63
Vanzetti, Bartolomeo, 229
Victoria, Queen, 37, 71, 147, 168, 173, 174, 253, 314, 320
Voisin, La, 135

Waitakere, City Council of, 40
Wakeford, The Venerable John, 157
Walsin-Esterhazy, Major Ferdinand, 70
Walworth, Sir William, 199
Ward, Nathaniel, 242
Watkins, Maureen, 91
Watts, Nigel, 192
Wednesbury, 58
Wehrmacht War Crimes Bureau, The, 190
Wehrmacht-Untersuchungstelle, 190
Weinstein, Jack B, 262
Wentworth, Charles, 62
Wentworth, Sir Thomas, 62
West Africa Squadron, 248
Westinghouse, George, 29
Weston, Sir Francis, 166
Whistler, James Abbott McNeill, 162
Whitaker Wright, James, 55
Wild, Jonathan, 34–36, 38, 42
Wilde, Oscar, 37, 121
Wilkes MP, John, 5

Wilkinson, General James, 88
William III, King, 34, 102
Williams, Thomas, 297
Williams, Zephaniah, 220
Willis, John Walpole, 278
Witley Park, 55, 56
Wolfe Tone, 224
Wolsey, Cardinal, 7
Wood, Thomas, 20
Woodville, Elizabeth, 7
Woolf, Lord, 327
Woolmington, Reginald, 85
Wright, John Michael, 316
Wyatt, Sir Thomas, 166

Yarn of the Nancy Bell, The, 333
Yelverton, Mr Justice, 331
Yippies, 95
Young, Stephen, 347

Zong, The, 246, 247

Printed in Great Britain
by Amazon.co.uk, Ltd.,
Marston Gate.